Understanding
Vulnerability and Resilience

This book offers an accessible and evidence-based approach for professional staff to improve their interactions with vulnerable people. Drawing upon contemporary research from a broad array of disciplines, including psychology, sociology, economics, biology and the neurosciences, it demonstrates how vulnerability and resilience are not fixed personality traits, as is commonly assumed, but rather fluid and dynamic states that result from inhibitory and developmental factors that reside within individuals and their external environments.

Each chapter focuses on factors that create vulnerability and those that promote resilience with reference to important subjects, such as child development, epigenetics, trauma, shame, addiction, poverty, emotional intelligence, personality, empathy, compassion and behaviour-change. Attention is given to the role of positive, early life experiences in creating an internal working model of the world that is based on trust, intimacy and hope and how the root causes of vulnerability often lie in the cyclical relationship that exists between child maltreatment, trauma and socially deprived environments that cumulatively act to keep people locked in states of inter-generational poverty. The author explores pressing and important workplace issues, such as occupational stress and burnout, and highlights the urgent need for compassionate systems of management that are functionally equipped to address human error, stress and trauma in complex professional arenas where staff are continually exposed to other peoples' suffering. The book also demonstrates how strategies and processes which coerce individuals and groups into changing their behaviour are generally counterproductive and it explains how resilient change is invariably supported by strategies that enhance trust, cooperation, personal control and self-efficacy.

This book will benefit professional staff, including health, emergency and social services, humanitarian workers, counsellors and therapists, as well as students who want to learn more about the conceptual frameworks that explain vulnerability and resilience.

Understanding Vulnerability and Resilience

A Guide for Professional Staff who Work with Vulnerable Others

Graham Russell

Routledge
Taylor & Francis Group
LONDON AND NEW YORK

Designed cover image: © Getty Images

First published 2023
by Routledge
4 Park Square, Milton Park, Abingdon, Oxon OX14 4RN

and by Routledge
605 Third Avenue, New York, NY 10158

Routledge is an imprint of the Taylor & Francis Group, an informa business

© 2023 Graham Russell

The right of Graham Russell to be identified as author of this work has been asserted in accordance with sections 77 and 78 of the Copyright, Designs and Patents Act 1988.

All rights reserved. No part of this book may be reprinted or reproduced or utilised in any form or by any electronic, mechanical, or other means, now known or hereafter invented, including photocopying and recording, or in any information storage or retrieval system, without permission in writing from the publishers.

Trademark notice: Product or corporate names may be trademarks or registered trademarks, and are used only for identification and explanation without intent to infringe.

British Library Cataloguing-in-Publication Data
A catalogue record for this book is available from the British Library

ISBN: 978-1-138-49030-7 (hbk)
ISBN: 978-1-138-49031-4 (pbk)
ISBN: 978-1-351-03554-5 (ebk)

DOI: 10.4324/9781351035545

Typeset in Helvetica
by codeMantra

I dedicate this book in memory of my bother Malcolm, who was born with haemophilia and died as a result of contracting AIDS from contaminated human blood products and to my wonderful children, Melanie and Dominic and grandchildren, Daisy, Miles and Bonnie.

Contents

Acknowledgements x

About the author xi

Preface xii

PART ONE
Vulnerability 1

1 Defining vulnerability 3

Definitions of vulnerability 3
How we manage our vulnerability 14

2 How vulnerability is created and maintained 18

Vulnerability, control and powerlessness 18
The need to belong 22
Poverty and vulnerability 24
Happiness and vulnerability 25
Blaming the victims 27
Vulnerability as a heritable condition 30
Temperaments, traits and vulnerability 32
Biological systems and vulnerability 35
Chronic stress 37

3 Vulnerability and childhood 40

Vulnerability and the social brain 40
The development of the self 44
Epigenetics and vulnerability 46

4 The psychological impact of vulnerability 51

Shame and vulnerability 51
Trauma and vulnerability 54
Addiction and vulnerability 60

PART TWO
Resilience 69

5 Defining resilience 71

A brief history of resilience 71
Defining resilience 73
The fixed model of resilience 73
The fluid model of resilience 76
The bioecological model of human development 78

6 The family environment and resilience 81

Parenting and resilience 81
The role of the family 84
Trust and intimacy 87
Attachment styles and resilience 89
Disorganised attachments 91
Disorganised attachments – building resilience 95
Attachments and construct validity 100

7 Intelligence, emotion and compassion 103

General intelligence 103
The development of emotion 106
Emotional intelligence 109
Intuition as emotional intelligence 113
Compassion 115
Self-compassion 117
Processes that disrupt compassion 119
Self-compassion and shame 121
Compassion mindfulness 123

8 When compassion fails 126

Stress and burnout 126
The prevalence of occupational burnout 129
Organisational failings and burnout 132
Compassionate organisations 135
To err is human 138

9 Resilience and poverty 142

Inter-generational poverty 142
Community resilience 144
Corruption and stigmatisation 147
The problem of motivation 149
Welfare sanctions 152
Tough on crime 153
School exclusion 156
Breaking the cycle of inter-generational poverty 159
Social support and resilience 164

10 Behaviour change and resilience 168

The principles of change 168
Health beliefs 170
Attitudes, intentions and change 173
Stages of change 174
Achieving change through dialogue 176

Epilogue 178

Bibliography resilience 180

Bibliography vulnerability 201

Index 211

Acknowledgements

To my dear wife Ea for casting an experienced, professional eye over the many formative drafts of this book and to Helen for her support and encouragement during periods of self-doubt and procrastination.

About the author

Graham Russell is a Chartered Psychologist, Fellow of the Higher Education Academy and Associate Fellow of the British Psychological Society. He spent two enjoyable decades teaching psychology to a wide range of health professionals, during which time he published the successful textbook *Psychology for Nurses and Other Health Professionals*. Graham has also been active in mental health research with a particular focus on the impact of social anxiety on students in higher education. Towards the end of his career in academia he became involved in collaborative projects with voluntary sector organisations in the United Kingdom and Europe. He started writing this book around the time that he reached the age of retirement.

Preface

The roots of this book are manyfold and closely bound to personal experiences in childhood, which shaped my interest in mental health and vulnerability.

My brother, who was fifteen months younger than me, was born with haemophilia, a rare blood clotting disorder, at a time when treatments were crude and still being developed.

He was often in severe pain and the fear and worry that he might, at any time, develop a fatal, internal bleed, permeated family life. Such fears were wholly justified. Average life expectancy for people with haemophilia in the late 1950s was only eleven years, and although this had increased to twenty years in the 1960s with the advent of blood clotting treatments, it felt like the wolf was always at the door.

As a consequence, life was never completely normal. Vulnerability and apprehension cast a long shadow over our daily lives and left an indelible mark on me as a growing child.

At the same time, my brother was incredibly resilient. Like so many children with chronic, life-threatening illness, he coped remarkably well and was never quick to complain. However, I don't think I fully appreciated this until much later in life, when I found myself wanting to learn more about the relationship between vulnerability and resilience.

The other motivation for writing this book stems from the long-held conviction that knowledge drives change. Indeed, during the course of my career I have observed that insights gained from research can motivate creative and clever people to develop new ways of working and thinking that enhance and improve other people's lives.

During the course of the book, I hope to show that vulnerability is a fundamental human condition that shapes our emotions and behaviours throughout the course of our lives, and that contrary to popular opinion, vulnerability and resilience are not polar-opposites, but rather more akin to binary stars that are intrinsically locked into each other's orbit, in a symbiotic relationship where changes in the state of one inexorably alters the condition of the other. Likewise, I hope to demonstrate that vulnerability and resilience are not fixed traits that we inherit and pass on to our children, as is often commonly thought, but are best described as dynamic, shifting states that are, in large part, a product of our environments and life experiences. In illustrating this, I will explore central topics like child development, poverty, powerlessness, stress, trauma, shame and addiction and illustrate the importance of compassion for oneself and others and the sometimes tragic consequences that arise when systems and organisations treat people as dispassionate objects.

In terms of presentation, the book is divided into two parts: Part one, takes a broad look at how we may best understand vulnerability and the key factors that render individuals and communities susceptible to vulnerability, which lays the groundwork for understanding the resilience. Part two, teases out what resilience is and is not, and explores the manyfold factors that create and maintain resilience.

I elected to look at vulnerability and resilience separately and to start with the former, because much of what we know about resilience is based on the early research flowing from the study of vulnerability, which has allowed researchers interested in resilience to progress and pursue new avenues of exploration. The early study of learned helplessness, by psychologists, for example, showed the importance of perceived control for mental and physical well-being, and this has been subsequently developed and incorporated into the theories and models of resilience in areas as diverse as child and family development and humanitarian work in disaster zones.

The contents of the book are drawn from a wide range of evidence and multi-disciplinary research from differing countries across the globe. I have done this, because vulnerability and resilience cannot be properly understood without addressing research in important areas like the neurosciences, psychology, sociology and economics, and because traditionally research has been narrowly dominated by articles flowing from institutions in the United States and the United Kingdom (a trend that is thankfully being reversed by improved non-institutional access to global research via the world-wide-web),

I believe the book will be of interest to a wide audience, including, nurses, midwives, clergy, mental health workers, police, social care workers, prison staff, education worker, humanitarian and workers and last, but not least, people working or studying in academia.

In terms of content and presentation, I decided early on to present vulnerability and resilience as separate topics and whilst this has created something of an artificial divide, it was the most practical way of presenting the content.

However, it is important to note that it is not a self-help book that comes complete with illustrative examples of have theory may be applied. Whilst this might have been desirable. I decided at an early stage that it was not practical. If you are humanitarian worker supporting clients in the field, your needs will be very different to that of a social worker engaged in child protection work, or a teacher looking to better- support vulnerable students with special educational needs or a health visitor seeking to promote the well-being and development of children and families. Moreover, each individual and community has clients with differing needs. For some people who are vulnerable, support may necessitate tertiary, therapeutic interventions for trauma or the toxic effects of chronic shame or addiction. For others, escape from cyclical vulnerability may necessitate the injection of material capital into a run-down neighbouring to develop essential infrastructure that boosts people life chances and opportunities for education, health and employment. Alternatively building resilience may involve developing parenting skills, or positive role models in the community or exploring how to promote the internal motivation to engage in life-affirming change.

For these reasons, my intention in writing the book has been to restrict my aims to drawing the reader's attention to important ideas, theories and concepts that demonstrate how vulnerability is created and maintained and how resilience may be promoted and developed, on the basis that this will provides a solid, conceptual platform for the development of new ideas and effective strategies for working vulnerable individuals and groups.

In addition, you will find that the book has a copious bibliography that will enable you to delve deeper into topics that are of relevance to your area of interest and occupation. So without further ado, let us begin by exploring vulnerability.

Part One
Vulnerability

Chapter 1
Defining vulnerability

Definitions of vulnerability

At one level, vulnerability is a simple thing with which we are all experientially familiar. At another, it is a complex conceptual phenomenon that defies simple definition.

Vulnerability, for example, is variously viewed as an elemental human condition that flows from the physical and psychological frailties that we all possess and the many risks that we negotiate as we go about our normal lives, and as a self-inflicted condition associated with the existence of negative personality traits, attitudes and behaviour, and as a phenomenon that can be directly traced to the impact of factors that lie external to individuals, such as insufficiencies, inequities and flaws in people's social, economic and geographic environment that undermine their ability to cope.

In addition, vulnerability is commonly used to refer to a state that is associated with the presence of factors that result in an immediate state of harm and to a state of susceptibility that increases the likelihood of vulnerability at some point in the future. A road traffic accident victim, admitted for emergency treatment with life-threatening injuries, can be said to be in an acute and immediate state of vulnerability, whilst an individual who contracts rheumatic fever in childhood is susceptible to developing heart valve failure in later life.

Definitions of vulnerability also vary depending on the area in which they are developed and operationalised. In humanitarian spheres, for example, the United Nations Educational, Scientific and Cultural Organisation (UNESCO), operationally divides vulnerability into a normative, elemental state associated with the human condition and a state of special vulnerability emanating from adverse factors in people's environments. Whilst people working in information technology commonly use the term vulnerability to refer to a specific software weakness that leaves the operating system vulnerable to malicious, external attack. In the field of health, it is common to distinguish between acute and chronic forms of vulnerability, whereas vulnerability may be defined in quasi-legal terms to enable specific protective or preventative measure to be put in place. In social work, case workers engaged in child protection work can designate a child as being 'at risk' and place them on a Child Protection Register, whilst a vulnerable child in education may be defined as a child with special educational needs and disabilities.

Moreover, vulnerability is commonly treated as both a subjective phenomenon that can only be understood from the perspective of the individual and as objective one that can be directly measured and assessed. In psychology, for example, it is recognised that individual perceptions of vulnerability are heavily influenced by personal perceptions relating to experiential factors and perceived capacity for coping. Whilst, in economics, vulnerability is often viewed through the lens of quantifiable metrics that measure extrinsic social and geopolitical factors, such as social and educational inequality and marginalisation, unequal hierarchies and power imbalances and poor governance and corruption.

In a similar vein, epidemiologists engaged in the field of public health commonly employ statistics and health metrics, such as prevalence, incidence and relative-risk, to gauge a given population's vulnerability from exposure to disease and other communicative forms of harm.

When taking these varying perspectives into account, it is of little surprise that no single definition or method of measurement has been found that satisfactorily captures the complexity and scope of vulnerability. However, as we will learn during the course of this book, vulnerability can be productively explained as a broad dynamic entity that varies in response to the synergistic interaction of factors that are internal to individuals and factors that are external to individuals, which have the cumulative effect of eroding an individual or community's capacity to adapt and cope with adverse events and demanding change.

The aim of the first section of this book is to identify and show how these factors contribute to the development and maintenance of vulnerability in individual and groups, but first I want to turn to the idea that human vulnerability is a universal phenomenon, that is part of the human condition.

Vulnerability as a *condition humana*

Viewed from a historical perspective, the idea that vulnerability exists as an essential human phenomenon, or a *condition humana*, can be traced back to the time of the ancient Greeks. According to the American professor of philosophy, Marina Berzins McCoy, for example, the Greeks viewed vulnerability as an integral element of the human condition and believed that recognising one's frailties and mastering them was a feat of achievement on a par with overcoming serious wounds and injuries. Indeed, acceptance of vulnerability as an essential or universal human condition is reflected in many philosophical works and religious articles of faith. In Christian teachings, Jesus is born into a poor family in precarious circumstances, but his human vulnerability is depicted as a strength that allows him to forge an intimate connection with his fellow beings who live in poverty and suffering. Similarly, the Chinese professor of religion and philosophy, Ellen Zhang, draws attention to Buddhist philosophy and the belief that personal enlightenment, and relief from anxious self-concern, flows from recognition and acceptance of suffering as an unavoidable part of life that binds us in mutual compassion and vulnerability.

Many of these ideas are reflected in modern psychology. The Dutch neuroscientist, Christian Keysers, for instance, proposes (in an echo of Buddhist philosophy) that our encounters with vulnerability, loss and hardship create an experiential template that allows us to empathically contextualise and understand other people's feelings and behaviours. Likewise, there is broad agreement among psychologists that anticipatory stress and anxiety commonly arise when we deny our own vulnerability or spend too much time fretting about life and events that have not yet happened. Indeed, the cognitive processes that support empathy and positive self-awareness can also work in reverse to create a template that supports harsh, self-denigrating evaluations of the kind that are commonly associated with stress and depression. As we will learn, the reasons for this are manyfold and include factors that have a significant impact on individuals and groups, such as maltreatment in childhood and social marginalisation.

However, according to the American neurobiologist, Robert Sapolsky, human vulnerability also has its roots in primary biological processes. In his book *Why Zebras Don't Get Ulcers*, he contrasts the origins of stress in humans and our mammalian counterparts. Zebras, he argues, don't suffer from stress-related illnesses, because they live entirely in the present and lack the cognitive capacity to ruminate about past failures or to fret about what future threat might lie around the next corner. When a zebra experiences fear, it is a purely physical experience that results from the automatic release of the neurotransmitter's epinephrine and norepinephrine in preparation for extraordinary levels of activity when a threat is detected in the animal's immediate environment.

Humans, like zebras, also experience physical fear. Indeed, it is the release of these same neurotransmitters that we associate with the pounding heart and jelly legs that occur immediately after we have instinctively leaped to avoid an oncoming car or startled in response to a loud noise in the street that sounds like an explosion. However, where we differ from our mammalian counterparts is that we also experience fear and other forms of emotional and social vulnerability that are cognitive in origin, courtesy of the development of powerful cognitive systems in the neocortex (literally the new brain), which have given us the ability to conjure up worst-case scenarios and engage in negative, self-other comparisons that give rise to powerful, negative emotions, which include, not only fear, but also anger, embarrassment and shame. This does not mean that the development of these cognitive capacities has created a condition of human suffering in humans that is biologically inevitable, because these same faculties also enable emotional literacy and other resilient processes, as we will discover later in this book. What it does mean, however, is that the human brain has developed the unique propensity to generate and perpetuate states of vulnerability that are to some degree independent of factors that exist in our immediate environment.

Vulnerability as weakness

In contemporary western culture, we have a strong tendency to focus on the negative aspects of vulnerability that are associated with unpleasant states, such as stress, anxiety and depression, rather than embracing the positive aspects of vulnerability, such as the idea that personal experience of hurt, loss, betrayal and anger builds empathic capacity and acts as springboard for engaging in processes of change that ultimately improve personal resilience and well-being. As a consequence of this, we have come to regard vulnerability as a source of emotional weakness that is best ignored, denied and avoided.

Yet if we delve deeper, we find a curious paradox, because we are also fascinated by human vulnerability and drawn to it, like moths to a flame. This is evident in the prominent role that vulnerability plays in works of fiction, starting with the humble comic book and ending with the great tragedies of literature. In comic books, for example, the mild-mannered scientist, Dr David Banner, alias the Incredible Hulk, has an incurable anger-management problem. Spider Man, alias Peter Parker, is forced to juggle mundane, everyday tasks with the responsibilities of being a superhero, whilst doing battle with an innate shyness and self-consciousness that renders him awkward around women. Likewise, what makes the plot of Superman stories interesting is not so much the existence of his super-human abilities, but his vulnerability to the fictional element, Kryptonite. Indeed, when we engage with these characters, we are reminded that even the most powerful of beings has an Achilles' heel and this basic theme is played out in the many of the great works of literature. In Scott Fitzgerald's' *Tender is the Night*, for example, the central protagonist and rich socialite, Dr Dick Diver, is consumed by a narcissistic, self-loathing that leads to rampant alcoholism and that fuels his eventual fall from grace. In a similar manner, Shakespeare's play *Macbeth* invites us to observe how unconstrained ambition leads to paranoia, and a bloody reign of terror and revenge that ultimately results in the suicide of his wife, Lady Macbeth.

We are captivated by these tails, because they afford us the opportunity to vicariously experience the darker sides of human vulnerability and mortality from a safe distance.

Yet, many authorities have argued that however much we might wish to suppress awareness of our vulnerability, it cannot be completely erased and exists at a level just below conscious awareness. The French philosopher, Gabriel Marcel suggested that this awareness periodically gives rise to existential angst, which may be broadly defined as state of fear relating to our non-existence or death. Angst is a Dutch-German word that is used to describe a state of being that goes beyond the common experience of anxiety, apprehension or stress. It is a state of terror and dread that occurs when events conspire to remind us of the impermeant nature of our existence. Such events include powerlessness, serious illness, loss and death, and events that instil a sense that ones' life is bereft of significant meaning or purpose.

The nature of existential angst in the human psyche provides another clue as to why we commonly associate vulnerability with weakness, but there are other factors at work too.

Research, for example, has shown we tend to view vulnerability as weakness of character and/or a state that people have brought on themselves. Evidence for this comes from research conducted by the American psychologists, Edward Jones and Victor Harris back in the 1960s, which revealed that we have a strong tendency to ascribe vulnerability to undesirable, traits and qualities that are intrinsic to individuals rather than to extrinsic, factors, events and circumstances that lie outside of the individual's control. Through this narrow lens, vulnerability in all its forms can be traced back to the existence of negative personality characteristics like laziness or lack of willpower. The Danish public health specialists, Ebbe, Nielsen and Allan Andersen, for example, found that 74% of the Danish general public polled in a survey expressed the belief that clinically obese patients should be compelled to shoulder some of the costs of weight-loss surgery, because they were perceived to be wholly or partially responsible for being overweight. Likewise, an attitudinal survey regarding poverty-beliefs conducted by the Kaiser Family Foundation in the United States found that approximately half of those surveyed expressed the belief that poverty and unemployment were self-inflicted conditions. The collective inference from findings such as these is that people would not find themselves in a vulnerable state requiring the administration of public benefits or medical interventions were it not for the presence of undesirable traits and weakness of character.

Chapter 1: **Defining vulnerability**

Such views ultimately reinforce the negative view of vulnerability that we hold in the highly individualistic west and make it harder for us to view vulnerability through a positive lens.

We can observe this effect in the way we utilise common synonyms for vulnerability, such as exposed, defenceless, feeble, gullible and helpless. Whilst we readily employ these terms to describe vulnerable individuals, we rarely use them to describe organisations or structures that are vulnerable, ineffective and at risk of failure. True, we might use the term 'exposed' to describe a financial institution that is at risk from questionable, sub-prime loans, dodgy share-dealings or global, economic depression, but we rarely, if ever, refer to a failing organisation as weak, feeble, gullible or helpless. These are terms that we reserve, almost exclusively, to describe people, which have the effect of reinforcing the notion that vulnerability is a thing of human weakness and the reflexive expectation that organisational failure is always the fault of individuals rather than, say, problems relating to poor management, communication and governance.

Moreover, the attribution of vulnerability to dispositional traits also extends to common social stereotypes that relate to variables, such as age, gender, ethnicity and class. These stereotypes are manyfold but include the assumption that children and the elderly as more inherently vulnerable than adults. Men are generally viewed as being more physically resilient and less emotionally vulnerable than women. We embellish the upper classes with qualities of leadership and resilience that are deemed to be absent in the lower classes and we continue to view ethnic minorities are culturally inferior, and powerlessly incapable of managing without the benefit of external support and instruction.

Yet, these stereotypes crumble on closer examination. At either end of the age spectrum, we find that children and the elderly are superbly resilient and adept at coping with change. Numerous studies have shown that adults are as vulnerable to stress and common mental health problems as those in any other age group. Research has shown that the excess rates of depression and anxiety in women that have been used to assert that women are more fragile are, in fact, linked to the excess female exposure to gender-based violence, lower social status and income, and gender biases in the diagnosis of common mental health problems (rather than emotional frailty). Reporting in the

Scandinavian Journal of Mental Health, for example, the Spanish public health researchers, Amaia Bacigalupe and Unai Martin, found that women were nearly twice as likely to receive a diagnosis of anxiety or depression than their male counterparts presenting with similar symptoms. In a similar vein, the belief that women are less constitutionally robust than men has recently been given short-shrift by the announcement that the female Nepalese Sherpa, Lhakpa Sherpa, had successfully scaled Mount Everest for the tenth time. Likewise, the belief that people from lower social status are less adept than their affluent peers at managing their resources has failed to stand up to scrutiny. The charitable organisation, Stand Together, for example, has reported that people living in poverty are generally extremely resourceful and routinely able to manage on meagre resources that would thwart their affluent counterparts. In addition, we are learning that many so-called 'primitive cultures' have coexisted for millennia in sustainable harmony with their environment, whilst this remains little more than a distant aspiration for the 'superior', post-industrial countries across the globe.

Vulnerability and cultural intolerance

The American shame researcher Rene Brown suggests that in our struggle to achieve self-perfection we have become intolerant of vulnerability in ourselves and critical of weakness and human error in others, and as we have just learnt, this can extend to victim-blaming people who find themselves struggling with conditions, like poverty and obesity.

In a similar vein, the Australian researcher Adam Fraser makes the point that our fixation with strength and resilience is responsible for promoting widely held beliefs that people are to blame for organisational failure, rather than systems and structures, which promote unrealistic goals and expectations. These beliefs and attitudes appear to be deep-seated and culturally rooted in the west. According to the Argentinian Bioethicist, Florencia Luna, for example, when people start to fail or function ineffectively our knee-jerk response is to attribute ineffectiveness and failure to personal frailty and weakness rather than the cascade effects that can result from multiple systemic failures. I will examine these issues in detail in the second section of this book and show that organisational failure is often linked to factors such as null

Chapter 1: Defining vulnerability

tolerance of human error, inadequate reporting systems for recording and rectifying mistakes and hierarchical decision-making structures that do not sit well with multi-disciplinary team working that typically characterises areas of work that involve supporting vulnerable people.

Cultural intolerance of vulnerability can also have undesirable cohort effects. The New Zealand psychologists, Sarah McKenzie and her colleagues, for example, state that cultural machoism in male cohorts is often associated with intolerance of 'feminine emotions', like anxiety and sorrow. Such attitudes have been found in working-class areas of the United Kingdom, where they are associated with low rates help-seeking for mental health issues, and high rates of stress, depression and alcoholism. Whilst in upper-class cultures, it may be manifest as a 'stiff-upper lip' and emotional illiteracy. Moreover, the British social psychologist, Antony Manstead has provided evidence that those who inhabit the upper echelons of society (which has traditionally prized the traits of stoicism and self-reliance) have greater difficulty than their working-class counterparts in engaging in compassionate perspective-taking and are more likely to attribute faults in others to internal attributes rather than situational factors.

Likewise, differences in tolerance for vulnerability can be found cross-culturally. The Canadian psychologist, Loren Toussaint, for instance, states that collectivist cultures tend to be more tolerant and compassionate and more likely to engage in emotional forgiveness than individualistic cultures, which tend to place greater emphasis on decisional forgiveness. Emotional forgiveness involves a high degree of empathic, perspective-taking and the replacement of negative emotions like anger and jealousy with positive, compassionate ones, whilst decisional forgiveness tends to focus on specific deeds and acts without attending to the accompanying emotions. Emotional forgiveness has been shown to be more beneficial for well-being, because negative emotions is addressed rather than ignored.

Taken as whole, these perspectives show that vulnerability is an essential part of the human condition, and we all have some form of Achilles' heel, though the form it takes varies greatly from person to person. This is not to say that some people aren't simply more unlucky and more vulnerable than others. In one of my favourite songs, *Some Folks Lives Roll Easy*, the musician Paul Simon notes that whist some people's lives seem to drift through life without being beset by major hassles, others are dogged by difficulty that seemingly occurs through no fault of their own. Indeed, many people struggle with disability and chronic illness all their lives or find themselves, seemingly, in the wrong place at the wrong time, whilst others are born with a silver spoon yet in their mouth. Yet, in many instances, vulnerability results directly from human actions that render people powerless and disenfranchised or struggling to cope in conditions of poverty with limited access to the services and resources that you and I largely take for granted. I want to move to examine the factors that are known to create and maintain human vulnerability shorty, but before we get there, I want to look at vulnerability as a psychological construct in order to debunk the idea that vulnerability is a fixed, negative personality trait or set of traits that reside within individuals.

Vulnerability as a fluid versus fixed construct

A construct is a psychological concept that is invented (constructed) to help us describe and explain the things that can be observed, but not directly measured (like physical entities, such as sugar and salt). A good construct allows scientists to accurately explain human behaviour in line with theoretical predictions.

Vulnerability is a human construct, and it is generally construed in two diametrically opposed ways, namely, as a fixed entity that is explained by the presence of stable, trait-like characteristics that reside within individuals (or groups) or as a fluid entity that is a product of continuous interaction between an individual's personal characteristics, their personal circumstances and the environments in which they live.

Of these two ways of looking at vulnerability, the former is the most prevalent, but also the least accurate. In explaining this, the American psychologist, Carol Dweck, and her colleagues, proposes that people commonly hold implicit theories about human behaviour, which centre on the belief that behaviour is driven primarily by personal characteristics, which include traits, age, gender, social class, disability and mental illness. Moreover, whilst she describes these beliefs as psychologically naïve, she states that they frequently coalesce to form negative stereotypes that result in individuals and groups being

Chapter 1: **Defining vulnerability**

erroneously labelled as helpless, incompetent and lazy. The French social psychologists, Odile Rohmer and Eva Louve, for example, found that employment attitudes towards disabled people in the workplace frequently cluster around stereotyped assumptions of dependency and incompetence, which result in disempowering condescension and pity.

Dweck argues that such views are psychologically simplistic and at odds with the alternative perspective, which portrays human behaviour and vulnerability as dynamic, fluid phenomena that result largely from the effects of situational factors rather than personal characteristics per se. Indeed, as we will learn in this book, vulnerability often has its roots in adverse situations and environments that promote powerlessness and stressful cascade effects that have little to do with personality. People who have a physical disability or psychological disability, for example, often struggle to deal with negative societal attitudes, relationship problems, unemployment and the loss of state benefits, which create new levels of vulnerability. Similarly, research shows that the environment people inhabit is often *the* determinant factor in the creation and maintenance of vulnerability, and for this reason, many economists, social scientists and humanitarian organisations now elect to define vulnerability in terms of human capital (i.e., social support), material capital (i.e., schools and hospitals) and economic capital (i.e., wealth), because their presence promotes resilience in the face of adversity, whilst their absence often has the effect of locking people into entrenched and cyclical states of powerlessness and vulnerability.

However, vulnerability is not an all or nothing condition. There are degrees of vulnerability that are, in part at least, determined by how individuals perceive their situation relative to the availability and effectiveness of support systems and structures. Drawing on modern stress theory, vulnerability is increasingly being viewed as the product of a negative imbalance between the perceived demands of a given situation and the individual's perceived ability to cope, which adds weight to the idea that vulnerability should be viewed as a dynamic construct that is in large part determined by how people, groups and communities perceive themselves and their environment. Indeed, throughout this book, you will find that we return again and again to the idea that vulnerability is best viewed as fluid and dynamic construct that is a result of interaction between intrinsic and extrinsic factors with the latter often being the major determinant of vulnerability.

How we manage our vulnerability

We do not like to be reminded of our common vulnerability and many people invest a considerable amount of time and energy avoiding the unpleasant feelings like fear and anxiety. However, despite our best-efforts, events inevitably occur that forcibly bring our vulnerability back to the fore of consciousness. Such events often include the loss of a family member or serious personal illness or relational problems, like divorce and employment and, more laterally, the advent of the SARS-CoV-2 (COVID-19) pandemic and the recent war in Ukraine, which have both served to remind us of the fragile and impermanent nature of the world that we live in.

Yet, despite these recent events, many of us who are privileged to live in the affluent west have been suffered from calamitous, large-scale events that wreak havoc on civilian populations. Indeed, until quite recently, severe poverty, famine, and geo-political disasters linked to war, earthquakes, hurricanes, floods and endemic diseases like malaria have appeared as things that occur only to people in third-world countries far removed from our experiential event-horizon.

Yet, occasionally, this illusion of vulnerability is punctured, and we are exposed to these horrific events on television or social media that trigger what psychologists call vicarious vulnerability. If, like me, for example, you watched the unfolding terrorist attack on the Twins Towers in New York in 2001 or 2004, Boxing Day Tsunami in Indonesia, or the enormous shock waves that resulted from the ignition of thousands of kilos of fertiliser in the centre of Beirut, you may have experienced a sense of horror and disbelief as though the events unfolding before your eyes were too awful to be real. In metaphorical terms, it as though the genie has seemingly escaped from the bottle labelled 'existential angst', and we find ourselves confronted with the brutal reality that life can be harsh, unforgiving and unpredictable.

Viewed from a philosophical perspective, existential angst is the primal source of all vulnerability – a unique, human condition that exists as a deep-rooted state of fear and horror that waxes and wanes over time, depending upon events and circumstances. Under normal conditions, it exists as little more than background noise, akin to the sound of traffic in a city as we go about our daily lives. However, when our angst

Chapter 1: **Defining vulnerability**

is re-awakened by adverse events, we may find ourselves temporarily overwhelmed by feelings of fear and dread or chronically disabled by trauma or we may find ourselves in the midst of an existential crisis characterised by degenerative self-doubt or a sense that life no longer has any coherent sense of purpose or meaning.

Because angst is deeply unpleasant and unsettling, we have developed various ways of protecting ourselves. The simplest, and most common method of avoiding anxiety entails conscious and deliberative actions that are designed to keep our minds busy and occupied. If that fails, we may resort to self-medicating our anxiety with alcohol or other addictive substances or behaviours, such as gambling, shopping or sex. However, we have also evolved more subtle ways of managing awareness of our fragility. The American social psychologist Melvin Lerner, for example, has proposed that children are socialised from a young age to believe that the world is a safe, predictable place that is characteristically fair and just. According to this world view, goodness is always rewarded, and bad things only happen to wicked people who bring adversity upon themselves. Lerner referred to these as *Just-World Beliefs* which he argued are intrinsic to classic fairy-tale classics, like *Snow White*, and more, laterally contemporary works, such as *Harry Potter*, which serve to create an implicit social contract that encourages all of us to be good citizens and to abide by the rules. Of course, fairy tales are not the only vehicle for such social contracts. Religion, for example, has a similar formative function in providing a moral imperative and comforting, explanative for events that we normally associate with loss and existential angst. According to the Norwegian philosopher, Peter Wessel Zapffe, for example, the rules, laws and rituals that are embodied in the mechanisms of state, society and religion give life a coherent sense of meaning and purpose in the face of adversity, a process he referred to as anchoring. Whilst the rule of law helps to prevent us descending into a state of chaos where the strongest prevail, rituals mediate angst and stress by giving our lives a sense of structure and purpose, and an external focus of attention that offers relief from intrusive thoughts and anxieties.

Such rituals take two basic forms. There are the informal rituals (or if you like routines) that we commonly employ to start and end the day and there are the formalised rituals that are culturally rooted in hierarchical structures and institutions, such as the monarchy, military, universities and the church. According to the Canadian psychologist Nicholas Hobson and colleagues, these formalised rituals, and the structures and hierarchies that accompany them, help us cope with highly stressful activities and support us in making sense of difficult and perplexing events, such as death and loss. When studying adult bereavement, for example, the British Psychiatrist, Collin Murray Parkes found that the ritualised procedures surrounding death provided a sense of meaning and comfort for the bereaved and their families. The highly formalised rituals associated with burying the dead were found to provide a sense of order in the presence of chaos, whilst the funeral wake marked the beginning of the formal process of mourning, and an important opportunity for social connection and emotional support.

Rituals have also been found to increase in frequency during periods of stress and can take the form of magical or superstitious thinking. Magical thinking is broadly defined as an act that is performed to ward of bad luck or evil spirits and it is a phenomenon that is deeply engrained in the human psyche and culture. The American psychologist, Alison Brooks and her colleagues, for example, found that Melanesian sailors putting to sea in dangerous and capricious ocean waters performed elaborate rituals prior to leaving, but such rituals were absent when launching into waters that were predictable and well-known. Brooks also reports on research which showed that Israeli civilians living in areas subject to incoming missile attacks were more likely to engage in magical thinking than their counterparts living in safe areas. Ritualistic behaviour is also found in elite sport where stress-management is paramount. These rituals can have an obsessive-compulsive quality. It has, for example, been reported that during competitions, the top-flight tennis player, Rafael Nadal always lays his water bottles out in a specific way and consistently drinks from one bottle and then the other, but never from the same bottle twice in a row. Whilst such rituals sometimes appear senseless or even odd, it is noteworthy that during the early days of the SARS-CoV-2 pandemic with its frequent lockdowns, one of the things that people commonly lamented was being excluded from the normal routines and activities that were woven into the daily fabric of their lives.

Chapter 1: **Defining vulnerability**

Beyond rituals, we know that the human brain has developed a range of cognitive coping strategies that act like a cerebral volume control which can turn down negative emotions like anxiety. The American psychologists, Shelley Taylor and Jonathan Brown, for example, published a seminal paper back in the 1980s which identified a range of common, illusory self-perceptions that provide us with an inflated sense of optimism and personal control. They noted that we routinely over-estimate our personal abilities. We habitually nurture the belief that the future will be better than the past and, when engaged in activities like gambling, over-estimate our ability to control the forces of chance.

Rather interestingly, these illusory self-perceptions are largely absent in people who are clinically depressed. In an equally thought-provoking paper, the American psychologists, Lauren Alloy and Lyn Abramson found that people who were clinically depressed were more accurate in their self-appraisal than their non-depressed counterparts, leading to a *chicken-or-the-egg* type debate about whether the absence of illusory self-perceptions leads to depression or whether depression leads to the absence of illusory self-perceptions. To date, the jury is still out on that one.

Viewed from a traditional perspective, illusory self-perceptions have taken their place alongside unconscious, Freudian defence mechanisms, like denial and repression, which are believed to stem from the automatic, unconscious processes that are designed to the self from angst and other forms of vulnerability. Moreover, scientists at Israel's Bar-Ilan University have provided evidence which suggests that the brain may have learnt to protect itself rather than *the self* from knowledge of its own mortality. In an experiment, they hooked volunteers up to a neuro-imaging monitor and asked them to watch a series of facial images accompanied by words relating to death. They found that brain activity was supressed when words like 'funeral' or 'burial' were paired with images of the participant's own face, but not when paired with the face of a stranger.

It appears that there is a lot that we still have a lot to learn about the psychological mechanisms that evolved to protect us from vulnerability.

Chapter 2
How vulnerability is created and maintained

Vulnerability, control and powerlessness

What rituals, routines and cognitive biases in perception have in common is the power to equip us with a sense of order and control as we go about our daily lives. Indeed, the importance of these factors is well documented in psychological research. We are happiest and healthiest when our environment is predictable and safe, and we feel able to exercise a high degree of control over the various aspects of life that are important to us. Conversely we are most stressed and unhappy when we feel powerlessness to affect meaningful change.

The importance of control, and its antithesis powerlessness, was vividly illustrated in two seminal pieces of research conducted in the 1970s by two American psychologists, Jay Weiss and Martin Seligman.

Weiss exposed genetically identical laboratory rats to painful electric shocks in two experimental conditions that were designed to examine the effects of powerlessness on physical well-being. In the first condition, rats received a series of painful electric shocks that were immediately preceded by a warning light. In the second condition, rats received an identical series of shocks, but without any form of warning. What Weiss found was both illuminating and disturbing. The rats that had received a warning remained free from major physiological damage, whilst those that had received no warning rapidly developed ulcers and died of exhaustion. Weiss reasoned that the physiological damage

Chapter 2: **How vulnerability is created and maintained**

to rats in the second condition was due to acute, unremitting stress caused by exposure to an environment that was fundamentally unpredictable and unsafe. In a related experiment, Seligman placed dogs in a cage and exposed them to a series of painful and inescapable electric shocks. After a short period of time, he found that the animals made no attempt to escape from the cage even when they were afforded the opportunity to do so. Seligman reasoned that the dogs had become passive, because they had learnt that they were powerless to control their environment. They had entered a state that he named Learned Helplessness.[1]

These early experiments demonstrated that stress and helplessness are both closely associated with powerlessness. Helplessness occurs when we learn that we are unable to affect meaningful change in our environment and stress results from loss of control and exposure to unsafe and unpredictable environments. However, whilst the evocation of powerlessness sometimes relates to intentional and malevolent acts, it can also result from actions that are intended to be entirely benevolent. The Victorian Mental Health Asylums, for example, were established to create a safe-haven for vulnerable people with chronic mental health issues, but their rigid routines and hierarchical structures created a dependency culture that inadvertently fostered helplessness and institutionalisation, with the result that many of the in-patients were unable to fend for themselves in the community when the asylums were closed in the latter part of the last century. In a similar vein, the Canadian psychologist, Tiana Rust reports that relatives caring for loved ones with Alzheimer's disease often do too much and unknowingly induce a dependency script that robs sufferers of vital motor skills and self-belief. Likewise, the Scottish social activist, Darren McGarvey argues that well-intentioned charities and non-governmental agencies are often guilty of doing things to vulnerable communities rather working with them to draw on available strengths and skills, which creates a state of dependency and apathy that readily feeds into pre-existing beliefs that such communities are incapable of helping themselves.

Whilst the ability to wield control over oneself and one's environment promotes resilience; loss of control sits at the centre of many models that seek to explain how vulnerability and powerlessness is created and maintained. If we go further and unpick the concept that we call control, we find that it is commonly employed in two discrete ways, namely to refer to a literal state of control in which people have the power and authority to make and execute decisions and a perceived state of control that is associated with positive beliefs, expectations and a sense of self-agency. Conversely, powerlessness relates to the inhibition of literal control, associated with pressing, external factors, such as socio-economic deprivation, poor governance and manmade or natural disasters, and internal beliefs and expectations that result in a perceived state of helplessness of the type identified by Seligman or a state of incapacity resulting from mental health problems, such as chronic depression or shame.

The distinction is an important one and I have drawn attention to it, because of the ramifications for how vulnerability is addressed. The remedy for vulnerability that is linked to personal perceptions of loss of control may involve treatment and therapy for underlying conditions like chronic stress, depression and shame, whilst vulnerability relating to the literal loss of control is more likely to necessitate interventions that are specifically geared to improving material resources and financial capital. However, it should be noted that the vulnerable people and communities often suffer from the effects of literal loss of control due to extraneous factors, such as poor governance and high corruption, *and* the effects of perceived loss of control due to the disempowering effects of marginalisation, discrimination, chronic depression and internalised shame. Indeed, it is now widely accepted that powerlessness, more often than not, emanates from a combination of intrinsic and extrinsic factors.

Powerlessness and loss of control are closely related to stress. According to the Transactional Theory of Stress, for example, stress occurs when the perceived demands of a given situation exceed an individual's perceived ability to cope. Viewed from this perspective, stress happens when we feel overwhelmed and out of control, and emphasis is placed on the term *perceived*, to signify that control is a function of individual perception rather than events per se. At first sight, this might feel counterintuitive, especially when thinking about people's responses to traumatic, large-scale disasters. However, the logic is revealed when we examine some of the problems that arise when we try to give common, significant life events a nominal or if you like 'average' stress rating.

Chapter 2: **How vulnerability is created and maintained**

Back in the 1970s, for example, the American psychiatrists Thomas Holmes and Richard Rahe designed an inventory of stressful life events to help clinicians predict the relative stressfulness of common, untoward events. At first sight, the inventory, (which can be readily accessed on-line) appears intuitively sensible. It is comprised of forty-three items that are rated on their level of stressfulness via a scale that runs from 0 to 100. At the top of the inventory, we find the death of a spouse, which is afforded a maximum score of 100, followed in second place by divorce with a score of 73, then marital separation with a score of 65. These seem to make intuitive sense. The loss of a spouse, for example, is commonly regarded as one the most stressful events that we can experience, and research shows that it is eclipsed only by the loss of a child. However, if we proceed down the Life Events Scale, we find an item placed third from the bottom, relating to major dietary change that scores a meagre 15 points and another below that relating to major holidays, which has an even lower stress score of 12. Now, if you happened to be suffering from an eating disorder, such as anorexia or bulimia, or were clinically obese due to an endocrine disorder, you might want to place the item relating to major dietary change at or the near the top of the stress inventory. Similarly, the UK mental health charity Mind reports that major holiday times, such as Christmas, are inherently stressful for people with chronic mental health problems, who feel left out, isolated and lonely. In a similar vein, although death of a spouse (which you may recall, scored a maximum of 100 points) is generally very stressful, there are exceptions. The death of one's partner in a marriage that has been lacking in intimacy or punctuated by episodic violence may result in significant relief rather than distress and viewed from an individual perspective, might warrant a relatively low stress score.

In short, life events are not fool-proof predictors of stress, because of contextual factors that affect individual perception. However, the British psychologists Ruth Spence, Lisa Kagan, and Antonia Bifulco argue that events *can* be useful in contextualising stress, when they take into account the presence of factors that are associated with universal stress, such as the severance of cherished emotional bonds, threats to our personal identity and threats to our physical and social security. Likewise, research has shown that certain conditions invariably give rise to stress. The American psychologists, Irving Janis and Leon Mann, for example, have shown that severe stress results from decisional conflict, a psychological condition that arises when we are compelled to choose between two or more unfavourable outcomes that each have potentially severe consequences. A family forced to choose between remaining in a dangerous war zone or fleeing to a refugee camp where disease and sexual exploitation are rumoured to be rife face decisional conflict as does as a woman who is forced between choosing a disfiguring, radical mastectomy or early death from stage three breast cancer. In a similar vein, some life events involve cascade effects that can overwhelm our capacity of coping. Patients who suffer an intracerebral haemorrhage (stroke), for instance, often have to cope with multiple stressors, such as hemiplegia and dysphasia, which may lead to loss of employment and financial problems, relationship difficulties and a crisis of identity.

Conversely returning to the Transactional model, research has shown that when we are exposed to untoward situations and events, our perceived capacity for coping is enhanced by the availability of good quality social support. In the literature on stress, support is typically broken down into instrumental or practical support and personal or emotional support. As a rule, we tend to associate the provision of emotional support with family, friends, colleagues, and the provision of instrumental support with statutory and non-statutory agencies that are designed to offer advice and practical assistance to those in need, and, whilst there may be exceptions to this rule, in all cases, support works by buffering us from the worst effects of stressful life events and stress by increasing our perceived capacity to cope.

The need to belong

Whilst social support works to enhance personal control, the same is true of the concept that sociologists and humanitarian organisations refer to as social inclusion. According to the United Nations' Department for Social and Economic Affairs, for example, social inclusion describes processes that ensure equal opportunities for all irrespective of social background, class or ethnicity, and it incorporates concepts, such as social cohesion, which refer to a communities' shared sense of values and purpose and the various processes that enhance active participation in democratic decision-making.

Social inclusion also relates to our deep instinctive need to belong to a social group and is closely associated with feelings of belonging, trust, control, and personal legitimacy in the sense of being liked and valued by those whose opinions we cherish. Social exclusion on the other hand invariably generates considerable anxiety and stress. Viewed from an evolutionary perspective, psychologists have proposed that we find social exclusion is innately stressful, because, if we go far enough back in time, to be ostracised from one's social group was tantamount to a death sentence. Likewise, the British social psychologists Paul Hutchinson, Dominic Abrams, and Julie Christian state that social exclusion is associated with intolerable feelings of rejection, ostracism, but also anger, hostility and self-defeating behaviours that are associated with self-harm, criminality and problems of addiction. In fact, the need for social affiliation and group identity and the problems that arise when these are absent were famously described by the French sociologist Emil Durkheim, who proposed that exclusion from our peers and mainstream society ultimately results in anomie, a state of powerlessness and abjection that arises when individuals or groups feel fundamentally out of kilter with their social milieu. Indeed, anomie has been used to explain the high rates of alcoholism and suicide in many disenfranchised indigenous groups that have been effectively ostracised from mainstream society.

Social exclusion is also closely linked to the concept known as marginalisation, which the Israeli academics Michal Razer and Victor Friedman define as a state of being in which people lack access to key benefits and activities afforded to people in society and which the Scottish researcher Joan Mowat states is associated with low levels of community trust, powerlessness and reduced motivation to engage in positive, life-affirming change.

These two concepts, marginalisation and social exclusion, disproportionately affect people who sit on the perimeters of society, including those from poor backgrounds, those who belong to minority ethnic groups and those who suffer from a physical or mental disability. Indeed, people from socially deprived backgrounds are routinely subjected to marginalisation and discrimination that create the conditions for powerlessness, poor education and health. Taking some examples, ELDIS, an offshoot of the United Kingdom's Institute of Development Studies, reports that social exclusion frequently deprives socially marginalised children of education and development opportunities, which lock them into cycles of inter-generational poverty. Likewise, Hutchinson, Abrams and Christian note that the high adult morbidity and mortality rates and excess infant deaths found in black and ethnic minority groups living in the affluent west can be directly traced to the effects of poverty, marginalisation and sub-optimal access to health and education. Additionally, Israeli Professor of Nursing, Maayan Agmon and colleagues report that the routine marginalisation and social exclusion of people with disability often results in their being infantilised as individuals without adult, sexual needs.

Poverty and vulnerability

There is an indisputable link between poverty and vulnerability, which is most starkly evidenced in the high rates of excess morbidity and mortality that are found in many poor communities across the globe. Yet, poverty has proved to be a surprisingly difficult construct to define, and people hold differing views about what poverty really constitutes. Those of you who are old enough to remember the horrific images of starving children in the BBC's 'biblical famine broadcast' from northern Ethiopia in 1984, for example, will recall iconic scenes of deprivation and human misery that set the bar for how many people in the affluent west envisage poverty. As a consequence of this and other high-profile, humanitarian disasters, many people in the affluent west have come to equate the concept of poverty with profound, abject misery and are dismissive of the idea that local phenomena, like foodbanks, are genuine indicators of economic hardship.

This raises several questions. How should poverty be defined? Does real poverty only exist in third world, developing countries, and if it exists in the affluent west, what baseline measures should be applied in defining it? The answers to these questions are complex. Whilst financial indicators are frequently employed to define poverty, they are problematic, not least because the baseline measures that are applied in affluent countries differ markedly from those employed in impoverished parts of the world like sub-Saharan Africa. The World Bank's baseline for poverty in third world countries, for example, is defined as earning less than $1.90 per person per day, whilst in the affluent, United States, the baseline is defined as earning less than $12,000.00 per year plus $4,000 for each household member (which works out at $54.00 per day for a household with two children).

These types of disparity have led some authorities to evoke the concept of absolute poverty, defined by the British economist Richard Layard, as not having the basic means to support yourself or your family. However, even this definition is problematic, and some authorities advocate that absolute poverty must take account not only of material deprivation, but also marginalisation and powerlessness and quality of life as defined by objective measures, such as access to good health and education and subjective factors, such as how happy and satisfied people are with their lot. In theory, for example, a community might live in relative poverty (compared to the affluent west), but still be reasonably content and happy with their lot. This perspective has been adopted by the United Nations, which combines fiscal measures with measures gauging people's perceived quality of life and happiness when assessing poverty. Explaining this, Jörg Schimmel, who is a senior programme officer at the United Nations Development Agency, states that happiness and well-being are complex constructs that cannot be adequately defined with reference to the abundance of material wealth. Happiness research, he states, consistently shows that well-being is more closely related to how individuals judge their overall quality of life rather than the accumulation of personal wealth. In a similar vein, Layard proposes that happiness and quality of life are best defined by factors, such as the degree of autonomy that people enjoy, the levels of community cohesion and social trust and the quality of the political systems with particular reference to inclusive and effective governance.

Happiness and vulnerability

To complicate things further, research shows that there is an inverse relationship between wealth and happiness. The accumulation of personal wealth does not necessarily increase a person's subjective well-being. In his book, *Affluenza*, the psychologist Oliver James argues that in our constant pursuit of wealth and gain, we have lost sight of the importance of social affiliation, friendship, trust and intimate relationships, and this has resulted in a psychological malaise that people believe can only be resolved by accumulating more wealth. Layard echoes this in stating that there is a point at which the accumulation of wealth results in diminishing returns. Indeed, the literature indicates that extreme wealth is often accompanied by extreme unhappiness. The American psychologists, Daniel Kahneman and Angus Deaton, for example, found that whilst rich people who earn more than one million US dollars a year subjectively report higher levels of happiness, their self-perceptions are not supported by objective measures of emotional well-being.

It has been suggested that this paradox can be explained by the idea that affluence erodes our sense of social connectedness and common humanity. The psychologists Paul Piff and Jake Moskowitz, for example, state that research shows that richer people tend to be more independent and self-orientated, and less likely to engage in prosocial behaviour than their poorer counterparts who (perhaps through economic expediency) are more inter-dependent and other-orientated on measures of compassion and concern. This matters, according to the psychologists Louise Hawkley and John Cacioppo, because our basic need for social affiliation and loneliness is not readily assuaged by the accumulation of wealth.

In consideration of these complexities, many authorities prefer to employ the construct of socio-economic deprivation, rather than poverty per se, because socio-economic deprivation is a universal concept that can be accurately defined and assessed.[2] According to the American Psychological Association, for example, socio-economic deprivation can be measured directly through indices, such as financial security, employment, educational attainment and literacy, social status, quality of life, psychological well-being and levels of personal aspiration. In a similar vein, negative indices, such as financial insecurity, chronic unemployment and low social status, have been reliably shown to keep people locked into poverty from one generation to the next.

In order to provide a definitive understanding of what powerlessness means to be people that are locked in poverty and social deprivation, the World Bank commissioned a report at the turn of the last century, which gathered information about the experiences of over 60,000 poor women and men from sixty countries around the world. The study, called *The Voices of the Poor*, found that powerlessness was deemed to arise from multiple, interwoven disadvantages that make poverty difficult if not impossible to escape. Poverty-evoked powerlessness was associated with social marginalisation and stigmatisation, abuse and social exclusion, the existence of weak and fragmented institutions, and through being unable to exercise control over one's environment and make things happen (not unlike the unfortunate creatures in Weiss and Seligman's experiments).

Closer to home, a study evaluating the UK's Troubled Families Programme, which was designed to tackle key factors associated with intergenerational poverty, such as child-maltreatment, drug abuse and crime, found that on average, families were grappling with nine different problems per household unit. The neighbourhoods concerned were often blighted by high levels of unemployment, abuse, neglect and domestic violence. Families were typically headed by a lone parent and many of the children concerned had special educational needs with high rates of school refusal and school exclusion. In addition, a significant number of families had chronic health problems at levels comparable or higher than that commonly found in elderly populations, and more than half of the families had been involved in crime or acts of anti-social behaviour with one in three children having a criminal conviction.

Blaming the victims

Despite copious evidence to the contrary, research has shown that many people believe poverty is something that people ultimately bring upon themselves. The Dutch social scientist, Dorota Lepianka's pan-European survey of attitudes to poverty, for example, revealed that 11% of those polled believed that poverty was attributable to laziness or lack of willpower and, whilst the British political scientist Peter Dorey found that the comparable rate in the United Kingdom was 27%, a survey conducted in the United States, by the Population Reference Bureau, found that a staggering 48% of respondents believed that those in poverty were not doing enough to help themselves.

There are many varying explanations for this. From a cultural perspective, people in the United States have traditionally placed a greater value on self-reliance than Europeans, and this is particularly true of the Scandinavian countries, whose political systems emphasise collective, social responsibility. As a consequence, in societies where self-reliance is esteemed and expected, events such as poverty and employment are more likely to be seen to be seen as a self-imposed deviation from the unwritten law that people are ultimately responsible for their own well-being and that of their family. Viewed from a psychological perspective, the belief that poverty is somehow self-imposed flows from cognitive biases, such as the Fundamental Attribution Error, that we encountered earlier, which are formed at a pre-conscious level together with implicit rules and assumptions that we automatically assume are a given. Conversely, the reverse holds true. Wealth and privilege are seen to flow from hard work and personal enterprise rather than some accident of birth. We tend to assume, for example, that people who make it to elite universities like Oxford, Cambridge and Harvard must be very intelligent, rather than stopping to consider whether their places at such prestigious institutions might be explained, at least in part, by their privileged backgrounds, which proffer access to elite coaching and small pupil-teacher pupil ratios, which are known to make a significant difference to learning outcomes. Professor Frederik Mosteller's classic study of class sizes in the US state of Tennessee, for example, showed that being taught in small classes in early grade education resulted in significant and persistent improvements in educational performance vis-a-vis pupils taught in larger classes. In a similar vein, we are inclined to assume that people who are obese lack the willpower to resist eating rich, sugary food, rather than considering the possible role of endocrine disorders or the deliberative actions of the food industry in purposively promoting hard to resist, fat-sugar-salt combinations that are designed to target the brain's innate, opiate reward systems.

In addition, it has been suggested that we happily engage in victim-blaming, because our brains prefer simple answers to complex problems. It takes time and effort to understand the myriad of complex, interacting factors that give rise to poverty or obesity or to explore how social class affects educational attainment, and it is so much simpler to attribute what we observe to personal traits and characteristics that

Chapter 2: **How vulnerability is created and maintained**

reside within the individual. However, there is another, equally powerful mechanism which can explain why we tend to attribute behaviour to people's innate characteristics, and it is one that we encountered earlier; namely our Just-World Beliefs, which stem from our fundamental need to view the world as a predictable and fair place where the good are rewarded and the guilty punished.

According to the logic of these beliefs, conditions like poverty, unemployment, obesity, alcoholism and even rape must in some way be self-inflicted and thus attributable to character flaws. Research conducted by the King's College Policy Institute in the United Kingdom, for example (conducted during the first SARS-Cov-2 lockdown), found that a significant number of people believed that unemployment was more likely to be caused by personal failure than chance. In a similar vein, Nielsen and Andersen's research, referred to earlier, showed that obese people were held to be at least partially response for their own predicament. Likewise, common defence strategies employed by defence lawyers in rape cases play on the idea that consent is somehow complicitly given if the victim was drinking alcohol or dressed in a 'sexually provocative manner' or was lacking in the decisional assertiveness required to unambiguously say no.

Some psychologists have referred to this effect as the Just World Fallacy, and whilst the associated beliefs might appear naive, fallacious, and child-like, when examined under a microscope, blaming the victim does has the power to make us feel safe and less vulnerable in what might otherwise be a world full of serendipitous threats and dangers. They allow us to reason that we won't get made unemployed if we are industrious. We won't get cancer if we exercise regularly and cut out foods that are high in fat and sugar and we won't fall victim to gender-based violence if we are cautious and sensible.

Causal explanations to one side, it is evident that many people simply have trouble believing that poverty exists in the affluent west. In fact, Professor William Wilson from Harvard University asserts that such beliefs are frequently bolstered by a media that is actively complicit in promoting and sustaining negative stereotypes and antipathy towards those who find themselves on the bottom rungs of society's ladder. Whilst I was researching material for this book, for example, it was evident that some parts of the British media actively sought to ascribe causality for the disproportionately high rates of SARS-CoV-2-related mortality in working class and ethnic minority groups to the moral failure of individuals to self-isolate and take self-protective measures, rather than to focus on identified, poverty-related factors that were reliably shown to increase exposure to the virus, such as front-line working, high density housing and inadequate sick pay to support self-isolation. On the positive side, however, the Joseph Rowntree Foundation, a major UK charity, has reported that attitudes towards the causes of poverty have softened somewhat since the 2008 financial crisis with more people prepared to countenance the role that situational factors play in creating poverty and vulnerability.

Vulnerability as a heritable condition

As you may know, many forms of serious illness and disease have a significant heritable component. Twin studies, for example, have shown that genetic factors can increase common cancer risk by up to 33%, whilst the overall burden of genetic risk for coronary heart disease has been estimated at 50%–60%. In a similar vein, recent heritability estimates for serious mental illness, such as schizophrenia, autistic spectrum disorder and depression, range from 79% for schizophrenia, to 38% for major depression to up to 80% for autistic spectrum disorder.

These estimates, however, are largely based on data from twin studies, which some authorities believe underestimate the true influence of environmental factors. The Canadian psychiatrist, Rudolph Uher, for example, argues that the heritable component of gene-environment interactions in biological research is almost certainly overestimated, because insufficient attention is paid to the role of the environmental factors in-utero, and to the reporting of data that are based on linear, statistical models, which are insensitive to the cumulative effects of crucial gene-environment interactions. Similar points are made by the American psychiatrists, Thomas Insel and Phillip Wang, who state that studies which show a high genetic component for mental illness highlight the inherent weakness in current genetic approaches; namely the failure to adequately account for the influence of factors that are known to adversely influence the development of the foetus in utero, which include vitamin D deficiency and alcohol misuse, and other factors that are suspected to negatively influence the gene expression in the developing foetus, such as infant parental stress and social deprivation.

Moreover, it is important to note that what we inherit from our parents is the genotype, which may be broadly defined as the sum-total of our individual genes. At a base level, the genotype modifies our risk of developing major disease. Through the genotype we inherit 'good genes' that protect us from disease and 'bad', variant genes that render us vulnerable to various physical and mental health problems. Variant genes, for example, are suspected of increasing the risk of high blood pressure and coronary heart disease in adulthood. Likewise, a variant gene is thought to inhibit the effective transport of the neurotransmitter, serotonin (5HT) in the brain raising the risk of adult depression.

However, just because we inherit variant genes does not mean they will be expressed. It is our phenotype that determines gene-expression, and everyone's phenotype is a cumulative product of their environment, personal lifestyle and behaviour and their temperaments and personality. It is, for example, the phenotype rather than the genotype that we observe in the middle-aged man who has developed insulin-dependent diabetes or the young girl whose failure to thrive in school has led to her being diagnosed with depression.

Indeed, convincing evidence for the role of gene-environmental interactions in promoting adult vulnerability for physical and mental illness comes from research associated with the Dunedin Longitudinal Study, which has followed 1,037 babies born in New Zealand between 1972 over five decades. Research that has employed the Dunedin study's data base has revealed that variations in the MAOI gene (which regulates the production of the neurotransmitters, non-epinephrine, serotonin and dopamine in the brain) appear to interact with life stressors to cause depression. Likewise, the 'breast-feeding gene', FADS2, affects how the body utilises fats and may account for the increases in intelligence that have been found in babies that are breast-fed versus formula fed, but only for babies that carry that gene. Similarly, research has found that a variation in the gene that produces the enzyme monoamine oxidase has been linked to anti-social behaviour in males, but only for those who were abused as a child.

It is important to note that some authorities regard these findings as speculative, not least because we currently lack robust, molecular models that can be employed to explain such effects. However, the British psychiatrist, Andrea Danese and his colleagues state that the Dunedin studies reliably show that three factors, low socio-economic status in childhood, child maltreatment (defined as harsh discipline, physical or sexual abuse, and frequent changes in the primary caregiver), and child social isolation (defined as neglect and low peer-acceptance), appear to significantly increase adult risk for metabolic and inflammatory disorders and emotional problems, such a depression. Moreover, the level of risk increases in proportion to exposure to adverse conditions. The children who experienced the greatest number of adverse experiences went on to develop the highest number of age-related diseases and emotional problems in adulthood.

These data tell us two important things about vulnerability. First that it is a product of our biological makeup *and* the environments which we are exposed and secondly that many of the pathophysiological change processes that drive physical and mental health problems in adult life have their roots in childhood.

This is a theme that we will return to later in this text, but for the moment I want to look at vulnerability from the perspective of our traits and temperaments.

Temperaments, traits and vulnerability

Back in the 1970s, the American psychologist, Jerome Kagan constructed an influential theory of personality, which proposed that we inherit broad temperamental dispositions rather specific personality traits. These temperaments are a function of biological differences in brain reactivity, which interact with environmental factors over time to shape and form an individual's traits.

Kagan discovered that these temperaments operate on two primary dimensions: namely, inhibition, and reactivity, with the former determining how innately comfortable or uncomfortable we are in situations that involve exposure to unfamiliar people and places and the latter determining how our nervous systems react to internal stimulation like discomfort and pain and external stimulation like noise and light.

Chapter 2: **How vulnerability is created and maintained**

These genetically determined variations in temperament are believed to account for the individual differences in behaviour that are readily observed in infants during the early weeks of life. It is not uncommon, for example, to hear of new-borns described as laid back and affable or as irritable and edgy and these differences are believed to emanate from individual differences in autonomic nervous system reactivity that determine a child's ability to tolerate stimulation that might otherwise result in stress. Research, for instance, has shown that children who are high in inhibition are more likely to become distressed when exposed to unfamiliar people, situations and environments, than those who are low in inhibition. Similarly, children who are low in reactivity are better able to tolerate aversive stimuli and are said to have a high stress threshold, whereas children who high in reactivity are said to have a low stress threshold, which decreases their ability to tolerate aversive stimuli and emotional discomfort. Moreover, inhibition and reactivity have been linked to the development of two important personality traits, introversion and neuroticism. Research, for example, has shown that people who score highly on the trait of introversion tend to be socially and behaviourally inhibited, whilst people who score highly on neuroticism, which is a measure of emotional instability, tend to be prone to stress and anxiety-related disorders.

According to Kagan these temperaments cast a life-long influence over the way that we react and respond to various environmental events and triggers in the sense that introverts tend to remain moderately shy, inhibited and uncomfortable around unfamiliar strangers and settings, whilst people with a neurotic temperament continue to be more prone than normal to stress and anxiety. However, although temperaments undoubtedly continue to shape our behaviours as adults, we need to factor-in the modifying effects of developmental and experiential processes in childhood and beyond. One of the key developmental tasks in childhood, for example, is mastery of internal distress. Many parents, for example, can bear testimony to the temper tantrums that occur around the age of two when children are unable to contain feelings of intense, irritation and frustration. Yet within a few years, the majority of these toddlers have learned to manage their emotions, courtesy of sensitive and attentive parenting, which enables them to recognise and tolerate uncomfortable emotion. Indeed, most children have become adept at regulating internal, emotional distress by the time they enter school. Likewise, as children gain confidence and social skills, they become less inhibited. So it is, perhaps no coincidence that 68% of all adults are classified as *ambiverts*, indicating that they are neither particularly prone to inhibition nor neuroticism (a term that I personally dislike because of its negative connotations).

However, research has shown that the relatively small percentage of children (circa 15%) who sit on the severe end of the spectrum of inhibition and reactivity are at increased risk of developing conditions, such as school refusal in childhood and social anxiety in adolescence. Similarly, whilst the acquisition of skills required to regulate affect is a normal part of child development that is well under way by the time children enter school, a small, but significant proportion of children continue to remain emotionally dysregulated. Research conducted by Avshalom Caspi, an American professor of neuroscience, and Phil Silva (the founder of the Dunedin Study) revealed that 10% of the children who had problems regulating their emotions at age three (which they referred to as an uncontrolled temperament) went on to have problems in later life associated with risk-taking and impulse control, including gambling, and drug and alcohol addiction. Whilst a smaller proportion (7%) went on to develop anxiety-related problems, including school-refusal (defined as persistent, prolonged absence from school) and social anxiety (a phobia fuelled by inhibition, fear and avoidance behaviour). Indeed, the Columbian lecturers in psychological medicine, Sunera Fernando and Hemamali Pereq, found that school refusal was strongly associated with timidity in school and other public settings and a tendency to get easily distressed.

In the clinical literature temperamental vulnerabilities go under the guise of many names, including temperamental fear, irritable distress, uncontrolled temperament, social inhibition and stress-reactivity, and their effects are explained by the stress-diathesis model developed by the American psychologist Michael Zuckerman, which predicts that pre-dispositional vulnerability (i.e., high inhibition and reactivity) lowers the biological threshold that triggers stress, depression and even psychoses. In this model, individuals that have a high stress threshold are less vulnerable to the effects of adverse situations, events and environments, whilst the reverse holds true for their vulnerable counterparts, who are especially sensitive to untoward events, circumstance and life transitions, such as school and adolescence (virtually all cases of social anxiety arise between the ages of 12 and 19).

However, the stress-diathesis model does not explain why only a relatively small proportion of children go on to develop mental health problems associated with temperamental vulnerabilities. One possible explanation is that individuals who develop problems are exposed to the cumulative effects of dispositional inhibition *and* autonomic nervous system reactivity (neuroticism). In a similar vein, the American psychologist, Alexander Shackman and his colleagues suggest that negative, biological dispositions may skew stress-regulatory systems, to create hypervigilance and debilitating levels of anxiety.

What these explanations don't take into account, however, is the role of developmental and experiential processes in shaping and mediating the effects of the temperaments that we inherit. For this we must look to the Goodness of Fit theory, which was developed by the American psychiatrists, Stella Chess and Alexander Thomas. In this model, innate dispositional factors are deemed to interact with contextual/ environmental factors in ways that modify the effect of inherited temperaments (i.e., increasing or decreasing the influence of biological temperaments). In this context, we can look to research conducted by Andrea Danese and her colleagues, which highlights the importance of the child's socio-economic environment, the quality of the parental milieu and access to positive peer-networks as key factors in promoting the child's ability to regulate and master emotional distress. Conversely, as we will learn shortly, negative factors, in the developing child's milieu, such as child maltreatment and the stressors associated with severe, social deprivation, can increase vulnerability by amplifying the effects of the biological temperaments that are inherited.

Biological systems and vulnerability

The body's nervous system is ultimately controlled by the brain and is comprised of two overarching systems: the parasympathetic nervous system, which triggers hormones that promote rest, digestion and repair; and the sympathetic nervous system, which prepares us for extraordinary levels of activity.

When the brain encounters a real or imaginary threat, the incoming information is sent to the amygdala, a small structure in the mid-brain that is often referred to as the brain's fear centre, and the hippocampus, an adjacent structure that works with long-term memory to check whether the threat is genuine. If a threat is confirmed, the brain activates the hypothalamic-pituitary-adrenal axis (or HPA for short), which is responsible for orchestrating a cascade of events that lead to the release of hormones from the hypothalamus, the renal gland and the pancreas. The HPA is the brain's primary stress-regulation mechanism, which primes the release of the fast-acting neurotransmitters, epinephrine and norepinephrine, that increase heart rate, blood pressure, muscle tone and attentional vigilance, and a group of slower acting 'stress-hormones' called glucocorticoids (the best known of which is cortisol), which help the body deal with the physical demands of stress and, which also function as anti-inflammatory agents in preparation for potential tissue damage. In addition, the pancreas is stimulated to release the hormone glucagon, which raises the levels of glucose in the blood to support the extraordinary levels of energy that are required for what we know colloquially as the flight or fight response.

Professor of neurobiology, Robert Sapolsky states that this response system evolved in mammals to provide a transient, emergency response to situations that require exceptional levels of activity in order to promote survival in the face of one-off threats. As a consequence, frequent or chronic activation of these systems leads to physiological damage, as was noted in the earlier reference to Wiess's experiments where rats were placed in an unsafe and unpredictable environment.

The Austro-Hungarian physician Hans Selye is accredited with being the first scientist to develop a working model that set out what happens to the body when we are stressed. He called this model the General Adaption Syndrome, because it is based on the premise that there is a universal reaction to stress that always occurs in three sequential stages. In the first stage, stress results in an alarm reaction, which is experienced as a pounding heart and dry mouth as the sympathetic nervous system is activated and stress hormones are released. In the second stage, termed resistance, the immediate and obvious physical signs of stress disappear,but the body remains in a heightened state of high alert with abnormally high levels of circulating stress hormones that insidiously damage the cardiovascular and immune systems, leading to what Selye termed, Diseases of Adaptation, which include heart disease, diabetes and asthma. The third stage, which results from prolonged stress and heightened levels of reactivity over months or years is termed exhaustion, an end-state that is associated with events such as myocardial infarction (heart attack) strokes, emotional burnout, depression, fatigue and ultimately death.

Chronic stress

Sapolsky offers a detailed insight into one of the mechanisms that are involved in depleting the body's resources, namely how chronic stress overloads the body's normal processing and storage of fats and sugars. Under normal conditions of homeostasis, our bodies digest foodstuffs and break them down into their constituent parts: amino acids, and simple sugars like glucose and starches. The amino acids are converted to protein to build tissue and muscle, the sugars and starch are converted to fat and stored in the body's cells and the simple sugars are converted into long chains to form glycogen, which is stored in the liver and muscles ready for future use when we require a burst of energy. These are the 'rest and digest' processes associated with activation of the parasympathetic nervous system. Conversely, when a threat is detected, the sympathetic nervous system is triggered. Glycogen is broken down to provide glucose in the bloodstream for immediate energy use and the release of glucocorticoids blocks the uptake of fat into long-term storage, ensuring that fat is available to provide energy. When the parasympathetic nervous system is reactivated, the process is reversed, and the glucose is converted back to starch and stored for later use. Under normal circumstances this cycle works in harmony with the body's metabolism. However, in the case of chronic stress, this cyclical activity consumes considerable energy, leading to depletion of fats and eventual fatigue and myopathy (muscle loss). To make matters worse, the repeated release of free-floating fats into the bloodstream to provide energy for the flight-fight response can result in fatty atheromas, which adhere to blood vessels and increases the risk of heart disease, clotting and stroke.

In a similar vein, frequent and repeated activation of the HPA, involving the release of epinephrine and norepinephrine, can lead to chronic hypertension, which increases the risk of inflammatory diseases, such as fibromyalgia and cardiovascular disease.

Because of these processes, chronic stress is recognised as one of the major risk factors for early-onset cardiac heart disease, ranking alongside the likes of obesity, smoking and alcohol.

However, the problems don't stop there because, chronic stress can also compromise our immune systems. There is a known link, for example, between the persistent release of corticosteroids and inflammation and, whilst acute inflammation is a normal, adaptative response to acute infection or injury, chronic inflammation can act to suppress the body's immune-protective cells and antibodies, leaving us vulnerable to infection and tumours.

Chronic stress also has the potential to alter the overarching architecture and systems that govern the body's response to threats. Repeated exposure to abuse in early childhood, for example, can cause the HPA to develop an abnormally low response threshold for stressors (also known as the 'set-point') with the result that relatively low levels of stress are required to trigger the HPA's cascade response, so that the whole system becomes highly reactive and indiscriminative.

This cascade response is, in large part, governed by the amygdala and the hippocampus, which process and store information about events involving threats to well-being. Under normal circumstances, the amygdala and hippocampus have complementary roles. The amygdala triggers the HPA response when a threat is detected, and the hippocampus attenuates the response once the threat is deemed to have passed. However, this homeostatic system can fail when an organism is repeatedly stressed. The neuronal connections in the amygdala may become hyper-excitable, triggering the HPA indiscriminately and if the neurons in the hippocampus sustain damage, they can inhibit the system's ability to attenuate (switch-off) the body's stress response.

As we will learn later in this book, this effect is implicated in the abnormal responses to fear that are observed in psychological disorders associated with trauma.

Notes

1. When drafting this book, I originally inserted a statement to the effect that for ethical reasons these two experiments had not been replicated in humans. However, in 2014, the American newspaper, The Washington Post published an article, which alleged that the American, Central Intelligence Agency operatives, had employed interrogation techniques, based on learned helplessness theory, on terrorist suspects in secret rendition sites dotted around the globe.
2. In practice, the terms poverty and socio-economic deprivation are often used interchangeably.

Chapter 3
Vulnerability and childhood

Vulnerability and the social brain

Experiences in early childhood shape not only the body's stress response architecture; they also affect the development and maturation of the social brain and the way that we come to see ourselves and others. The social brain is a psychological construct that is employed in neuroscience to describe several discrete regions of the neocortex that facilitate the processing of contextual information that relates to social information and emotion.

Whilst the social brain is typically treated as a cognitive entity, it also processes emotional information, relating to our own internal states together with what psychologists call Theory of Mind, which is commonly defined as the ability to imagine what others are thinking and feeling.

Theory of Mind (also known as mentalisation), a concept developed by the American psychologists David Premack and Guy Woodruff, back in the late 1970s, is made possible by specialisation of the neocortex, which allows the brain to utilise experiential learning to understand and predict others' intentions and motivations. Theory of Mind also embraces empathic processes, which at primitive level, involves the reflexive, inherited component seen in neonates who instinctively mirror the distress of other babies crying, but also sophisticated forms of cognitive empathy, which draws on awareness and inferential understanding of the motivations for other people's behaviour.

The ability to mentalise, or if you like to read other people's minds, may be reliably observed in children around five to six years of age and

Chapter 3: **Vulnerability and childhood**

arises when it is manifest as the ability to grasp the relatively simple idea that people behave in particular ways when they are motivated to achieve some form of reward or avoid some form of punishment. Over time, this ability develops and increases in sophistication, so that by the teenage years, young people are able to understand complex and abstract concepts, such as the notion that people can have conflicting motivations for behaving in given ways, which may include hiding their true beliefs and feelings.

Many psychologists believe that the human brain should be viewed, first and foremost, as a sophisticated tool for social communication with the evolutionary driver for this specialisation being the development of the social group.

Whilst social groups offer many practical advantages in terms of shared protection, shared planning and shared responsibility for weaker members of the group, such as infants, the elderly and those who are incapacitated, they necessitate that group members are empathically sensitive and responsive to others' needs and willing to engage in pro-social, altruistic behaviours that may involve putting the needs of the social group before before that of individual members.

Whilst many of the higher species of mammal show evidence of such behaviour, human prosocial behaviour has evolved (courtesy of an sophisticated neocortex) to embrace advanced forms of social cognition and affect that include moral reasoning and the self-regulatory emotions, pride, embarrassment, guilt and shame. Moreover, relative to other species of mammal (some of whom have bigger brains by mass and weight) humans have the largest neocortex and most developed frontal lobes, which are closely associated with social cognition.

In addition it is now generally acknowledged that infant human brain and the structures and systems that facilitate social cognition and empathic awareness are highly plastic and dependent upon rich, external stimulation for their proper development. These structures include the limbic system (also known as the emotional brain), which regulates emotion and stress, and the neocortex and associated structures that facilitate mentalisation and empathic awareness. In reviewing the literature on child maltreatment and neurobiological functions, for example, the British psychologist, Eamon McCrory and his colleagues found evidence that child maltreatment, which includes emotional neglect (a form of under-stimulation) and abuse (an extreme form of over-stimulation), negatively affects the development of the structures and systems that support emotional regulation in the midbrain and the structures and systems in the upper brain that support social cognition. Children that are subject to maltreatment are more likely than their non-maltreated peers to have an enlarged amygdala, a smaller hippocampus in the middle brain, which adversely amplifies the body's stress response, a reduced volume of the corpus callosum, which hinders right and left-brain hemispheric communication, and reduced volume in the prefrontal cortex, which hinders the development of social cognition. Likewise, the British psychiatrist, Danya Glaser argues that whilst the sequence of brain development in childhood is genetically predetermined, development of the systems and neural pathways that facilitate social cognition are heavily dependent upon the quality of stimulation provided by the child's immediate environment, which has led many experts to believe that early infancy should be regarded as a sensitive, if not critical period[1] for development of the structures in the social brain that govern cognition and emotion.

Critically, these structural deficits in brain development, together with the psychological and emotional impact of maltreatment and neglect, are believed to affect not only the child's ability to read other people's minds, but also their ability to regulate internal distress, which is an essential precursor to emotional literacy and well-being, the effects of which extend well beyond childhood.

In explaining these processes, the eminent, American child psychologist, John Bowlby proposed that the neonate is born with a strong, instinctive drive to form a close physical bond with the mother (or primary caregiver). This bond serves two primary functions. It provides the infant with physical comfort and security, and it stimulates the development of pathways in the brain that support social and emotional development.

This bond and the factors that coalesce to create it are genetically primed. Nature, for example, has sought to maximise the infants' chances of survival by endowing the new-born with attractive, large eyes and 'cute' sounds and smells that elicit a powerful, maternal, instinct to nurture and protect. These physical attributes trigger care-giving behaviours, which result in the release of the feel-good hormones, oxytocin and endorphins, which act to sooth and calm the baby and the release of oxytocin, vasopressin and serotonin in the mother, which reinforces the parental bond.

Under normal circumstances, these phenomena provide a mutually rewarding experience that reinforces development of a strong mother-infant bond that supports the child's development and well-being. However, when this process fails, the mother may experience a state of disconnect often associated with post-natal depression and the baby may struggle to thrive emotionally and physically.

Sadly, history has served up graphic examples of what can occur when these bonding processes fail. Following the collapse of communism in Romania during the early 1990s, up to one hundred and twenty thousand young children were discovered neglected and institutionalised in state-run orphanages. These children weighed significantly less than their peers and were found to suffer from profound intellectual and emotional retardation. In another study, conducted by scientists at the Centre of Neuroimaging Studies in London these neglected children, were found to have brains that were significantly smaller than normal. Similarly, the Romanian psychiatrist Nathan Fox and colleagues found that these children had a mean intelligence quotient of around seventy, which is normally associated with mental retardation.

Bowlby's work also emphasised the importance of infant bonding as a necessary pillar for the development of a deeper emotional attachment, which facilitates an inner, working model or template that the child uses to view itself and its relational place in the world. In this template the self and the world may be guided by a deep sense of well-being, trust and comfort and intimacy or the child's world view may be contaminated by anxiety and insecurity and a fundamental mistrust of others.

Although Bowlby's work has remained extremely influential in affecting how we view the relationship between the early years and the development of child-well-being and its anti-thesis, psychopathology, a related strand of work was development by the American-Canadian child psychologist, Mary Ainsworth that led to the development of attachment theory. This flowed from a research paradigm called the Strange Situation Experiment, which demonstrated that young children exhibited reliable differences in the extent to which they were securely attached to their mother or primary care giver.

In the Strange Situation paradigm, infants aged between twelve and eighteen months are temporarily left in an unfamiliar (strange) environment without the presence of their mother and introduced to a friendly stranger (a researcher) who attempts to engage the child through the medium of play. What Ainsworth found was a remarkably consistent pattern of results. Whilst the majority of toddlers (around 70%) were comfortable when separated from their mother for short periods of time, a significant minority showed signs of distress and avoided eye contact with their mothers on their return. In explaining these differences, Ainsworth reasoned that the relaxed, confident babies were securely attached, whilst those displaying apprehension were insecurely attached.

Ainsworth's assumptions have been empirically validated by years of research and findings from clinical practice. Mothers that are sensitively attuned to their child's needs tend to have children who are securely attached and vice-versa. However, we also need to remember that dispositional differences in infant behaviour shape the way that infants respond to unfamiliar people and environments. A toddler with an inhibited temperament is very likely to appear insecure and ill at ease in the presence of stranger in an unfamiliar university-baby-lab and their reaction may well have little do with the quality of mother's receptiveness to the child's needs. Moreover, whilst the German psychologist, Gottfried Spangle argues that dispositions almost certainly shape attachment behaviours, we should not forget that they may also be a reflection of insecurity and stress relating to child-rearing in high-risk environments where there are abuse, neglect, violence and poverty.

Indeed, as we will learn we revisit attachments in the context of resilience, there is compelling evidence of a strong relationship between these factors and insecure attachments.

The development of the self

Whilst experiential learning plays an important role in the development of the social brain and the neural pathways that regulate emotion and social cognition, the early years of childhood also shape the child's developing concept of self.

Chapter 3: **Vulnerability and childhood**

The self is a complex psychological construct that is predicated upon higher cortical processes, which allow us to be an object of our own knowledge and to reflect on what we know, think and feel. It is associated with how we see ourselves and our relational position in the world, which influences our self-esteem, and it incorporates perceptual dimensions, such as our body image and cognitive beliefs about our ability to act and achieve mastery of tasks and problems, which psychologists variously referred to as self-efficacy and self-agency.

We are not born with a concept of self, or at least not in the cognitive-affective sense of being aware of our thoughts, feelings and motivations. These appear later in childhood as a cumulative product of experiential learning and development of the neocortex and the emotional brain. Neonates are born with a relatively crude sense of self that is primarily sensory rather than cognitive. Evidence suggests that newborns are aware that they are entities that exist separately from their mothers and their immediate environments. They know where their toes end, and space begins, and they will actively try to mimic the facial expressions and sounds that their mothers make. However, children don't begin to show reliable signs of self-conscious awareness before the age of two when they display behaviours that are synonymous with embarrassment and the social masking of errors, and evidence of mentalisation associated with the development of theory of mind does not emerge before the age of five to six years.

In fact, the development of the self evolves in parallel with the social brain during the formative years of childhood and appears to be a product of experiential learning and specialisation of the neocortex and the limbic system (the emotional brain).

Evidence for this position comes from multi-stranded elements of research in developmental psychology and the neurosciences. However, theories about how the self develops can be traced back much further in time. The American sociologist, Charles Horton Cooley, for example, developed the Looking Glass Self theory back in the 1900s, which posits that humans are not born with a concept of self, but rather with a mind that resembles a 'tabula rasa', which is Latin for a clean slate or if you prefer a modern computer-analogy, an empty hard drive that is waiting to be populated with information.

Crucially, he proposed that everything we know about ourselves is learnt and flows directly from how we are treated and regarded by others. When others' responses are positive and encouraging, we develop a positive self-concept and when their responses are dismissive, critical and disapproving, we develop a negative concept of self that is characterised by low self-esteem and an internalised sense of shame.

According to Cooley, these self-other perceptions form an enduring template that is our concept of self. Moreover, it does not take a great leap of the imagination to imagine how these self-other mirroring processes might leave us vulnerable to abuse, neglect and indifference. If others' reactions towards us are overwhelmingly positive and we are shown love, regard and respect, we learn that we are loveable and valued. If their reactions are harsh and critical or if we are ignored and neglected, we learn to judge ourselves in a similarly harsh light and our self-concept develops in the skewed and disabling direction.

Broadly speaking, Cooley's ideas about how the self develops are reflected in modern-day developmental psychology. During the early months and years, children's principal sources of self-referential feedback are the parents with this shifting to school, friends and peers as they enter school and head towards puberty. Moreover, Cooley's theory is reflected in contemporary research which shows that harsh, critical parenting is a pivotal factor in the development of chronic, internalised shame and the propensity for developing anxiety-related disorders and depression in later life (as we will discover in the chapter dealing with shame).

Clearly then, the early years are of critical importance for the development of social cognition and the self. However, as we will learn next, an emerging field of neuroscience and biology called epigenetics appears to show that exposure to toxic environments (which include not only physical toxins like alcohol, but also maternal stress and trauma) can affect the foetus at an even earlier stage of development, namely the peri-conceptual period, which embraces the period when the egg is fertilised and implanted in the uterus.

Epigenetics and vulnerability

It has been known for some time that the genes we inherit alter our lifetime risk for developing illness in positive or negative direction. However, it is less commonly known that changes in our behaviour or our environment can alter the way that genes are expressed through a process called methylation in which a methyl group (comprising one carbon atom and three hydrogen atoms) is added to a candidate gene. This process does not lead to the creation of new, variant or mutant genes. Rather it alters the way that a gene behaves by switching it on or off or by turning gene expression up or down (much like the volume control on a radio).

Early evidence that environmental stimuli might directly affect gene expression came from the study of Dutch Civilians who were subject to mass starvation during the Nazi blockade of 1944–1945. Scientists initially observed that women affected by the famine were more likely than normal to give birth to children who went on to develop obesity and heart problems in adulthood. On exploring this phenomenon further, investigators found that only women who were exposed to the famine during the peri-conceptual period of pregnancy were affected, which you may remember is the period immediately before and after conception. This led to the hypothesis that exposure to famine during this sensitive period had resulted in the creation of a 'hunger gene', which had increased the body's basal uptake of lipids and other fats. Whilst this hypothesis sounded tenable, it was later discredited when Elmer Tobi and his colleagues from Leiden University in Holland showed that methylation had simply altered the existing gene's ability to metabolise and store fats.

Meanwhile other research had provided tantalising evidence that appeared to show that gene expression could be altered by changes in behaviour that were subsequently passed from one generation to the next. Michael Meaney and his colleagues at McGill University in the United States, for example, examined the effects of individual differences in maternal rat behaviour (attentive licking and grooming) during the first week of life that were believed to modulate gene methylation in brain receptors that release soothing corticosteroids that reduce stress. Meany found that rat pups whose mothers were maternally inattentive had higher levels of stress reactivity than rat pups whose mothers were maternally attentive. Moreover, these differences in stress reactivity were passed down to the next generation.

The implications of these studies for our understanding of how stress and other environmental teratogens might affect infant development are potentially profound: Namely, they suggest that toxic environments (be they physical or emotional) have the potential to alter the way that our genes are expressed and second, that, the changes in gene expression may be passed from one generation to the next, adding a totally new perspective on inter-generational abuse, poverty and stress.

Yet, extrapolating from animal studies, like Meaney's to humans is fraught with difficulties. Yes, we share a large percentage of our genetic architecture with rats and other mammals, but rats have much smaller brains with higher levels of pre-programming and reduced brain plasticity, so direct comparisons are simply not plausible. As a consequence, studies that have sought to explore the effects of gene methylation on humans have had to rely on retrospective, correlational studies that do not prove cause and effect. Just such as study was conducted by Zachary Kaminsky and his colleagues at the John Hopkins Department of Psychiatry in the United States.

Comparing the brains of healthy individuals and the brains of those who had committed suicide, Kaminsky found that the suicide group had higher levels of gene methylation in a protein called SKA2, which has the function of suppressing negative thoughts in the pre-frontal cortex. To understand the logic of this finding, you need to know that lower methylation *increases* gene expression, leading to higher levels of SKA2, which suppresses negative thoughts, whilst higher methylation *weakens* gene expression, leading to lower levels of SAK2 which increases negative thoughts. The implication being that the higher levels of SKA2 gene methylation found in the suicide victims may have lowered the brain's capacity to suppress negative thoughts, leading to suicidal ideation.

In a similarly intriguing study, Rachael Yehuda and her colleagues at the Veterans Affairs Medical Centre in New York studied the children of mothers who had survived the Holocaust, and found that the mother's trauma appeared to have altered the expression of a specific 'stress gene' called FKBP5, which regulates the expression of the class of stress hormones known as glucocorticoids,[2] but in the *opposite* direction to that which had been anticipated. Whilst the mothers had higher methylation of FKBP5, leading to a decreased corticosteroid stress response, their offspring had a lower level of FKBP5 methylation, leading to a higher corticosteroid stress response than control subjects whose parents had not been subject to trauma, leading Yehuda to conclude that their parent's experiences had rendered their offspring more

Chapter 3: **Vulnerability and childhood**

resilient to future trauma (echoing the experiences of the Dutch hunger victims' offspring whose bodies were better able to store fat to cope with potential famine).

However, the story does not end there. Yehuda also conducted studies of women who were pregnant when directly exposed to the horror of the Twin Towers terrorist attack in New York in 2001. The women were initially invited for screening to test for exposure to toxic materials, but what Yehuda found led her on a detective-trail, which revealed that women who had been witness to the Twin Towers attack during the third semester of pregnancy had higher-than-normal levels of the stress hormone, cortisol and an enzyme called 11β-HSD2, which has the protective effect of deactivating cortisol, which is toxic to the developing foetus.

Yehuda also found that the babies were born with low salivary cortisol and whilst this might be taken to suggest that, like the children of holocaust survivors, epigenetic processes had led the babies to be born with a lower, but functionally adaptive level of stress reactivity, the real picture is less clear cut. Numerous studies, for example, have linked low levels of blood cortisol to *increased* vulnerability for stress and depression, and one school of thought is that low cortisol reduces glucocorticoid receptor sensitivity, which inhibits the body's ability to dampen stress.

Hence, whilst Yehuda's research might well provide a plausible epigenetic model for the transmission of stress susceptibility across generations, caution is required, because we don't yet understand the direction of causality. Lower levels of cortisol in the offspring of mothers who have been exposed to stress and trauma during pregnancy may help their children fair better in unsafe environments by increasing their threshold for stress or it may have the opposite effect by lowering the body's ability to recover from stress.

Notes

1 From a biological perspective, a sensitive period refers to a window of developmental opportunity in which an organism is especially receptive to stimuli that elicit developmental processes. With a sensitive period, development may be delayed, but plasticity permits some development at a later

stage. With a critical period, the developmental window of opportunity is fixed, so that future development is precluded.
2 Glucocorticoids are involved in many aspects of the body's stress response that can be confusing. They are often referred to as 'stress hormones', not least because cortisol, which is a glucocorticoid is involved in supporting the primary flight-fright mechanism that readies the body for extraordinary levels of action; however, glucocorticoids are also involved in slowing the body's primary stress response, post-threat and reinstating the homeostatic, rest and digest processes.

Chapter 4
The psychological impact of vulnerability

Shame and vulnerability

One of the more insidious effects of harsh, critical parenting and other forms of maltreatment in childhood is the internalisation of shame, which is one of a small group of 'self-consciousness emotions', which arise out of self-other evaluations, which also include embarrassment, guilt and pride. Evolutionary psychologists believe that these have evolved for the purpose of promoting prosocial behaviour that broadly conform to societal norms and standards, and for constraining egoistical behaviour that might be otherwise detrimental to the welfare of the wider social group. Indeed, each of these emotions has a positive valence that promotes behaviour and a valence which inhibits behaviour. When we experience pride, for example, and are praised by others for our efforts, we feel good about ourselves and the brain releases the feel-good hormone, dopamine, which reinforces the associated behaviours. Conversely when we experience embarrassment, guilt or shame, we experience cognitive dissonance (an uncomfortable emotional state that arises when our actions lie at odds with our values and beliefs) and are motivated to avoid future repetition of the offending behaviour or behaviours.

Of these latter states, shame is the most toxic and enduring. Embarrassment, for example, is normally associated with minor transgressions of social rules or etiquette (like grabbing the biggest piece of cake at a party or blurting out something that is indiscrete) that are usually forgiven and forgotten quite quickly. In a similar vein, guilt generally

DOI: 10.4324/9781351035545-5

takes the form of a transient state, which is relieved when we engage in reparative behaviour, such as saying I'm sorry or offering to make good damage to a broken pane of glass.[1]

Shame, on the other hand, is associated with acts that are regarded as morally or ethically wrong and which are not easily forgiven or erased from memory, such as acts of extreme violence and abuse towards others, like rape and child-abuse.

Like virtually all aspects of the social self, we are not born with these emotions. We acquire them in childhood, and they shape not only our behaviour, but also our sense of self. When a child is scolded for, say biting and parents take the time to explain why biting is abhorrent and how it makes others feel, the child is encouraged to feel empathy and to make amends for their behaviour, which relieves their guilt. If, however, the *child* is scolded rather than the behaviour and the parental responses are consistently punitive rather than restorative, the scolding may be internalised as shame – a deeply rooted sense of being bad or not good enough.

The American psychologist and expert in guilt and shame, June Tangney argues that the root causes of internalised shame can invariably be traced back to childhood and are usually a product of family dysfunction and child maltreatment. There is a clear link between the development of internalised shame and harsh, critical parenting for example; and likewise, children who are consistently punished, scolded or made to feel guilty for experiencing normal feelings (such as anger, fear, jealousy, joy and normal sexual drives) learn that because such feelings are abnormal, they must be inherently bad for possessing them.

In a similar vein, children who are exposed to sexual abuse often harbour shameful beliefs that they have in some way been party to encouraging the abuse and such beliefs may persist into adulthood as a complex mix of shame and trauma.

Research also suggests that there are individual differences in the extent to which children are susceptible to the effects of shaming and maltreatment. Tangney, Youman and Stuewig, for example, state that a small proportion of children are dispositionally vulnerable to shame, because they have particular difficulty regulating and tolerating unpleasant emotion. Such effects may be attributable to individual differences in a person's biological threshold for stress-tolerance, associated with dispositional temperaments (as we learnt earlier). However,

Chapter 4: **The psychological impact of vulnerability**

shame is also more prevalent in people with conditions, such as autistic spectrum disorder (ASD). People with ASD are frequently particularly sensitive to criticism, and contrary to the popular misconception that people with ASD lack insight into their own behaviour, the American developmental psychologist, Carrie Masten and her colleagues have presented evidence which solidly refutes this position. Similarly, research conducted by the British psychologists Catherine Sebastian and Sarah-Jayne Blakemore shows that people on the autistic spectrum divert an abnormal amount of time and energy reading and anticipating other people's reactions towards the self, not least because the high prevalence of late, ASD diagnosis, results in many children growing up with a sense of being different, which they negatively attribute to a (shameful) failure of the self.

In a similar vein, the American psychologist, and shame researcher, Rene Brown suggests that children who are repeatedly exposed to shame and humiliation in childhood are often driven to present an image to the outside world that is far removed from that which they privately feel inside. This is often referred to as 'masking behaviour' and shaming in childhood is known to be associated with lifelong perfectionism that drives chronic social anxiety and conditions, such as imposter syndrome – a condition where people feel like fraudulent actors regardless of how they much achieve.

It has been argued in some quarters, that shame has a healthy, regulatory function in shaping social behaviour, which is based on the idea that the aversive nature of feeling ashamed can motivate people to change their errant ways and/or that people can be publicly shamed into changing behaviour. If you have ever seen the film *Patten*, for example, you will recollect that the General infamously slaps a soldier (who is probably suffering from traumatic stress) in front of his buddies, because he believes he can shame the soldier into 'shaping up'.

Such attitudes were not uncommon during Patten's time and existed a decade later when it was common practice in Scottish primary schools to correct abhorrent behaviour by making offenders stand in the 'Dunce's Corner' (in Scotland the word dunce is used to describe a slow-witted idiot). Moreover, the ideology behind such practices has continued unabated. It is not uncommon, for example, to find newspapers and other media outlets proclaiming loudly that those guilty of misdemeanours should be 'named and shamed'.

Whilst such actions may have an intuitive appeal, Tangney states there is no scientific or clinical evidence to support the idea that publicly shaming people leads to positive behaviour change. Rather, she shame is an overwhelmingly destructive emotion that is associated with immobilisation of the self and the evocation of psychological processes, such as avoidance and denial that run counter to positive self-change and development. In other words, shaming people can entrench behaviour rather than elicit change.

Shame also has other undesirable effects that are not immediately obvious. The British psychologist, Paul Gilbert states that one of the most powerful forms of shame is humiliation, which is associated with anger and lust for vengeance.

Many experts in the field believe that the humiliation of shame can give rise to uncontrollable anger and rage, which may put the self and others at risk. The trauma researcher, Helen Block Lewis, for example, states that trauma victims, who have been subject to rape and subjugation, often act in self-destructive acts that provide an outlet for suppressed rage. This happens because the humiliation associated with shame can be so aversive and intolerable that victims feel compelled to engage in risky or self-destructive behaviours in order to achieve a sense of temporary agency and control. Indeed, it is notable that in his book on the causes and consequences of aggression, the American psychologist Leonard Berkowitz states that the likelihood of engaging in aggressive acts towards others is greatly enhanced when we feel bad about ourselves.

However, shaming has other dark sides, as revealed in so-called 'honour-killings' that result when an individual's actions are deemed to have brought shame and disrepute on a family's standing and reputation. In a similar vein, expressions of denigration, such as 'slut-shaming', 'mom-shaming' and 'body-shaming' into common vocabulary, have made their way into common vocabulary and contributed to the victimisation of people and groups in society who are vulnerable.

Trauma and vulnerability

According to the American psychiatrist, Judith Lewis-Herman, psychological trauma occurs when a victim is rendered helpless and terrorised

Chapter 4: **The psychological impact of vulnerability**

by some overwhelming force that incapacitates the normal human responses to threat. Such events may include rape and other forms of sexual and emotional abuse or being caught in the horrors of war or a car crash. In addition, professional staff, such as child protection case workers, emergency response personnel and humanitarian aid workers who are vicariously exposed to other's suffering, may also succumb to trauma, which can be manifest as emotional detachment and cynicism.

Trauma is also synonymous with post-traumatic stress disorder (PTSD), which the Dutch trauma expert, Bessel Van der Kolk states was not formally recognised as a psychiatric disorder before 1986. Indeed, prior to this period, expert opinion had it that people could only develop PTSD following exposure to extraordinary events that lay outside of normal human experience. However, it is now commonly accepted that people can become traumatised by events that are tragic, but relatively commonplace, such as a stillbirth and serious illness.

Trauma is often manifest as a chronic condition, precipitated by changes in the brain's fear processing structures that may last for years. Van der Kolk, for example, states that neuroimaging studies have indicated that during exposure to traumatic events, the left side of the brain is deactivated, leaving the right side of the brain, which contains the fear-processing centres, in a state of hyper-arousal. This results in the abnormal processing of memory that keeps the precipitating events and circumstances locked into the forefront of consciousness in a state of chronicity. Likewise, the American psychiatrist, Douglas Bremner asserts that studies examining the stress-response of people who have been subjected to trauma show that they have an increased activity in the amygdala, which plays an important role in triggering the body's flight-fight response, and a decreased volume in the hippocampus, which normally attenuates the body's stress response.

This state of trauma may also be exacerbated by the violation of the individual's Just-World Beliefs, leading to existential angst and a pervading sense that the world is an unsafe, unpredictable place that is full of of danger. For victims of trauma, it is as if danger lurks around every corner and attentional processes go into overdrive. The brain continually scans the environment for potential threats and reacts strongly to stimuli that were associated with the original trauma. Particularly, sensory stimuli, such as sounds, images and smells.

Beyond this, trauma may trigger a crisis of the self, as in survivor guilt, which is relatively common in combat veterans and emergency personnel, who see their colleagues killed or injured in action and as shame in survivors of child or adult sexual abuse, who hold erroneous beliefs about self-complicity.

The technical criteria that are used to diagnose PTSD and trauma are complex, and there are two competing diagnostic systems: Namely, the American Diagnostic and Statistical Manual (DSM) and the World Health Organization's International Classification of Diseases (ICD). However, these diagnostic systems broadly agree on the core criteria for PTSD.

Namely, the presence of three, cardinal, cognitive-affective states referred to as *hyperarousal*, where the systems that normally regulate the body's stress response go into overdrive, resulting in intense fear and anxiety. *Intrusion*, where conscious awareness is randomly punctuated by flashbacks (vivid, life-like, images, smells and sounds), chronic insomnia and nightmares and *depersonalisation*, defined as feelings of being emotionally detached from the traumatic events and/or the surrounding world, and problems with attention, concentration and memory, which can include dissociative amnesia for events preceding the trauma. In addition, the latest version of the International Classification of Diseases (ICD11), distinguishes between 'simple PTSD', occurring after exposure to a single horrific incident and complex PTSD, arising out of exposure to multiple traumatic events occurring a period over time.

In explaining the intrusive phenomena associated with PTSD, Lewis-Herman states that it is as though time and the normal processes that facilitate the processing of events associated with fear and anxiety have been frozen at the point of trauma, which gives the events and stimuli associated with the traumatic event an abnormal, invasive quality that is absent in normal memory. This phenomenon was first formally observed by the pioneering French psychotherapist, Pierre Janet, over one hundred years ago, when he noted that the memories of soldiers who had been traumatised in combat had an unusually vivid quality that appeared to set them apart from normal memories.

Indeed, recent research has shown that trauma memories are not consolidated into the long-term memory networks that are normally employed to categorise and record everyday experiences. Memories

Chapter 4: The psychological impact of vulnerability 57

associated with trauma are primarily iconic (visual) and lacking in contextual information and verbal coding and are, in fact, closely reminiscent of the somatic (body) memories for events that occur in pre-verbal stages of infancy (the period before children have the capacity to explain and record the world in terms of language and verbal comprehension).

In explaining these phenomena, Van der Kolk refers to in-vivo, neuroimaging studies of trauma victims undergoing an induced flashback, which revealed enhanced activity in the amygdala, the fear processing centre in the right side of brain, and reduced activity in the thalamus, which normally acts to filter our extraneous sensory information and the dorsolateral prefrontal cortex in the left hemisphere of the brain, which acts as the brain's timekeeper and storyteller, providing a contextual narrative for events that are stored in long-term memory.

Van der Kolk suggests these findings are significant because scientists believe that when the brain's language processing centres are deactivated, we revert to a pre-verbal, child-like state that results in memories that are primarily somatic and difficult to articulate or describe.

Evidence for this supposition comes from studies of brain damaged patients that have shown that when the dorsolateral prefrontal cortex is deactivated or dysfunctional, patients experience a sense of time slowing down or a feeling that time has stopped completely. Likewise, studies have shown that problems with the thalamus are linked to impairment in executive dysfunction, memory and attention problems.

Van Der Kolk suggests that the cumulative effects of these changes may explain why trauma victim's brains seem to be locked into the past and beset by intrusive memories and emotions that typically are difficult to verbalise.

The third cardinal feature of trauma is constriction, a concept first defined by the American psychologist George Kelly, who defined this as a narrowing of a person's perceptual field. Constriction is commonly observed in animals that are subjected to overwhelming force and it closely resembles the learned helplessness that Seligman observed in his captive dogs, who were subject to inescapable electric shocks.

An antelope, for example, pinned down by a lioness, will enter a frozen, immobilised state of helplessness, which studies have shown is linked to the flooding of the brain with the neurotransmitters, serotonin and dopamine. Similarly, qualitative studies of rape victims and combat veterans who have had traumatic, near-death experiences have revealed that victims often report entering a trance-like state in which time appears to slow down. In this state events are still registered in consciousness, but they are accompanied by a sense of calm and emotional detachment in which terror and pain dissolve.

The psychological term for this distancing of the self from reality is dissociation and it is common in people that have been subjected to trauma. Dissociation may thus be viewed as protective mental state in which there is a degree of disconnect from the outside world.

Dissociation differs from psychosis where there is a complete break with reality. In dissociation, people feel emotionally numb and separate from their body, personal identity and physical pain, but they are still conscious and aware of their surroundings.

Like most other mental defence mechanisms, dissociation is manifest as an automatic and unconscious response to overwhelming threat and is witnessed in children and adults who have been subjected to persistent abuse. In such circumstances, victims may learn to readily dissociate in response to direct threat or the presence of environmental triggers. These dissociative periods may occur sporadically and last from minutes to days or can take the form of a chronic, disabling condition that prevents trauma victims from engaging in normal life.

Whilst these forms of psychological numbing have an ego-protective function, they also come at significant personal cost. Constriction affects not just negative emotions like anxiety. Positive emotions are similarly blunted, and trauma sufferers may complain of feeling numb and going through the motions without the capacity to feel joy or hope. It is as though the constriction binds them in an emotional straitjacket, which can be deeply distressing. The American psychiatrist, Meredith Warshaw and her colleagues, for example, found that patients with a diagnosis of trauma or PTSD functioned poorly in many areas of life and were significantly more likely to suffer from clinical anxiety, depression, suicidal ideation (thoughts of suicide) and suicide attempts.

Trauma is also associated with avoidance, which may involve keeping oneself busy, avoiding places and things associated with the original trauma or consciously suppressing intrusive thoughts. Avoidance is a classic response to fear and whilst it can function as a useful short-term strategy for circumventing uncomfortable emotions, it tends to be self-defeating in the longer term. Misplaced beliefs relating to survival guilt or self-complicity in sexual abuse may remain entrenched and unchallenged, and the contingent fear-relationship that was formed at the point of trauma may remain frozen in place in perpetuity if the victim is denied the opportunity to place the traumatic events in the context of the here and now.

In fact, research shows that although spontaneous recovery from trauma is possible with the passage of time, a significant number of victims continue to have problems with post-traumatic stress without formal treatment. The German psychologist, Nexhmedin Morina and his colleagues, for example, found that only 44% of patients with PTSD spontaneously recovered over the course of forty months. However, treatment can be very effective, even to the point of modifying the biological processes and structures that are believed to be involved in creating and maintaining trauma. Using magnetic resonance imaging (MRI) techniques to observe what was happening in the brains of PTSD sufferers, the American psychiatrist Fonzo Gregory found that patients in receipt of fear-exposure techniques, which involved in-vivo exposure to fear-stimuli (for instance, revisiting the place where the original trauma occurred or guided, imaginary exposure), showed reduced brain activity between the amygdala and the frontal lobes in a manner that was consistent with fear reduction.

Before, we leave the topic of PTSD and trauma, I would like to draw attention to the presence of trauma in workers whose roles can expose them to vicarious trauma. Lewis-Herman states that this can include anyone who is a direct witness to the abuse, mutilation or death of others, including first responders, emergency personnel and humanitarian aid workers.

In a survey of volunteering staff, for example, working in South Sudan (one of the most dangerous and volatile areas in Africa) the Dutch psychiatrists, Hannah Strohmeier and Willem Scholte found evidence of post-traumatic stress in 24% of staff together with high rates of depression, anxiety and hazardous levels of alcohol consumption. Similarly, the American trauma expert, Olga Phoenix, who specialises in vicarious trauma and resilience, estimates that rates of vicarious trauma in front-line staff, such as social workers, therapist, hospice personnel and intensive care nurses, have been shown to range from 40%

to 80% over the course of someone's working life. In a similar vein, Lewis-Herman states that such staff are particularly vulnerable to the effects of long-term exposure to repeated trauma, because there is a point (referred to as a 'dosage effect') where the cumulative effects of exposure invariably exceeds the influence of protective factors, such as experience, training preparation and trauma-debriefing.

Addiction and vulnerability

Addiction is a complex psychological state of dependency that is characterised by a compulsive and overwhelming desire to engage in behaviours that bring relief from emotional tensions and stress. It is generally manifest as a cycle, involving a craving stage, characterised by an obsessive pre-occupation with the addictive activity, an impulsive binge-intoxication stage that brings feelings of pleasure, well-being and relief from physical and emotional tension and stress, and a withdrawal stage that involves strong and unpleasant symptoms that are both physical and emotional in origin.

In this cycle, addicts may attempt to break free from their addiction, but the powerful cravings and unpleasant symptoms associated with withdrawal invariably lead to renewed addictive activity in order to gain relief.

The behaviours associated with addiction are frequently harmful. The misuse of chemical substances, such as drugs, alcohol and solvents, can be physically damaging to organs, such as the liver and the brain, whilst the intense obsession and preoccupation associated with the addictive activity is often relationally damaging, as it typically takes precedence over intimate relationships and work and family-related commitments. In addition, the body commonly develops a degree of physical tolerance and psychological habituation[2] over time, which results in greater dosage effects being required to achieve an affect.

Addiction can involve physical and psychological dependency to chemical substances, such as the sedative drugs morphine, fentanyl, ketamine and heroin, and stimulants, such as cocaine, amphetamines and methamphetamine (crystal-meth), alcohol, tobacco and solvents or it can involve dependency relating to a wide range of behavioural

Chapter 4: The psychological impact of vulnerability

activities, that include gambling, internet addiction (including gaming and the use of pornography), shopping, working, eating and physical exercise. Both types of addiction are relatively common. A study conducted by the British psychologist Steve Sussman and his colleagues, for example, found that population estimates for non-chemical addiction lay in the range of 2% to 10%, which was not far behind the prevalence estimates for alcohol and drugs, which lay at 10% and 5% respectively. Moreover, evidence suggests that all forms of addiction, regardless of whether they are chemically or behaviourally based, involve shared neural reinforcement pathways in the brain, exact the same deleterious effects on impulse control, judgement and memory and are similarly subject to psychological habituation and physical tolerance.

The causes of addiction are complex and multifactorial with genetic, social and emotional factors all playing a contributing role. In reviewing the data from twin studies, for example, the American psychiatrists, Arpana Agrawal and Michael Lynskey have estimated that the heritable component of addiction lies in the range of .30 to .70, depending on the gender and age of those involved and the substances being used. Heritability also appears to play a more prominent role in the development of addiction in males and particularly with reference to hard drugs, such as cocaine and heroin. However, they also note that despite intensive efforts, research has failed to identify specific candidate genes, for addictive behaviours, which weakens the genetic-addiction hypothesis.

Rather, as the American psychologist, Annabelle Belcher and her colleagues have noted, genetic studies have tended (somewhat speculatively) to focus on the role of dispositional variables or temperaments of the type we encountered in earlier in this book. It has been proposed, for example, that dispositional problems with impulse control, delay-gratification and emotional regulation may make it more difficult for certain people to resist drugs and alcohol. Likewise, you may recall that research associated with the Dunedin longitudinal study found that a small percentage of the children, who had problems regulating their emotions at age three (referred to as an uncontrolled temperament), went on to have problems in later life associated with risk-taking and impulse control, which included gambling, and drug and alcohol addiction. Yet the link between genetics and addiction has remained tenuous and some authorities believe that genetic studies have tended to overestimate the influence of heritable factors in addiction, whilst underestimating the impact of environmental factors, such as the quality of parenting and the adverse environments in childhood. Professor Wayne Hall, who is a former Director of the Australian National Drug and Research Centre, for example, states that the disease model of addiction (which draws heavily on the genetic link to addiction) has not been borne out by animal or neuroimaging studies. In a similar vein, the American psychologists, Tiffany Mueller and Zoe Peterson note that the problems of impulse control, impaired executive control and emotional dysregulation seen in addiction are better explained by the robust association that has been found between child maltreatment and trauma and addiction, a point to which I will return shortly.

Viewed from a biological perspective, addiction derives its power by targeting three innate, biological systems that are central to our survival, namely, the dopamine system, which is responsible for reward, energy and motivation. The opioid system which regulates emotional gratification, bonding and relief from pain and discomfort, and the systems in the upper and middle brain, relating to emotional regulation, impulse control and decision-making.

Of these systems, the dopamine-reward system is the most phylogenetically primitive, being linked to the brain's chemical reward system that is associated with motivational behaviour.

Dopamine is a chemical messenger that regulates many aspects of human functioning, such as motivation, energy and motor activity. When we experience success, receive praise, complete a marathon or listen to a great piece of music, the body's innate dopamine receptors are activated and the chemical floods into brain's synapses in two important regions of the brain: Namely, the ventral tegmental apparatus in the mid-brain, which is associated with reward and behavioural reinforcement, and the nucleus accumbens in the lower forebrain, which produces a feeling of elation, often described as a 'high'. Stimulant drugs, such as cocaine, readily bind to receptors in this part of the brain to produce an artificial high that can be extremely pronounced, particularly in the case of crack-cocaine and crystal meth. Likewise, common activities, such as browsing a shop counter full of sweets and

Chapter 4: The psychological impact of vulnerability

chocolates can increase dopamine levels by 50%, whilst sexual arousal can increase dopamine levels by 100%, but these pale into insignificance when compared with the effects of powerful, artificial stimulants. The American addiction expert, Gabor Mate, for example, states that ingestion of cocaine can raise the brain's levels of dopamine by 300% and crystal meth by a staggering 1,200%.

Stimulant drugs work by inhibiting the reuptake of dopamine at the synaptic cleft so that there is a delay in the reabsorption of dopamine back into the host receptor site, meaning that more dopamine is available for longer. Modern anti-depressants, called selective serotonin reuptake inhibitors (SSRIs), make use of the same molecular technique to increase the synaptic levels of the mood-enhancing neurotransmitter, serotonin. However, powerful narcotic stimulants are less selective in their action. Whereas SSRIs target only the receptors for serotonin, narcotic stimulants are less discriminating and are believed to have a more global and pervasive effect on brain chemistry. As a result, repeated exposure to high levels of dopamine results in enhanced sensitisation to the environmental cues associated with the addiction, meaning that mere exposure to so-called drug paraphernalia, or simply thinking about 'the hit' can stimulate the release of dopamine.

This also creates the phenomenon known as craving, which can lead to a loss of impulse control. Prolonged and repeated exposure to excess levels of dopamine, however, also has the effect of reducing the number of dopamine receptors in the brain (because the brain has detected, what is regarded as an unnecessary surplus), which leads to the phenomenon referred to as tolerance. When tolerance occurs, the person needs to have more of the drug to achieve the original effect, which may lead to an escalation of the existing additive behaviour(s) and/or efforts to seek new, novel highs with consequences that may be risky and/or illegal.

The American experimental psychologist, Michael Nader and his colleagues state that evidence from animal studies suggests that those who go on to develop addictions have fewer dopamine receptors from the outset and it has been hypothesised that this renders them particularly susceptible to the effects of artificial dopamine stimulation. However, this has remained a speculative hypothesis, and there is no conclusive evidence that people who have an inherited condition associated with acquired dopamine deficiency, such as Parkinson's disease, are more likely than the general population to develop an addiction.

The second neuro-chemical system that is targeted by addiction is the opioid apparatus, which provides, not only the brain's natural defence against pain, but also the chemical basis of emotional gratification that facilitates important processes, such as attachment and bonding. The chemical messengers in the opioid apparatus take the form of proteins that latch onto natural opioid receptors in the brain and central nervous system. These proteins include enkephalin and dynorphin, but the principal molecules of interest in addiction are the endorphins. When the opioid apparatus is activated, the released endorphin molecules act as natural analgesics to relieve pain, lower anxiety and emotional distress. They are the body's 'natural or endogenous opiates', pain killers and soothers. When a mother, for example, responds in a sensitive and caring way to her infant's fear of separation or pain following a fall, stomach upset or hunger, her actions activate the body's innate opioid apparatus and the infant's brain is flooded with endorphins, which provides a sense of comfort and well-being. These processes cement normal attachment and bonding, and notably, the synthetic opiates, opium, morphine, heroin and fentanyl work by latching onto the same, innate opioid receptors, which are located throughout the brain spinal cord and core organs, creating similar, but more powerful effects.

These effects function not only as analgesics that quell physical pain. They also relieve emotional discomfort, in a way that is thought to be reminiscent of the soothing that we experience as infants when held by our mothers. Indeed, Gabor Mate quotes one of his patients, a heroin addict, as describing the effects of the drug as being like a 'soft warm hug'.

These are the short-term gains associated with the ingestion of chemical substances like cocaine and heroin. The long-term effects, however, are both insidious and deleterious.

Long-term addiction appears to affect not only the brain's chemical processes, but also its very structures. The American neurobiologist, Colm Connolly, for example, reports that imaging studies have shown that long-term exposure to frequent, high doses of opiates and

Chapter 4: The psychological impact of vulnerability

stimulant drugs results in the loss of white brain matter, called myelin (which is responsible for connectivity between neurons) and grey, brain matter in the cortex (which comprise our brain cells or neurons). Moreover, the higher the frequency and dosage, the greater the deleterious effects, which are not limited to addiction associated with chemical substances. The same deleterious consequences have been found in people with long-term addiction to pornography and people with chronic alcohol addiction. The American psychologist Kendra Muller, for example, reports that loss of grey matter in people addicted to pornography closely mirrors that of people addicted to chemical substances, with the pre-frontal cortex, which is associated with decision-making and self-control, particularly affected.

The net effect of activation of the dopamine and opioid centers provides a temporary, yet powerful physical and emotional release from intolerable internal distress, which is often referred to as 'self-medication'.

However, relief from emotional tension and the disturbing, intrusive phenomena that are associated with trauma may also come via a process that psychologists refer to as associative learning. A child subject to shaming or sexual abuse, for example, may come to discover that the feeling of pleasure derived from playing with his or her genitals creates a temporary release from tension. This association may then be registered in long-term memory and reawakened by re-exposure to trauma or tension occurring during the onset of pubescence (where there are marked hormonal changes associated with the adult sex-drive). If this occurs and the earlier relief from tension and stress is re-experienced, it may, with the passage of time, come to be manifest as a chronic addiction to sex, characterised, for example, by a compulsive drive to masturbate or engage in sex with another person or to look at pornography.

Many researchers and authorities regard trauma as the principle, causal factor in the development and maintenance of addictive behaviours. Gabor Mate, for example, makes a powerful case for rethinking addiction as a primal response to trauma and vulnerability. Addiction, he argues, invariably flows from trauma and he points to evidence that rates of alcohol and substance abuse are significantly higher in individuals who have been exposed to trauma and in communities that have been disenfranchised and marginalised.

Studies of combat veterans, for example, have found that higher than normal rates of alcohol and substance abuse dovetail with post-traumatic stress disorder and depression. Writing in the *American Journal of Drug and Alcohol Abuse*, the American psychiatrist, Stanton Peele states that whilst as many as one in five enlisted soldiers were estimated to have routinely used heroin to combat stress during the Vietnam War in the 1970s, only 5% of those went on to develop a heroine-addiction on their return to civilian life. Similar findings have been reported for combat veterans involved in the 1991, Gulf War and follow-up studies revealed that addiction was most likely to occur when there were co-factors present, such as pre-existing psychological problems. Likewise, the American psychologist, Matthew Tull, who specialises in addiction, states that approximately 46% of people who are diagnosed with chronic post-traumatic stress disorder struggle with problems related to alcohol or drug addiction.

Other studies have found a similarly strong association between reported childhood incest, rape and subsequent substance abuse, which typically begins in adolescence. The American psychologists, Dawn Szymanski and Stewart-Richardson, for example, found that 72% of young men addicted to pornography had experienced physical abuse in childhood, whilst 81% had experienced sexual abuse, and 97% had experienced emotional abuse. Similarly, the Australian researchers, Frederick Cohen and Judianne Densen-Gerber found that 84% of a sample of adults with drug or alcohol addiction had a history of parental violence and abuse, including incest and rape. Likewise, the American psychologist Susan Mason found that women who were subjected to physical or sexual abuse in childhood were significantly more likely to develop the food addictions, anorexia nervosa and bulimia, as adults.

Societal and cultural factors are also known to influence vulnerability to addiction. The renowned French sociologist, Emile Durkheim proposed that rapid societal change could result in a profound loss of cultural identity and purpose, leading to a phenomenon that he called anomie, which has subsequently been used to explain the disturbingly high levels of drug, and alcohol abuse found in marginalised communities. The American researchers, Patrick Abbott and Duane Chase, for instance, state that excessive reliance on chemical substances like alcohol is particularly likely in communities during periods of rapid and

Chapter 4: The psychological impact of vulnerability 67

significant cultural change and upheaval (particularly among groups where there has traditionally been no/or limited prior exposure). Likewise, such processes have been employed to explain the high rates of alcoholism and substance abuse found in indigenous societies around the world. Abnormally high levels of addiction, for example, have been reported in indigenous North American Indians, the Australian aborigines and the Inuits in Greenland. To take a specific case, the Aboriginal Healing Foundation in Canada reports that the death due to alcohol abuse in Canadian indigenous communities lies at 43.7 per 10,000 compared to the national norm of 23.6, whilst incarceration in the penal system for indigenous youth (which is frequently for drug and alcohol-related crimes) lies as 64.5 per 10,000 compared to 8.2 per 10,000.

Interestingly, however, lower social status and income is not a reliable predictor of addiction. The UK's Social Metrics Commission has reported that middle class communities typically consume *more* alcohol than their counterparts in poorer communities. Likewise, several authoritative newspapers, including the *Wall Street Journal*, have periodically run articles that reported what appears to be the frequent usage of cocaine amongst wealthy commodity traders, which (perhaps understandably) has not been the subject of formal research.

Vulnerability to addiction is also closely linked to the co-existence of depression, and conditions, such as autistic spectrum disorder (ASD, attention deficit hyperactivity disorder (ADHD) and social anxiety (SAD). The German psychiatrist, Martin Ohlmeier, for instance, found that ADHD was a significant risk for both alcohol and substance abuse, whilst the Swedish researcher, Agnieszka Butwicka and her colleagues reported that the risk of substance use-related problems was the highest among individuals with a dual diagnosis of ASD and ADHD. In a similar vein, the American psychiatrist, Franklin Schneir reported that significantly higher rates of alcohol problems have been reported in young adults with ASD versus their counterparts in the general population.

In addition, the misuse of alcohol has long been associated with emotional impact of stress, grief and loss following bereavement across cultures. The Hungarian psychologist, Janos Pilling, for instance, found that bereaved men where almost twice as likely as their non-bereaved counterparts to be clinically at risk from excess consumption of alcohol.

Similarly, the Norwegian public health researcher, Solveig Glestad Christiansen found that alcohol-related mortality in parents who had lost a child was significantly higher than for the general population, whilst the Finish psychologist, David Teye Doku found the risk for alcohol-related mortality in parents following the death of a child was higher for mothers than for fathers.

Notes

1 Guilt can also arise as chronic condition alongside clinical depression, grief and trauma, and particularly when the perceived cause of harm to those cannot be reversed (for example as in survivor guilt associated with trauma).
2 Habituation refers a diminished response to a given stimuli. People who live a busy town quickly habituate to the background noise caused by traffic and habituation also occurs with drug use and novel activities, with the behavioural high requiring a more frequent and intense dosage to achieve the same effect.

Part Two
Resilience

Chapter 5
Defining resilience

A brief history of resilience

When I was an undergraduate back in the late 1980s, the concept of resilience was just starting to appear on the psychological radar. Huge strides were being taken in fields such as child-development, cognitive psychology, social psychology and biological psychology, but wisdom gained from these disciplines tended to exist in academic silos. When knowledge was pooled and applied to human behaviour, it tended to be in the context of the disease-based model of human behaviour with its focus on deficits in human behaviour. In the field of health, for example, the leading undergraduate textbooks of the time were firmly focused on abnormal development, and common topics included disorders of personality and childhood, the biological basis of abnormal development and, mirroring psychology more generally, these books had relatively little to say about the normative factors that promote resilience, health and well-being.

However, that is not to say that research *relating* to resilience did not exist. Two longitudinal studies were in progress that were already shedding light on the role of traits, parenting and the environment in mediating outcomes relating to adult health and social success.

The Harvard Medical School Grant Study, which began in 1942, had tracked nearly 300 students over a period of seventy years and revealed that success in relationships and employment was predicted by sensitive maternal care, an empathic coping style and self-confidence.

DOI: 10.4324/9781351035545-7

Men who had warm, caring mothers were found to earn $87,000 more per year on average than those who did not, and whilst this study was criticised for focussing exclusively on white, privileged males, who were students of an elite educational establishment, another study, named the Kauai longitudinal study was in the process of tracing developmental outcomes in children of mixed gender, race and social class.

This study led by the American developmental psychologist, Emmy Werner followed a cohort of 698 children over a period of forty years, commencing in 1955, and produced findings that had echoes of its Harvard equivalent. The existence of a close relationship with an emotionally stable adult (such as a parent, family member, or a mentor, teacher or coach in the community, school or church) appeared to buffer children from the worst effects of parental discord, social deprivation, alcoholism and trauma. In a similar vein, children who were described by their mothers at age one as easy-going and sociable[1] experienced fewer life problems and had better, overall health. Conversely, children who were described as pessimistic and quick to blame others for their one own mistakes and behaviours were significantly more likely to experience poorer health in later life, and to be involved in teenage delinquency.

Yet, in keeping with the disease model of human behaviour, which was prevalent at the time, the findings that were identified in these two studies did not awaken the interest of mainstream psychological until the late 1990s when a seed change in psychology heralded the arrival of two, new disciplines: the Positive Psychology Movement, spearheaded by Martin Seligman, with its explicit focus on the study of human strengths rather than deficits, and emergence of Health Psychology, with its emphasis on health promotion and quality of life. Not only did these new disciplines act to shift the focus of psychological research away from the investigation of human deficits, they also acted as catalysts that encouraged researchers to look *across* disciplines when developing theory and practice guidelines and *outside* of psychology in order to embrace diverse scientific fields, such as biology, neuroscience, sociology epidemiology and economics.

These developments were, for psychology at least, quite revolutionary and as we will learn shortly, contributed to interest in resilience as a multi-dimensional construct that determines human health and behaviour.

Defining resilience

If you do a web-search for resilience, there is a high probability that you will find that it treated as personality trait (or set of traits) that gives people the ability to bounce back from adversity. You may also come across an oft-cited quote from the British author P.G. Wodehouse, which drily observes that 'there is in certain men…a quality of resilience, a sturdy refusal to acknowledge defeat, which aids them as effectively in matters of the heart as in encounters of a sterner and more practical kind'.

Although there is almost certainly more than a hint of sardonic humour in this proclamation. It does, nevertheless, accurately reflect our predilection for viewing resilience as a trait, which has drawn us to believe that people can be readily divided into two camps: Those who are robust and resilient and those who are vulnerable and weak.

This world view is also reflected in sections of the British media which encourages us to believe the current generation of young people (the so-called millennials) are vulnerable 'snowflakes', who lack the stiff resolve required to be true leaders of men.

However, the idea that resilience can be attributed solely to the presence of certain personality traits does not sit well with research, which has shown that resilience is more accurately described as a dynamic, composite phenomenon that may be acquired, nurtured and developed or conversely, undermined and destroyed.

For simplicity, I will refer to these two ways of conceptualising resilience as the fixed model that is predicated on the belief that resilience is a personality trait (or set of traits) and the fluid model that draws on the premise that resilience is a dynamic phenomenon that can developed and enhanced (and, in some circumstances, impaired).

In explaining these differences, I would like to guide you through some of the problems that render the fixed model of resilience untenable.

The fixed model of resilience

The literature on resilience shows that our capacity for dealing with adverse events and stress is influenced by a relatively small number of personality traits, which include the traits of self-efficacy, optimism and locus of control, and a cluster of traits referred to as the Big Five.[2]

Self-efficacy, optimism and locus of control are all indirect measures of perceived personal control. People who are high in self-efficacy are typically confident in their ability to master challenging tasks and acquire transferable skills that bolster resilience. As a consequence, they are less likely than people who are low self-efficacy to succumb to stress when faced with complex issues. In a similar vein, people who are high in the trait of optimism tend to believe the future will be better and view problems as temporary obstacles that are short-lived, whilst people who are low in the trait of optimism tend to view problems as complex and enduring and have a future-view that is often contaminated by things that have gone awry in the past. Likewise, people that have a high internal locus of control tend to believe that the solutions to life's problems typically lie within their own grasp, whilst those with a strong external locus of control have a fatalistic tendency to believe that they have little control over their environment because the acts that befall them are matter of luck (or bad luck as the case may be).

The cluster of traits named the Big Five are also widely associated with resilience and comprise the traits of openness, conscientiousness, agreeableness, extraversion and neuroticism.

These traits were distilled from multiple sources of research during the 1980s by the American psychologists Paul Costa and Robert McCrae, and are widely regarded as having good explanatory power in terms of resilience and human behaviour more generally. Indeed, it is easy to envisage how each of these traits might positively influence the outcome of adverse events. Being open and responsive to new ideas, for example, can help people reframe problems and prevent them getting stuck in old patterns of behaviours that are ineffective. In a similar vein, people who are high on the trait of conscientious tend to persist in the face of obstacles and are meticulous about problem-solving and planning for change, which is helpful when dealing with problems that are complex and enduring. Likewise, people who are extroverted tend to enjoy a larger peer-network than their introverted peers, which in theory at least, enables them to draw on support when in times of need.[3]

Similarly, people who are high in neuroticism (a trait associated with low emotional stability, and high anxiety and guilt) are more prone to stress than people who are low in neuroticism and are more likely to externalise negative emotion (i.e., blame others for their feelings of anger and guilt), which can have the effect of driving people away when social and emotional support is most needed.

So taken at face value, these traits clearly have something important to tell us about resilience. However, if we dig a little deeper, we find that collectively they only account for a relatively small proportion of what psychologists refer to as variance in individual behaviour. Variance is a quasi-statistical term that refers to the extent to which a given trait or cluster of traits can explain and predict individual differences in behaviour. Put crudely, the higher the variance the better a trait is at predicting behaviour and vice-versa. A variance of one hundred in, say the relationship between optimism and resilience, would mean that the trait of optimism explained all the individual differences in resilient behaviour that could be observed and measured through research, whilst a variance of null would indicate that no meaningful relationship existed. In practice, however, it is common to find that traits are at best, moderately good at explaining individual differences in behaviour and this is what we find when we examine the aforementioned traits. If we look, for example, at the traits called the Big Five (conscientiousness, agreeableness, neuroticism, openness and extraversion), we find that they collectively account for a maximum of 30% of the variance in resilience and virtually all of this is explained by three traits, neuroticism, conscientiousness and extraversion. The data for the other leading personality trait, optimism are not dissimilar, with studies showing that it accounts for no more than 20% of the variance in resilient behaviour.

What these data tell us is that taking a best-case scenario, these personality traits collectively explain only 50% of individual differences in resilience, and whilst is impossible to know exactly what accounts for the remaining 50% of variance in individual behaviour, good candidates (as we will learnt shortly) include the biological temperaments that we inherit from our immediate family, the quality of parenting and education during childhood, the neighbourhoods in which we live and more.

However, there are other problems too. Personality theorists have traditionally regarded traits as fixed, stable and enduring. After all the trait of honesty would not be a very useful construct if it were found that individuals varied in honesty, depending on the situation they found themselves. Put another way, traits should be stable and consistent across time and place, but they are not. Self-efficacy, for example, is known to be highly domain specific. An individual may be high on self-efficacy in respect of work-related tasks, but low on self-efficacy in terms of parenting or romanticism. Likewise, a person's sense of optimism may be greatly affected by events that involve major loss, like serious illness or social displacement, and by traumatic events that alter their Just-World Beliefs. In a similar vein, people's emotional stability (neuroticism) can be radically undermined by extrinsic factors that create powerlessness, dependency and helplessness.

An additional problem for trait theory is that vary in their expression across an individual's lifespan and particularly during life-transitions. It is not uncommon, for example, for teenagers to experience a big dip in self-efficacy as they transition, sometimes chaotically, into the world of adulthood. Moreover, a run of stressful events, like serious illness leading to cascade effects, such as unemployment and loss of health insurance can foster pessimistic beliefs and a sense of powerlessness that fundamentally alter an individual's self-efficacy.

What this tells us in practical terms, is that, collectively and individually, the traits of openness, conscientiousness, agreeableness, extraversion and neuroticism, optimism and self-efficacy have less explanative power than the statistics might suggest, because situational factors have a significant effect on how they are expressed over time and place.

Viewed from this perspective, resilience *cannot* be a fixed, trait-like entity, for the simple reason that resilience is shaped and modified by factors that are themselves fluid and subject to change. In other words, resilience is less a trait and more, as we will learn next, a fluid construct that is influenced by a person's internal characteristics, significant life events and their social and economic environment.

The fluid model of resilience

In 2013 a panel of experts gathered together at a conference hosted by the *International Society of Traumatic Stress*, to define resilience and identify pathways for future developments in research and practice. The

Chapter 5: **Defining resilience**

panel chaired by Professor of Psychiatry, Steven Southwick, proposed that resilience is a dynamic construct that describes an individual or community's ability to cope and adapt with adversity and significant sources of stress. It was noted that resilience fluctuates over time in response to significant life events involving transitions, loss and trauma, and the experience of adversity was regarded as being central to the development of resilience.[4]

Moreover, resilience, it was argued is not, as is commonly believed, and all or nothing phenomenon that may be conveniently linked to an individual's personality traits, but rather a fluctuating thing that waxes and wanes in response to life circumstances.

Indeed, one the panellists, the child psychologist, Ann Masten stated that her favourite definition of resilience centred on the idea that resilience is the capacity of a dynamic system to successfully adapt to the disturbances that threaten its viability. Indeed, Masten echoed the points that there were made in the first part of this book: Namely that vulnerability and resilience are common bedfellows and adaptive resilience flows from our experiences of vulnerability and the knowledge and skills that we acquire from mastery. It is easy, for example, to imagine how adversity begins at a young age. Infants must learn to master anger and frustration and find alternative way of using their emotional energy in a positive way. As young people enter puberty, they must negotiate the often difficult transition from childhood to adulthood and as adults they must learn to cope with illness, loss and the life-long responsibility of being a parent. In addition, the panel argued that resilience should be viewed as a product of complex interacting systems that are influenced by social, biological, genetic and psychological factors, which act in a cumulative manner.

These factors exert a maximum effect during the developmental years of childhood, as the cumulative effect of positive and negative experiences creates a template that is influential in shaping our response to adverse life events in adolescence and adulthood.

The processes involved are eloquently described in one of the most influential models of child development: Namely, the bioecological model, developed by the Russian born, psychologist Urie Bronfenbrenner in 1994, which sheds light on how social, biological, genetic and psychological factors act to shape personal resilience and or vulnerability.

The bioecological model of human development

The bioecological model employs a systems-based approach that sets out the interactive factors and conditions that influence the development of resilience (and vulnerability) in childhood, and these are placed within the context of a chronological framework that takes account of maturational processes relating to major life-transitions, personal development and loss. In the model, biological processes are deemed to create innate, dispositional characteristics (traits and temperaments) that are developmentally generative or developmentally inhibitive and these drive child development through interaction with proximal resources that include the quality of parenting and distal resources, such as the quality of the child's wider environment. These resources act with the child's dispositional characteristics in a cumulative manner to promote or constrain growth and development.

The biological processes that shape child development include the many processes that we encountered in the first part of the book: the epigenetic effects of toxic environments, for example, that affect the baseline reactivity of the developing foetus's stress response system or the nurturing impact of sensitive parenting or the deleterious effects of abuse or neglect on the developing architecture of the infant's social and emotional brain. In respect of developmentally generative factors inherent in the child we might look to a biological predisposition towards low stress reactivity and the acquisition of positive temperaments and traits, such as extraversion and optimism that facilitate resilience and openness to change. At the other end of the spectrum, developmentally inhibitive characteristics might include a biological predisposition towards high stress reactivity, the acquisition of temperaments and traits, such as neuroticism that trigger anxiety and resistance in unfamiliar situations and inherited vulnerability for serious mental health problems (including anxiety and depressive disorders, attentional disorders, such as attention deficit disorder and autistic spectrum disorder and psychotic disorders of perception and cognition, such as schizophrenia).

The proximal resources referred to in the model include factors present in the child's immediate environment that promote development, such as warm, sensitive parenting and the presence of positive role-models (other family members, teachers, mentors and coaches), whilst distal resources refer to the wider societal milieu that lies outside of family, including access to supportive peers, high-quality education, health and other such resources that facilitate development and wellbeing. Likewise, the model also takes account of factors in the child's proximal and distal environment which may be developmentally inhibitive, including maternal depression, family dysfunction and conflict, environmental pollution, poor- quality housing and schooling and factors associated with powerlessness, such as socio-economic poverty, marginalisation, racism and stigmatisation.

The bioecological model emphasises, not only the sensitive nature of the interface between the child's innate biology and the quality of the environment in which the child resides, it also asserts that the processes that drive development are bi-directional and subject to the principle of reciprocity. Each child's behaviour elicits a response in parents that is experienced as rewarding and reinforcing or stressful and aversive. Likewise, parents may act in ways that promote comfort and security or they may act in ways that result in distress and discomfort. To take an example, parenting a child, with what Jerome Kagan identified as an uninhibited and socially laid-back temperament, is likely to be a pleasant and rewarding experience that will resonate emotionally with the child in a positive way. Whilst rearing a child, whose insecure disposition leads to frequent emotional meltdowns may well generate parental stress that is recycled in ways that further amplify the child's unease.

In considering the principle of reciprocity, we might also wish to add the concept of Goodness of Fit that we encountered earlier in this book. A child with a low, innate tolerance for stress born into a family environment that is characterised by tension and conflict is likely to fair worse in developmental terms than a child born into the same family, who has a high, innate tolerance for stress. Moreover, things may get even more problematic when we look to the reciprocal impacts of parenting a child with an inherited developmental disorder, such as autistic spectrum disorder (ASD). Children with ASD, for example, tend to be emotionally distant, hypersensitive to environmental stimuli and prone to distressing and difficult to manage emotional meltdowns when things deviate from predictable routines. This can have a devastating impact on parent's well-being and their ability to parent in a developmentally generative manner. Reporting in the *Australian Journal of Guidance and Counselling*, for example, Vicki Bitsika and Christopher Sharpley found that half of the parents sampled who had children with a diagnosis of ASD reported high levels of anxiety, nearly two-thirds were clinically depressed, and 90% reported that they often felt unable to parent their child effectively. Moreover, research conducted by the American child psychologist, Pamela Ventola and her colleagues found that parents of children who had ASD were more likely than their counterparts to employ parenting methods that were intrusive and controlling (a problem that is almost certainly exacerbated by late diagnosis).

Given the proven relationship that exists between developmental delay, parenting stress and untoward outcomes, one would expect to see enhanced, available support for parents struggling to raise a child with a development disorder, severe physical illness, handicap or trauma. However, Bitsika notes that support for struggling parents is frequently inadequate or non-existent. Moreover, Bronfenbrenner states that viewed from a historical perspective, families in distress have frequently been viewed as part of the problem rather than the solution and tarred with dysfunctional, trait-like qualities without due regard to the problems and circumstances that they face.

Fortunately, things have improved somewhat with the advent of systemic models of child and family development (such as the bioecological model), which have focussed attention on the importance of identifying and understanding the patterns and behaviours within families that facilitate resilient development, as we will discover next.

Notes

1 There are echoes here of Kagan's dispositional temperaments.
2 Resilience is also closely associated with intelligence, but I will deal with this separately as many researchers do not regard intelligence as a trait.
3 This is just one of the many problems with the Big Five theory of personality. Recent, research, for example has shown that the idea that introverts have reduced access to friends and high-quality social support is false.
4 The exception being life events and circumstances that overwhelm our ability to adapt, as in trauma and powerlessness.

Chapter 6
The family environment and resilience

Parenting and resilience

Many scientists believe that the human brain has evolved to become a sophisticated tool for social communication, empathy and cooperation, which allows us to thrive in social groups and collectively adapt to environmental threats and opportunities. To achieve this, nature has largely ditched the fixed, pre-programmed behavioural responses that are found in species that occupy a lower niche on the evolutionary chain and adopted developmental processes that support neuronal plasticity as the key to adaptation. As a consequence, whilst the systems and structures that govern behaviour in lower species, such as reptiles, are largely pre-programmed and fixed at birth, the human brain is highly dependent upon external, generative stimulation for optimal development of behaviour, cognition and emotion... together with other, important faculties, such as language and fine-motor control.

During early infancy the primary source of stimulation is the mother (or other primary caregiver), and the processes involved are laid out in the Transactional Model of Childhood Development, which was developed by the American psychologist Arnold Sameroff. According to this model the developments that we see in the infant brain are a product of continuous, reciprocal interactions that are predicated upon the child's innate, biological dispositions and the quality of parenting and the environment.

The processes involved are largely automatic and occur outside of the conscious awareness, but according to the model, everything a child feels, hears and sees during infancy is registered and imprinted in the developing brain's neural networks in the form of emotional memories and implicit rules that come to govern our thinking and patterns of behaviour in adulthood.

As in the bioecological model, these developments are subject to the principles of parental reciprocity and goodness of fit that were mentioned earlier. If we are fortunate and in receipt of developmentally generative inputs during the formative years of childhood, we emerge as resilient beings with a repertoire of cognitive and motor skills that support problem solving and communication and a healthy, confident sense of self, associated with good social skills and the ability to effectively regulate emotional distress.

If we are unlucky, however, and are exposed to developmentally inhibitive stimuli, such as parental abuse, neglect or inattention, we are likely to emerge from childhood in a state of vulnerability that is characterised by insecurity, poor social skills and emotional dysregulation (the chronic inability to manage emotional distress).

Indeed, research unanimously shows that the single most important factor in this chain of development is the capacity of parents to raise their child in a sensitive and caring manner that fosters resilience through support for emotional development, self-care skills, play and education. However, parental capacity can be affected by many factors, and one of the most important is the parents' own experiences of being parented. Of particular interest here is work emanating from the US Centers for Disease Control and Prevention and its study of adverse childhood experiences (ACEs), referred to as the *CDC-Kaiser ACE Study*, which collected data in two waves between 1995 and 1997, from more than 17,000 cooperating organisations.

In this study, childhood adverse experiences, referred to as ACEs were found to be mediated by a relatively small number of adversity factors, such as child maltreatment, domestic violence and parental conflict, and environmental factors, such as poverty and social deprivation and mediating, parental and family factors such as parental age, levels of education and family cohesion.

Moreover, these ACEs were found to act in cumulative, pyramidal manner, with the result that the risk of family dysfunction, cyclical, child maltreatment, and long-term illness could be accurately predicted by the number of stressors that households were exposed to.

Chapter 6: **The family environment and resilience**

The researcher Antonella Miccoli and her colleagues, for example, found that high parental ACE scores were associated with a heightened risk of intergenerational, childhood development delay and referral to penal, community service. Similarly, the American Professor of Psychology, Amanda Sheffield Morris and her colleagues found that low family ACE scores were correlated with nurturing parenting attitudes, higher parental income and education levels, whilst high ACE scores were associated with harsh, critical parenting styles of parenting.

These outcomes mirror child development research, which shows that parents who have had positive parenting experiences tend to arrive at parenthood with a blueprint for resilient child development that is characterised by positive expectations, reflective self-awareness and secure attachments, whilst those who were subject to maltreatment or neglect in their own childhood are at high risk of entering the world of parenthood frightened and insecure and saddled by emotional baggage, which adversely their capacity to parent effectively.

Likewise it is generally believed that parents who had positive role models as children have a greater capacity for emotional warmth and empathic perspective-taking.

The eminent psychologist, Carl Rogers, referred to this as unconditional positive regard, which describes a parent's capacity to tolerate and accept a child's, inevitable shortcomings, mistakes and dispositions. Rogers argued that this capacity is readily accommodated by parents who are secure in themselves, whilst those who are insecure are more likely to seek to forge the child in their own (idealised) image and reward only the behaviours that meet with prior expectations – a phenomenon that psychologists refer to as 'conditional parenting'.

In a similar vein, positive child-rearing is associated with authoritative styles of parenting that promote autonomy and independence within healthy, non-intrusive boundaries that are respectful of the child's need for privacy and growing autonomy. Authoritarian parenting, on the other hand, is associated with intrusive control and unhealthy boundaries that can put a child in danger and/or fail to create a sense of security and control and, which may act as developmental brake that inhibits the development of resilience.

The effect of boundary setting in childhood has been the subject of considerable research. According to the American psychiatrist, Kai

MacDonald and his colleagues, for example, people who have difficulty setting healthy boundaries often have personal problems relating to childhood trauma, insecure attachments and maladaptive childhood beliefs, which may be unconsciously played out through parenting. Moreover, whilst some parents are readily able to compensate for a less-than-optimal childhood by making a conscious decision not to repeat the mistakes that their parents made, this requires a high degree of self-awareness and reflection, which may be lacking in parents who experienced childhood trauma due to neglect or abuse that has been repressed. Indeed, unresolved emotional damage arising from childhood abuse, neglect and/or emotional trauma relating to problems such as domestic violence and alcohol abuse are readily carried into parenthood as boundary problems that have serious consequences for the next generation. Intrusive boundaries, for example, can arise when a parent has an unconscious need to resolve and play out earlier, repressed traumas that have been rekindled by the intimate nature of childbirth and child-rearing. This can result in the child being inappropriately treated as an adult confidant or subjected to physical or emotional harm and it can create an environment in which children feel chronically insecure and confused. Likewise, childhood exposure to harsh, critical parenting and shaming can result in authoritarian parenting involving boundaries that are overly restrictive, harsh and unyielding. Parents, for example, who were neglected and unloved during their own formative years may come to see their child's increasing independence as a threat and respond by seeking to control them in the manner that they were controlled by their parents.

The role of the family

According to the American clinical psychologist, Froma Walsh, who is an acknowledged expert on family resilience, families play an important role in buffering individual members from stress, during times of crises and are the main conduit for the transmission of values, mores and traditions that support resilient development.

According to Walsh, family resilience is characterised by a relatively small number of factors that centre on a family's beliefs, organisation and communication. Shared beliefs, for example, help families to find

Chapter 6: **The family environment and resilience**

meaning and purpose in untoward events and support transformational processes that enhance resilient growth. Similarly, a stable family structure and organisation provides a sense of connectedness and mutual support that facilitates flexibility and openness to change, born out of a sense of security and mutual support. Likewise good communication is characterised by ability to communicate with each other about practical issues, but also to share feelings and concerns that support emotional literacy and empathic understanding that allows families to celebrate triumphs and sympathise with failures and loss. Conversely, Walsh found that family resilience was stifled by secrecy and competing agendas, disunity of purpose and lack of willingness to seek support, particularly where masculine stereotypes fostered self-reliance.

However, families are not homogenous units. In the western, industrialised world, the nuclear family is the norm, comprising the mother and father and one to three children per household. Moreover, it is increasingly common to see households being headed up by a single parent. According to the UK's Office for National Statics, for example, in 2019 nearly of 22% of families in the UK were headed by a lone parent. Similarly, a survey of family life, published by the UK's Department of Work and Pensions dated 2006, reported that family breakdown and divorce has become increasingly common with 20% of children under one year of age living in a single-parent household, rising to 40% for children sixteen and over.

In developing countries, it is more common to see multiple generations of families, including grandparents, uncles, aunts and cousins living under one roof and, whilst it has been suggested that the extended family is best placed to offer parenting advice, practical help and encouragement during times of stress, research has produced a mixed picture. Extended families can suffer from inter-generational conflict, which can create stress rather than solve it. The British psychologist Edmund Sonuga-Barke and his colleagues, for example, report that generational differences in beliefs and values can lead to conflict, stress and depression in British Muslim families.

Research has also shown that raising children as a loan parent can be particularly taxing and it is not difficult to imagine how and why the added responsibilities of raising a child without the support of a partner might be stressful. Indeed, research shows that single mothers experience more stress than their counterparts in stable relationships and more economic hardship. Helen Graham from the Employment Research Institute at Edinburgh Napier University, for example, reports that lone parent families are more likely than couple families to experience poverty and have lower than average employment rates. Likewise, you may recall the Troubled Families Report, referred to in the first section of this book, which found that on average women in the study (nearly all of whom were single) were exposed to multiple major stressors relating to economic hardship, physical and psychological health issues and problems relating to their children, such as school exclusion and delinquent behaviour.

It needs to be noted that the women in the Troubled Families study were drawn from urban cohorts living in areas of high socio-economic deprivation, so clearly their experiences cannot be generalised to single parents that live in more affluent areas with steady jobs and a regular source of income. However, for a more representative view we can look to a German study, carried out by the psychiatrist Michael Franz and colleagues, which examined a cross-section of approximately 900 mothers from across a broad spectrum of social backgrounds, whose children where starting school for the first time. The study found that, on average, single mothers experienced more stress than their counterparts, who were in a stable, supportive relationship and were more likely to have a lower socio-economic status.

These findings aside, adverse life events, such as unemployment, severe illness and the death of child can prove overwhelming for even the most secure and well-adjusted of families. The months that precede the death of child, for example, and the period that follows it are stressful, emotionally exhausting and associated with significant marital stress that may be amplified by pre-existing relationship problems, which can lead to divorce. The American Emeritus Professor of social work, Grace Christ and her colleagues, for instance, reports that the experience of child bereavement is frequently associated with marital conflict, anger and misunderstanding, reduced intimacy and discordant patterns of coping, such as incongruent grief and misuse of alcohol.

In a similar vein, research has shown that refugee families often struggle to deal with the aftermath of torture or exposure to horrific events such as genocide, and the cultural trauma that is linked to displacement, long-term uncertainty and forced-choice outcomes that are stressful and disempowering. A Finish study, for example, of families living in an asylum centre, carried out by the child psychiatrist Andre Sourander, revealed high rates of depressive disorder and distress linked to fear of deportation and separation from members of family. Likewise, the Danish public health researcher, Signe Nielsen and her colleagues, found that nearly one-third of children living in asylum centres in Denmark were rated by their teachers as having a mental health and behavioural problems.

Problems linked to major life events, such as bereavement or displacement in the case of refugees, are exacerbated when families are unable to pull together, because of competing priorities or pre-existing issues, such as severe parental conflict. As Walsh notes, under normal circumstances, stress is mediated when families have shared unity of purpose and levels of intimacy that permit the free exchange and resolution of difficult emotions, such as anger and sadness. Conversely, research into family resilience conducted by the British civil servant, Anne Harold for the Department of Work and Pensions, concluded that unresolved parental conflict and family disunity was traumatising for children and increased the risk of childhood hostility and depression, anti-social behaviour and criminality, impaired educational attainment and school refusal.

However, crises and transitions can also have a silver lining. Froma Walsh also states that families who routinely manage adverse events, crises and transitions more often than not emerge scarred, but stronger. Reflecting the ideas suggested by the expert panel at the aforementioned conference organised by the International Society of Traumatic Stress, Walsh asserts that whilst crises often impact the whole family unit, they can act as a catalyst for resilient change and growth by forcing the members to take stock of their priorities and to decide what is really important.

Trust and intimacy

One of the most important processes in the development of resilience in childhood is the creation of a sense of trust and intimacy, which, according to John Bowlby, is grounded in the formation of a secure emotional attachment with the mother (or other primary care giver), which occurs when she is reliably attuned to her child's emotional and physical needs.

Indeed, Bowlby asserts that when children are comfortable and secure around others, it is because they have developed an internal, working model that is founded on experiential security, trust and intimacy rather than exposure to events that have created insecurity, mistrust and affective states like anger and shame that are associated with child maltreatment.

Moreover, this inner model acts as a cognitive and emotional template for the development of meaningful relationships with others throughout life, based on the capacity to trust one's feelings and intuitions and the self-confidence to engage with one's own personal vulnerabilities and shortcomings.

From the perspective of attachment theory, these internal working models are referred to as attachment styles, which we carry into adult life for better or worse. Whilst secure attachments are associated with trust and intimacy, insecure attachments stem from adverse childhood experiences that, in varying degrees, can leave children feeling insecure and mistrusting of others, particularly in respect of close relationships that normally involve intimacy. Moreover, these internal models may be carried over into adulthood affecting the parent's capacity to fully meet the needs of their developing child. In addition, it is not uncommon for adults who are emotionally handicapped by adverse childhood experiences, involving abuse, violence or neglect, to enter into relationships that are characterised by marital discord, relational violence or addiction, in an apparent replay of the childhood circumstances in which they themselves were raised.

Of course, to err is human. We are all fallible and it may surprise you to learn that researchers estimate that around one-half of all adults may be categorised as having attachments problems associated with relational trust in self and others. On the face of it that sounds rather alarming. However, put into context, whilst most of us exit childhood with negative baggage, we are generally adept at managing childhood's emotional scars and finding ways of coping that allow us to function as reasonably well-adjusted adults. Moreover, of the four primary attachment styles that have been reliably identified, only one is not obviously characterised by adaptive and resilient coping mechanisms.

In order to explain this further, I want to expand on the four primary attachment styles that were first identified by the American-Canadian psychologist, Mary Ainsworth.

Attachment styles and resilience

The four attachment styles identified by Ainsworth are the secure attachment style, which is associated with trust, intimacy, emotional self-regulation and healthy social relationships in childhood and adult life. The avoidant-dismissive and anxious-preoccupied insecure attachment styles, which are both associated with relational problems in later life and the disorganised attachment style, which I will deal with separately, because it is strongly correlated with emotional problems and life-long pathology.

As previously discussed, the development of a secure attachment flows from parenting that is sensitively attuned to the infant's emotional and physical needs. Through the repeated experience of being sensitively cared for, the securely attached child develops an internal working model of the world that facilitates confidence in the self and others.

In addition, the securely attached child learns to understand and manage troubling emotions like anger and jealousy, and they perceive the world to be a safe and predictable place, which helps to forge traits like optimism and openness that, in turn, enable the formation of healthy relationships based on trust and intimacy.

The second, avoidant-dismissive attachment style, broadly relates to people that we might think of as being somewhat aloof and self-contained. This attachment style stems from parenting that was not consistently attuned to the child's emotional needs, leading to recurrent anxiety and insecurity. In response, the young child learns the need for self-reliance, and discovers that they can avoid anxiety by constricting their emotions and avoiding situations where trust and intimacy are required. As a result, people with this attachment style are often very self-reliant and confident in their general abilities, but they tend to be wary of others and keep a tight rein on their emotions with particular regard to relationships that require emotional intimacy.

The third attachment style, referred to as anxious-preoccupied, broadly relates to people that we might regard as socially adept, but somewhat emotionally needy. They have a strong craving for love, affection and intimacy and are often overly reliant on others for nurturing needs that they cannot fulfil themselves (because they did not learn how to do this in childhood). Unlike people with an avoidant-dismissive attachment style, individuals with an anxious-preoccupied attachment style are more likely to be low on self-esteem. They do not readily tolerate being alone, are prone to worry about being negatively judged or ridiculed by others and tend to ruminate about past failures.

Now given that these two patterns of coping are referred to as *insecure* attachments styles, we might well be tempted to jump to the conclusion that people with an anxious-preoccupied or avoidant-dismissive attachment style would be relatively high in vulnerability and low on resilience, but that would be a false conclusion, because both attachment styles embody elements of resilient coping.

People with an avoidant-dismissive style may be emotionally constricted, but they tend to be self-reliant, low in anxiety, high in self-efficacy and generally proficient at looking after themselves. Moreover, they may go through life being successful in their careers, particularly in occupations where high levels of self-reliance, self-efficacy and a degree of detached, personal aloofness are prized above the ability to build and maintain the relationships. The American anthropologist, Willem Eduard Frankenhuis, for example, states that avoidant-dismissive individuals tend to be highly independent and good at working independently. Likewise, their relative disinterest in socialising can render then more job and task-orientated than their more sociable counterparts, which can be beneficial from an employer's perspective.

In a similar way, the anxious-preoccupied individual's need for social connectedness often leads to their being socially adroit and they may be successful in forging intimate relationships, providing they are fortunate enough to pair with someone who is happy to adopt a role that provides some succour for the unmet emotional needs of childhood. In addition, the American psychologist, Jeffry Simpson and his colleagues note that people who are anxious tend to be more empathically accurate and sensitive to others' distress than their non-sensitive counterparts, which may be valuable in occupations that necessitate a high degree of emotional tact and understanding.

In short, both of these insecure attachment styles involve resilient ways of coping that allow people to function socially and emotionally without being overwhelmed by feelings of anxiety or concerns about rejection. Regrettably, however, the same cannot be said of the fourth pattern of coping, which is commonly referred to as the disorganised attachment, which we will look at next.

Chapter 6: **The family environment and resilience**

Disorganised attachments

The fourth, attachment style, known as a disorganised attachment[1] was created to house disparate and problematic patterns of behaviour that did not fit neatly into the pre-existing attachment categories derived from Mary Ainsworth's Strange Situation paradigm, which was referred to earlier in this book. Using this method Ainsworth demonstrated that securely attached children were better able to tolerate the separation from their mother and exposure to unfamiliar people and environments than insecurely attached children, who showed clear evidence of emotional distress.

The individual differences in attachment behaviours that Ainsworth observed have been explained from interlocking biological and psychosocial perspectives. In explaining the biological origins of insecure attachments, for example, the British researchers, Carol George and Judith Solomon draw on Bowlby's assertion that attachment behaviours are driven by powerful, innate mechanisms, whose purpose is elicit care-giving behaviours that immediately sooth infant distress and which promote the neurological development of structures in the brain that enable self-regulation of emotional distress so that children are effectively able to manage stress in the absence of the parent figure.

Viewed from this perspective, individual differences in attachment behaviours in children and (adults) are a direct reflection of biological variation in the development of the structures and systems in the brain that support emotional regulation (which you may recall include the prefrontal cortex, the amygdala and hippocampal fear processing centres).

These differences exist on a continuum. At the one end, we find securely attached children who have successfully developed the capacity to self-regulate internal distress, whilst at the other end, we find a small proportion of children (estimated at 5%–15%), who cannot contain their distress and who bounce chaotically from one life crisis to another in a pattern that is consistent with what child psychologists refer to as a disorganised attachment style.

Children and adults who have a disorganised attachment style invariably suffer from chronic anxiety and insecurity, a low stress threshold, emotional instability and neuroticism, seemingly unpredictable emotional outbursts, low self-worth and fundamental lack of trust in others.

Viewed from a social-developmental perspective, these phenomena almost always stem from maltreatment in childhood, which *creates* emotional dysregulation and the development of a negative or (in the worst-case scenario)' fragmented self that is associated with chronic, existential angst, shame and mistrust of others.

Indeed, the link between disorganised attachments and traumatic maltreatment in childhood is a powerful one. The British sociological researcher, Sue White and her colleagues, for example, report that it has been estimated that approximately 80% of children and adults who present in clinical practice with a disorganised attachment style have been subject to severe physical, emotional or sexual abuse and/or have been moved from one care institution to another as a child and young adult. Moreover, research has shown that this attachment style is frequently associated with a childhood where intimacy has been absent, or inconsistent, where boundaries have been intrusive or non-existent and where fear of rejection has been juxtaposed with trauma linked to abuse, domestic strife or violence, criminality, or addiction.

The trauma expert, Judith Lewis-Herman, for example, argues that disorganised attachments arise when the primary care giver becomes a source of fear rather than comfort, as may occur when parenting is critical, hostile and shaming. Likewise, George and Solomon note that disorganised attachments are likely to occur when one of three conditions exist: The first being that the child is attached to a caregiver whose own disorganised attachment style elicits unregulated and unpredictable, distress, hostility and emotional constriction or physical and sexual maltreatment; the second being that there is a major and prolonged separation from the caregiver; and the third being that the child is exposed to chronic neglect. In addition, these authors state that any one of these conditions can result in 'fear without resolution', a form of primal trauma, which, if allowed to persist, morphs into a chronic fear of abandonment that is associated with an internal state of persistent distress and perceived powerlessness.

These assertions have considerable support. Research has shown that prolonged separation, abuse and neglect have an untoward effect on the body's stress regulatory systems. The researchers, Kristin Bernard and Mary Dozier examined the impact of parental separation on children with different attachment styles and found that those with a disorganised attachment had elevated cortisol levels, indicative of fear

Chapter 6: **The family environment and resilience**

and anxiety, that persisted following temporary separation from the primary caregiver and this result was not found in children with other attachment styles. These findings are of particular interest because chronically elevated cortisol levels are associated with conditions, such as high stress reactivity, dysfunctional fear-regulation, labile emotions and unpredictable behaviour, which may explain why people with a disorganised attachment style are prone to swinging erratically between withdrawal and emotional constriction and high expressed emotion, involving temper tantrums, rage and overt aggression.

Adding to this, Lewis Herman argues that disorganised attachments are also a function of deep, internalised shame, or what she calls a 'shattered states' that come to shape the child or young person's persona. It is, for example, not uncommon for children who come from traumatic backgrounds to experience a deep self-loathing that is associated with the shameful sense of not being loveable. Indeed, it is widely accepted that children who have been subjected to emotional or sexual abuse often develop irrational guilt and shame-based beliefs that they have in some way contributed to their own abuse. Children who are sexually abused, for example, commonly come to be believe that they were in some way complicit in the abuse that occurred, whilst children subject to domestic conflict and violence often conclude that they must be the source of parental conflict. In a further twist, parents who are stressed, helpless and frightened may externalise their anger and frustration and deflect it towards the weakest point, which is often the child, so exacerbating the child's feeling of shame, self-loathing and inadequacy, and tragically they may come to see themselves as 'damaged goods' beyond help or repair.

However, the dysfunctional patterns of coping that are associated with disorganised attachments may also be explained by conflict that exists between a person's innate need for intimacy and affection and their learned, fear of rejection. Children and adults with a disorganised attachment style have a compulsive need to be loved, to feel safe and to be loved, because this was missing in childhood.

However, this need exists alongside an equally strong fear of rejection and abandonment, relating to early experiences of neglect and abuse, and this juxtaposition results in a seemingly irreconcilable conflict between the powerful need to seek intimacy and the equally strong fear of the terrors that intimacy might bring. The American psychologist, Kurt Lewin called this the approach-avoidance paradox, and it is commonly observed in children and adults who passionately engage in intimate relationships that are abruptly and repeatedly terminated without apparent cause.

June Tangney and Ronda Dearing suggest that such behaviours may also be plausibly explained by the presence of internalised shame. There is, for example, a strong theoretical association between what are referred to as 'disrupted' attachments[2] and shame, and it is known that adults who carry deep-rooted shame are quick to see imaginary signs of rejection, which can lead them to terminate budding relationships, so they are afforded an illusory sense of control in rejecting the other rather than being rejected.

In addition, children and young people with a disorganised attachment style are prone to various forms of self-sabotaging behaviour that can be both distressing and perplexing. Karen Zilberstein and Eileen Messer, for example, refer to the case history of an eight-year-old, subjected to severe neglect, whose behaviour would alternate between withdrawal and demands for instant attentional monopoly and gratification of needs.

Such patterns of behaviour echo primitive survival instincts of the kind described by Bowlby and are reflective of a social brain that has not acquired the systems and architecture that are necessary to manage the powerful and aversive raw emotions that accompany fear, anger, shame and guilt. Children caught in this state of dysfunctional development are, in effect, required to cope with whatever life throws at them without the neural architecture to quell stress, nor the security blanket of a close, intimate relationship with a trusted other. They are instead often left to rely on their own inadequate and immature coping strategies and the net result is emotional and behavioural turmoil, the causes of which are often poorly understood in settings, such as education, the courts and penal system more generally.

Worse still, there is a clear cyclical element to all of this. The female prison population is significantly over-represented with people that were exposed to violence, abuse and neglect in early life. Similarly, children who have a disorganised attachment style are much more likely to find themselves incarcerated as young offenders and adults than those from the general adult population.

This cyclical nature of insecurity is also like to reverberate across generations. The eminent Italian psychiatrist, Giovanni Liotti, for instance has noted that disorganised attachment behaviours often involve patterns of responding that are normally associated with trauma, such as dissociation and emotional constriction, which would detrimentally affect the quality of maternal care (because the mother would distant and emotionally unavailable). Similarly, George and Solomon note that mothers of children with disorganised attachment frequently suffer from severe mental health problems, such as depression and border-line personality disorder and typically describe themselves as helpless, stressed and exposed to serious, chronic stressors, such as abusive relationships and financial hardship.

Given these factors it is not surprising that children and adults with disorganised attachment style struggle to be resilient. However, programmes and strategies for building resilience in such contexts do exist as we will discover next.

Disorganised attachments – building resilience

Initiatives that have been developed to increase resilience in people who present with problematic behaviours associated with disorganised attachments fall into three broad categories: Namely, those that are designed to prevent the parenting problems that lead to the development of insecure attachments in early childhood, those that seek to repair the damage caused by early life exposure to toxic environments in order to build personal resilience in childhood or later life and initiatives that focus of educating professionals that work with children about attachment theory and the consequences of problematic attachment styles.

In the case of the preventative approaches, several government-funded, programmes have been constructed to address parenting problems that are associated with attachment issues and/or poor outcomes in social educational and occupational domains. These include the United Kingdom's *Family Nurse Partnership Programme*; known as the Nurse Family Partnership in the United States and the *Sure Start Programme*; known as Head Start in the United States and Australia and the Early Years Plan in Canada.

Starting with the latter, Helen Roberts, who is a professor in community child health, states that the Sure Start programme was established in the United Kingdom in 1998 to provide local communities with a range of outreach services to parents from disadvantaged backgrounds to enhance parenting skills, strengthen the family unit and support for social and emotional needs and to provide opportunities for high-quality learning through play.

The Nurse Family Partnership (NFP) was originally developed by Professor David Olds from the University of Colorado and later adopted by the UK's Department of Health and Social Care in 2008 when it was rebadged as the FNP. The aim of these programmes is to is to improve the parenting skills, aspirations and self-efficacy of young, first-time mothers as a means of countering the cyclical problems that are commonly associated with urban deprivation, which include inter-generational poverty, high rates of teenage pregnancies and single-parent households, low achievement in education and employment, and prevalent criminality, drug and alcohol abuse.

The FNP utilises an intensive home visiting programme that employs specially trained nurses to deliver one-to-one support for first-time mothers. The programme aims to educate about first-time mothers about the importance of reciprocal mother-baby interactions, and improve their capacity for interacting with their baby in manner that promotes a secure attachment. In addition, the nurses are trained in motivational interviewing techniques that are designed to raise the mother's aspirations for themselves and their children in order to break the cycle of generational poverty. The programme is broadly based on the principles set out in Bronfenbrenner's bioecological model and is, thus, designed to take account of the many, social and domestic problems that commonly beset first-time mothers raising young children in impoverished communities, where it is common to find high levels of domestic violence and criminality associated with alcohol and drug misuse.

A further model worthy of note is the ARC model (the acronym stands for the Attachment, Regulation and Competency framework), which is aimed at providing support for children and adolescents who are suffering from the effects of complex trauma (a common feature of disorganised attachments) and support for birth parents, foster parents and adopted parents. The associated programmes focus on building parents and caregivers' knowledge and skills in order to promote healthy, secure attachments and to build young peoples' self-awareness and skills in respect of problems relating to emotional dysregulation.

In line with the approach adopted by the FNP, the ARC model focuses on promoting reciprocal infant-child interactions that facilitate emotional bonds and deepening the participant's understanding of children's behaviour and emotional needs. Unlike the FNP, however, it goes further in seeking to build trauma-informed responses to complex, challenging behaviour associated with disorganised attachments (i.e., emotional dysregulation and problems relating to broken trust and intimacy and shame).

A further intervention, the Attachment and Biobehavioral Catch-up (ABC) programme developed by the American psychologist Mary Dozier (which is based on attachment theory and their neuro-biology of stress) has been designed to reduce common barriers to the development of secure attachments. The programme is grounded in the principle that sensitive, attuned parenting is vital for development of the normal, systems and structures in the brain that support emotional regulation. Hence, the programme is designed to give caregivers' awareness and understanding of the developmental processes that promote emotional regulation, including the importance of following the infant's cues, and to improve the caregiver's sensitivity to avoidance and other ways in which rejection is commonly manifest.

These programmes are important for children and parents, but also for substitute caregivers and professional staff working with children and adults in supportive roles, who, research suggests, often know relatively little about the theory of attachment and bonding or the complex processes that lead to the development of disorganised attachments and the cognitive, emotional and behavioural sequelae. Research shows that this extends to people working in teaching and education, community and youth work, nursing, medicine and humanitarian work. Indeed, despite many years of research and applied practice, attachment theory and its implications remain poorly understood outside of a small number of specialist areas. As a consequence, the perplexing behaviours associated with severe attachment problems are easily misattributed to vague and unhelpful constructs that suggest the problem lies with the child rather than with the effects of abuse, neglect or trauma. Children, for example, may be diagnosed with oppositional defiance order – a diagnosis, which infers that problem behaviour is intentional and therefore best served by applying discipline in the form of sanctions and other forms of punishment that are likely to make matters worse.

One area where this issue is particularly problematic is child education. The British Professor of Social Work, Professor Elizabeth Harlow, for example, states, there is an urgent need to include attachment-theory in teacher training in order to improve teachers' knowledge of child relational problems and behaviour. However, the issue is not constrained to the teacher training. There are no recognised pathways to guide community mentors, social workers and teachers tasked with supporting young people with externalising problems relating to insecure attachment styles. Moreover, some authorities have argued that fiscal austerity has placed constraints on the teaching of 'soft subjects', such as pedagogy, which embraces child-development and learning with the consequence that children with attachments issues are often left to fend for themselves with limited personal resources.

In a similar vein, numerous studies have shown that sensitive support, mentoring and coaching delivered by people, outside of the immediate family, such as teachers and community youth workers, can have a significant effect in turning young people's lives round by providing safe boundaries and access to positive achievement-related activities, such as engagement in sport that build self-worth and self-efficacy.

Individual treatment for disorganised attachments can also be very valuable in helping young people (and adults) gain resilience, though it has to be said that cost and resourcing issues have resulted in levels of service-provision that typically range from poor to non-existent. However, trauma-informed interventions that employ techniques, such as compassionate mindfulness, are becoming more commonplace and I will return to these later in the book.

It goes without saying that authorities are reluctant to invest in preventative programme and strategies that individual treatments unless it can be proven that they are clinically effective *and* cost effective, and rather paradoxically, large-scale evaluations that employ randomised control trials (RCTs; regarded as the gold standard of research) are themselves expensive and time-consuming. As a consequence, the evidence-base for the effectiveness of interventions that are designed to build resilience in children and adults with disorganised attachments is quite slim and dogged by contradictory findings. Cohort studies of neglected children from the highly institutionalised Romanian orphanages in the 1980s that were adopted into Canadian families showed mix results. In one study, the American professor of child development, Megan Gunnar and her colleagues, for example, found that children quickly formed attachments to their adopted parents, but continued to show disorganised and conflicting patterns of behaviour that may well have reflected a fundamental lack of trust in others. In another study, the American professor of psychology, Charles Nelson and colleagues found that most of the orphans had significant developmental delays in executive functions and social skills that mimicked many of the patterns of behaviour that are associated with disorganised attachments.

Likewise, evaluation of the UK's Nurse Family Partnership, Sure Start Programmes their mirror-equivalents in the USA and Australia have received mixed reviews and varying levels of political support and commitment.

An RCT evaluation of the FNP programme, two years after its inception in the UK, conducted by Prof Mike Robling and colleagues at the Southeast Wales Trials Unit found that the programme was no better than standard, routine care at reducing smoking in pregnancy, improving birth weight, and reducing secondary pregnancies and rates of emergency admission to hospitals. On this basis, the study concluded that the small beneficial consequences identified were outweighed by the programme's extensive financial costs. However, writing in *The Lancet*, public health specialist, Jane Barlow expressed concern over the medically orientated outcome measures that were assessed in the trial, and the lack of psychological outcome measures, especially given that the FNP programme is designed to provide support for the development of crucial mother-baby bonds. In a similar vein, a follow-up FNP study, *Building Blocks 2-6*, published in 2021 concluded that although the programme led to improvements in child development, school-readiness and educational outcomes, FNP children were found to be *as statistically likely* to be referred to social care or to be placed on a child-protection plan as non-FNP children matched for social and educational criteria.

The ARC does not appear to have been subject to same level of rigorous assessment as the FNP and NFP. However, research published by the American clinical psychologist, Hilary Hodgdon and her colleagues, showed a significant reduction in post-traumatic stress disorder symptoms and externalisation of anger, which at least one other study associated with the reduced use of physical methods of restraint in institutional care settings post education.

According to Mary Dozier, randomized trials evaluating the ABC model have shown that the associated interventions significantly enhanced caregiver's sensitivity to infant distress and reduced levels of intrusive behaviour. Likewise, the US Department of Health and Human Services has published evidence showing that the programme had a significant effect with on improving child development, school readiness, child health and positive parenting practices.

Taken as a whole, these findings reflect the complexities involved in working with families where complex relational problems are juxtaposed with entrenched, cyclical poverty and low aspirations. However, evidence suggests that preventative interventions which target parents and children early on have the best outcomes. In gathering evidence from seventy-five early intervention programmes targeting young children and their parents that were designed to improve child outcomes based on child attachment security, behavioural regulation, cognitive development, and fostering parenting skills, Kirsten Asmussen and her colleagues, from the Early Learning Foundation, found that evidence of effectiveness was strongest for programmes that targeted children based on early warning signals, but that overall, work needed to continue to improve the efficacy of the programmes.

Attachments and construct validity

It is worth bearing in mind that an attachment, (as is the case with all psycho-social and diagnostic categories) is an imperfect, artificial construct that has been devised to help us make sense of the complex patterns of human behaviour that overlap with other disorders. In addition, the Irish psychologist, Michael Fitzgerald suggests that attachment disorders, like most psychological phenomena, almost certainly exist on a continuum of severity, which he suggests sits uneasily with the idea that people and their behaviour can be neatly slotted into different diagnostic boxes. Elsewhere, various authorities have complained that attachment theory places too much emphasis on the influence of parenting and not enough on the effects of the child's peers and social environment (a problem rectified by Bronfenbrenner's bioecological theory).

However, viewed from a practical perspective, the construct that However, evidence suggests that preventative interventions which target parents we call an attachment has high validity. It provides a satisfactory explanation for the discrete patterns of behaviour that emanate from parenting styles, which are sensitively attuned to the child's needs the patterns of behaviour that are closely associated with child maltreatment, neglect and trauma. In addition, attachment theory is supported by copious volumes of high-quality research and brain imaging studies which show that these patterns of behaviour are mirrored in differences in the physical structure of normal children's brains versus those who have been subject to abuse and neglect.

However, attachment theory is not without issues. The patterns of behaviour associated with disorganised attachments closely mirror those found in other common psychological problems and mental health issues. The *American Diagnostic and Statistical Manual* (5th Edition), for example, states that the behaviours used to diagnose reactive attachment disorder (the diagnostic name for disorganised or disrupted attachments) closely mirror those that are found in high functioning, autistic spectrum disorders, depressive disorders and intellectual impairment. Similarly, it has been noted that there is significant overlap between the criteria used to diagnose reactive attachment and the criteria used to define borderline personality disorder, which according to the American psychiatrist, John G Gunderson, include intense, unstable emotions, fear of rejection and abandonment and approach-avoidance behaviours.

Hence, given that these named constructs are associated with diagnostic and conceptual confusion there is a need to tread with caution, not least because an incorrect diagnosis can have serious ramifications for how people are supported. The treatments and methods that are employed to support individuals with autistic spectrum disorder, for example, which is an inherited condition that is associated with developmental problems that affect cognition, social communication and sensory perception, differ quite markedly from the methods of treatment and support that are commonly used to support someone with an attachment disorder arising from childhood experiences that have involved parental abuse and neglect.

In short, when working with nebulous constructs, we need to be wary of trying to fit people's behaviour into pre-conceived boxes and cognisant of alternative explanations for the patterns of behaviour, cognition and emotion that we observe.

Notes

1 In clinical spheres disorganised attachment is also referred to as reactive attachment disorder.
2 Disrupted attachment and disorganised are names for what are broadly the same phenomenon. However, the term disrupted attachment is sometimes employed to highlight the significance of disrupted emotional development during the early years of infancy.

Chapter 7
Intelligence, emotion and compassion

General intelligence

General intelligence is an important element in resilience. The ability to solve novel problems and to draw on experience, for example, are important tools in combating stress and dealing with the daily hassles that beset us all. In addition, various studies have found a link between high levels of generalised intelligence and longevity and even reduced susceptibility to trauma and whilst these findings may also be attributable to the differences in the social and economic milieus that people inhabit as children, there seems little doubt that intelligence predicts success and positive outcomes in many domains.

Yet for many decades the construct that we call intelligence taxed some of psychology's most eminent thinkers, and led to sometimes acrimonious argument about whether intelligence was inherited and fixed at birth or created through experiential learning. Fortunately, these arguments have been largely resolved and it is now generally accepted that intelligence varies according to the effects of inherited, genetic factors (which account for individual differences in speed of processing and domain-specific capacities like maths, music or language, memory) and the effects of experiential learning, practice, opportunities and environments in which to learn and hone such skills.

In other words, intelligence is a product of our genes, our environmental and experiential learning. Hence, the idea that if you set your sights on becoming a world class violin virtuoso or a formula one

DOI: 10.4324/9781351035545-9

racing driver, you will probably need to start early, put in at least 14,600 hours of practice, and have oodles of raw, natural ability.

There have also been long-running debates about intelligence and gender. Viewed from a historical perspective, women have been regarded as less intelligent than men, not least because early anatomical studies revealed that women's brains are smaller than men's and because it was commonly thought that women were more prone to using the right hemisphere of the brain associated with intuitive, emotional reasoning, whilst men were more disposed to employ the left hemisphere associated with logic and analytical reasoning.

Fortunately, the idea that women are less intelligent than men has been comprehensively debunked. The British neurobiologist, Professor Gina Rippon, for example, states that recent imaging studies have shown that there are no statistically significant differences in male and female brain size or anatomical structure. Women's brains are marginally smaller than men's on average, but the explanation lies in the simple fact that brain size covaries with body size, and women tend to be physically smaller than men. Indeed, if there was a plausible relationship between body size and intelligence, all brain surgeons, maths professors, chemists, and physicists would quite literally stand head and shoulders above the rest of the population. That said, gender differences in domains of intelligence do exist.

Research has shown that males tend to perform better than females on tasks related to mathematical ability, reasoning and spatial awareness, whilst females typically outperform males on tasks requiring language and verbal skills. Rippon, however, notes that these differences are more likely to be due to the effects of parental upbringing, systemic biases in the education system, which encourage girls and boys to choose different learning pathways, and cultural practices in shaping the child's developing brain rather than fixed, biological differences in male-female brain structure.

You may already have noticed that what is missing in these various ways of construing intelligence is any reference to emotion. Indeed, the study of intelligence during much of the last century was very much focused on the investigation of intellectual abilities associated with 'pure' sciences like maths and physics that rely heavily on logic, reasoning and abstraction. The reasons for this can be traced back to the way that western culture has traditionally prized rationale thinking and the pursuit of logic over other forms of intelligence. As a consequence, the study of intelligence relating to feelings states involving emotion and intuition was widely regarded as a scientifically irrelevant and given short shrift. This state of affairs was not helped by the dominance of behavioural psychology during the early part of the last century, which was exclusively concerned with things that could be directly observed and measured (like rats' behaviour in a learning maze). For radical behaviourists like the eminent psychologist, Burrhus Frederic Skinner, emotion was a fuzzy, abstract entity that only existed in the mind. In addition, emotion was regarded as feminine construct, unworthy of scientific pursuit and tainted by deeply entrenched, gender-based myths.

Indeed, the pursuit of intellectual knowledge had long been regarded as an area, off-limits to women, because they were regarded as intellectually inferior and prone to irrational thinking and behaviour. In addition, female reasoning was believed to be negatively coloured by emotion stemming from their natural biology. The words 'hysteria' and 'histrionic', for example, date back to the ancient Greeks and Egyptians, who used them to describe various states of emotive behaviour caused by an excess of female hormones. During the 1930s, Princess Alice of Battenberg, the mother of Prince Philip, had her ovaries irradiated under the instruction of the famous Austrian, psychiatrist Sigmund Freud to cure her of an excess of emotion that was thought to be the cause of her paranoia (she was in all probability suffering from complex trauma and unresolved grief relating to tragic incidents in her earlier life). Moreover, the use of terms that denote an excess of female hormones still exists in common language. To be hysterical is to be neurotic, overcited and irrational, whilst the term histrionics is used to describe gestures and behaviours that are excessively emotional and dramatic.

Similar ideas about gender and emotion also existed in mainstream science.

The French physiologist and psychologist, Paul Briquet coined the phrase 'somatisation' in 1859 to describe diverse physical symptoms arising from hysteria and neurosis, and although hysteria is no longer a tenable psychiatric diagnosis, the idea that an excess of emotion can lead to physical maladies stubbornly persists. Women, for example, are still more likely to have their physical symptoms explained by somatisation (the attribution of physical conditions to psychological factors like anxiety) than men. In conducting a literature review of gender-based differences in pain, the Swedish epidemiologist, Anke Samulowitz and her colleagues found that women's symptoms were more likely to be psychologised than men's. Similarly, men were more likely to be regarded as stoical and in control of their symptoms, whilst women were more likely to be perceived as overly sensitive.

Happily, as the myths about gender-based intelligence have declined there has been an increasing interest in the role of emotion in intelligence, which has dovetailed with recent developments in neuroscience and, very probably, the increasing numbers of female academic psychologists, who now outnumber men by three to one – which, I guess, says something rather poignant about gender and intelligence.

The development of emotion

Emotions are central to our being. They prompt us to react near-instantaneously to threats in our environment and they contribute to intelligence by shaping our preferences and choices and placing value on the decisions that we make.

However, like so many psychological constructs, emotions are complex, and to simplify matters and I want to start with the proposition that there are two basic classes of emotion: Namely, primal-instinctive emotion supported by the lower parts of the brain and cognitive-rationale emotion supported by the neocortex, which gives the emotions that we experience meaning.

Back in the 1970s, the zoologist Desmond Morris demonstrated that a small number of primal-instinctive emotions are common to all mammals and cross-culturally universal in humans. Infant primates are born with a repertoire of facial expressions that communicate fear, anger and disgust and these same expressions are mirrored in human body language across all human cultures. Put another way, we don't learn to grimace in disgust; it is an instinctive, inherited response.

These emotions are also primal in the sense that we experience them physically and reflexively. A loud bang or flash of light can trigger the surge of adrenalin, dry mouth and pounding heart that we associated with fear, and fear has a clear survival value. When we are threatened, fear causes us to flee or fight, or to freeze in a state of immobilisation. Fleeing a threatening situation may save your bacon if you are sufficiently fleet of foot and fighting may be an effective last resort if all else fails. Likewise, freezing and playing dead (AKA 'playing possum') can be a smart survival strategy, because some predators are biologically programmed not to consume dead meat. The primal emotion, disgust, on the other hand, adds an additional layer of protection, because we are programmed to instinctively avoiding things that make the stomach churn, so that we avoid the risk of being poisoned or contaminated. We reflexively avoid contact with people and objects that show visible signs of disease, for example, though an unfortunate side-effect of this response is manifest in people's, sometimes abhorrent, behaviour towards those who have facial disfigurement or suffer from medical conditions associated with disfigurement.

These emotions are also primal and instinctive, in the sense that they can occur without the 'top-down' intervention of higher-processing centres in the brain and they are initiated by centres in the bottom and middle layers of the brain.

Indeed, the bottom layer of the brain is the most primitive in evolutionary terms and is sometimes referred to as the 'reptilian brain', an idea spawned by the American neuroscientist Paul MacLean during the late 1950s. This part of the brain is comprised of the brain stem, which is responsible for the control of core life-functions, such as heart rate and breathing, whilst the basal ganglia is responsible for motor learning and fine motor control, and for generating pre-programmed patterns of behaviour and instinctive drives relating to sex and territorial defence, including the flight-fight response. The emotions emanating from this part of the brain are thought to be largely physiological in origin and crudely differentiated (meaning that the physical sensations associated with fear, disgust and anger are difficult to distinguish from one another) and largely devoid of cognition, a point to which I will return shortly.

Above this part of the brain, lies the limbic system, also known as the emotional brain, which you may recall, includes the amygdala, hippocampus and the hypothalamic-pituitary-axis (HPA).

These structures play an important role in processing information relating to fear and other emotions[1] and are connected to the cortex via neural networks that allow bottom-up and top-down processing of sensory information, which gives fear meaning. Their primary purpose is to elicit rapid, evasive behaviour in threat situations, vital-milliseconds before the cortex has had time to respond. A simple way of thinking about this is to imagine that you startle and jump back on seeing an object that looks like snake, before your cortex[2] has had time to inform you that it is actually a piece of old rope. Those few milliseconds may well have saved your life.

Although these primitive emotional responses are valuable, they are not without problem, because they can override rationale thought. We commonly talk about people 'seeing red', acting out of 'road rage' or being slaves to passion. In fact, the American psychologist, Leonard Berkowitz states that about 80% of all acts of aggression are emotional in origin, arising out of uncontrolled, primal emotions like fear and anger that do not involve premeditated deliberation. Indeed, up until the 1970s, France had a criminal defence of 'le crime passionnel' for crimes of murder committed in a moment of passionate madness (i.e., jealous rage) that was not premeditated, and, in a similar vein, (though no less controversially) the United Nations Entity for Gender Equality and the Empowerment of Women has advocated that passion be used as a defence in acts of homicide precipitated by severe emotional and physical abuse.

When our attentional processes detect a threat, the amygdala triggers the hypothalamic-pituitary axis into taking corrective action, whilst the triggering sensory data are simultaneously sent upwards to the neo-cortex where it is contextualised, evaluated and subsequently experienced as emotion.

This process is explained by the cognitive labelling theory of emotion, developed by the American psychologists Stanley Schachter and Jerome Singer, which rests on two assumptions. The first being that the physiological changes that occur when we experience emotions like fear, anger and disgust are too generalised and undifferentiated to account for the complex array of emotions that we commonly experience, and the second being that emotion is dependent upon cognitive appraisal and the contextualisation of feeling. Put another way, many of the emotions that we experience are a composite product of aversive or pleasant physiological arousal and negative or positive thoughts relating to the situation that we find ourselves in.

Chapter 7: Intelligence, emotion and compassion

Whereas we are born with primitive-instinctive emotion, contextualised emotion does not emerge until later in childhood. The American Professor of Psychiatry, Michael Lewis and his colleagues, for example, have shown that although the primitive-instinctive emotions, joy, anger, sadness, fear and disgust can be reliably measured in infants aged six months, the development of self-conscious, contextualised emotion, which includes embarrassment, pride, shame and guilt, does not emerge before the ages of two to three years, which dovetails with significant cortical expansion and the development of self-referential cognition based on conscious knowledge and awareness of what is socially right and wrong.

Likewise, although empathic emotion can be detected in neonates, it takes the form of an instinctive reflexive response that is designed to elicit caregiving-attention. Conversely the American-French neuroscientist, Jean Decety states that true empathic emotion, based on theory of mind and experiential memory that facilitates an understanding others' intentions and motives, does not emerge before the ages of five to six.

Emotional intelligence

Emotional intelligence has moved from being the backroom kid in psychology to take centre stage as one of the most important aspects of resilience.

The American psychologist Daniel Goleman, for example, states that the ability to know and act on what we feel, together with the capacity to control our impulses and make balanced, informed decisions, is now regarded as central to physical and psychological wellbeing. Moreover, whereas emotion was once regarded as a negative thing that clouded rationale judgment and reasoning, we are now coming to understand that emotion gives not only meaning and value to the choices that we make, but also underpins our ability to be empathically in touch with ourselves and others.

Emotions also play an important role in self-regulatory processes by encouraging us to reflect on events that have led to success or failure and to consider ways of ensuring future success or avoiding future repetition. We are motivated to avoid shame and guilt, for example, because they give rise to cognitive dissonance (an unpleasant affective state that occurs when our behaviour is fundamentally out of kilter with our core beliefs and values). Likewise, we are motivated to repeat behaviours that give rise to pride, because it feels good (it is associated with the release of feel-good hormones, such as dopamine and oxytocin), and because we associated it with hard work and perseverance.

In a similar way, our emotions also help us to communicate with others.

To be emotionally literate is to possess the ability to readily communicate our needs, desires, misgivings and concerns to others and to empathically understand and appreciate theirs in return. Likewise, emotions can help us to imagine a better future that can prime us to defer short-terms gains in patient pursuit of long-term goals.

Indeed, without the regulatory effects of emotion, we would probably resemble sociopaths locked very much into the here and now and grabbing whatever we could without too much thought or consideration for the future or the well-being of others.

Last, but not least, emotions also help us to place a value and preference on the decisions and choices we make. It has been argued that we would be cognitively paralysed if we had to make choices without the motivational and preferential nuances that emotions imbue. That said, there are circumstances where our emotions and desires lead to decision-making outcomes that are unhealthy, such as addiction, where emotion and desire take the form of cravings and compulsions that override rationale judgement and reasoning.

Emotional intelligence is also associated with empathic awareness, which as we have learnt flows in part from our ability to mentalise (imagine and predict) others' emotional states, intentions and motivations.

Evolutionary psychologists think that emotional intelligence probably evolved in line with the emergence of mammals and the demands of group living, which was supported by the development of the limbic system, which is also referred to as the emotional brain.

Whilst many lower species of animal live solitary lives and rely on pre-programmed instinctive behaviours for their survival (the exception being collectivist insects like ants and bees), higher mammals, such as wolves, dolphins, and elephants, cooperate to select and hunt their pray and share responsibility for raising and 'protecting the vulnerable young and old. Whilst these shared activities enhance the well-being of the social groups and its individual members, they require communication and planning and a degree of self-other referential awareness to enable group cohesion that is not present or required in lower-order species that rely on an instinctive reptilian brain.

Moreover, ethnological research suggests that higher-order mammals possess the capacity for complex emotion that cannot be satisfactorily explained by instinctive, reflexive mechanisms. Elephants, for example, show shared delight in the arrival of a new member born into the herd and, likewise, they display patterns of behaviours that we commonly associate with grief on the death of a herd member. Similarly, in a recent study led by the German biologist, Simone Pika, chimpanzees were found to apply an insect-based salve to other chimpanzees' wounds, in act that she describes as being akin to the prosocial behaviour we associate with humans. Likewise, the British behavioural researcher, Catherine Douglas and her colleagues provided experimental evidence that appeared to show that pigs raised in an enriched, physical environment displayed more optimistic bias in decision-making than pigs reared in a barren environment, suggesting they were happier than their counterparts. I mention this, not because I want to convert you to veganism, but to make the point that in evolutionary terms, emotion appears to play a central role in supporting the intelligent behaviours that are required to facilitate the complex, social and hierarchical structures that enable group-living.

Emotional intelligence can be broken down into distinct elements. The psychologists Peter Salovey and John Mayer, for example, state that emotional intelligence rests on five key skills or abilities: Namely, self-awareness – as in the ability to recognise and authenticate what we are feeling. Emotional management – as in the capacity to rein in emotions, such as anger, anxiety, irritability and over-exuberance. Self-motivation – as in the ability to marshal energy and overcome obstacles, such as procrastination and delay gratification in deference to the pursuit of long-term goals. Empathic recognition – as in the capacity to be in tune with our own and others' emotional states, and relational awareness – as in the capacity to act with tact and demonstrate compassion. These capacities are also reflected in a recent model of intelligence developed by the Greek psychologists, Athanasios Drigas and

Chara Papoutsi, which combines theories from generalised intelligence and emotional intelligence to create a nine-factor model, which incorporates elements of self-actualisation, along the lines of Maslow's hierarchy of needs.

As you might expect, individuals differ in their capacity for emotional intelligence, particularly with regards to self-awareness and self-regulation, and such differences appear to be a composite product of our genes, our upbringing, our exposure to cultural influences and, more controversially, gender. Research conducted at the University of Cambridge, led by Varun Warrier, for example, recently found that roughly 10% of individual differences in empathy can be accounted for by our genes. Conversely, the British neurobiologist, Gina Rippon argues that how we act and how we feel is, to a high degree, a product of the formative years of childhood. Indeed, as we learned earlier in this text, emotional regulation and self-awareness develop in tangent with emotionally attuned parenting that shapes the architecture of the infant's social brain. However, emotional intelligence is also affected by culture.

Research shows that people who live in collectivist cultures tend to have higher levels of empathy. The Australian psychologists, Miriam Heinke and Winnifred Louis, for example, found that Asian-Australian students were more collectivist in their outlook and higher in levels of empathy than European-Australian students. Such differences have been explained by ethnological research which shows that collectivist cultures place significantly more emphasis on the importance of interconnectedness and social harmony, than individualistic cultures that place value of individual uniqueness, motivation and personal success.

Empathy also varies with gender. Women tend to score higher than men on measures of empathy, interpersonal relationships and social responsibility, whilst men tend to score higher on areas, such as assertiveness and stress tolerance.

Empathic awareness and emotional intelligence have also been shown to predict success in life-domains, including interpersonal relationships, education and employment, where they appear to trump general intelligence. Daniel Goleman, for example, states that emotional intelligence is a more reliable predictor of career success than general intelligence, and people with a very high IQ (intelligence quotient) often find themselves being managed by someone who has a lower IQ, but better social skills. In a similar vein, research has shown that university degree classification is a relatively poor predictor of career success. Studies, for example, of Harvard University cohorts conducted in the 1940s (referred to earlier in this text) revealed that those with the highest IQs were the least likely to be successful in terms of eventual salary, productivity and social status.

In explaining these findings, many psychologists have pointed to research findings which show that people who are high on emotional intelligence tend to be socially skilled, good at motivating others in group-settings and high on resilient traits like extraversion and optimism.

However, other psychologists (who are admittedly in a minority), have suggested that business success might well be a product of sociopathic traits.[3] In a review of the literature, for example, the American psychologist, Sophia Wellons found evidence that 'Corporate Psychopaths' defined by traits associated with sociopathy are over-represented in the boardroom. Similarly, whilst the American clinical psychologist Martha Stout has estimated that about 4% of the general population have sociopathic traits, the Australian, forensic psychologists, Nathan Brooks and Katarina Fritzon found that around one in five CEOs (21%) had destructive, psychopathic personalities – which is equivalent to the typical rate of psychopathy found in general prison populations. Moreover, it has been suggested that sociopaths do particularly well in business because they are intelligent, extremely good at manipulating people and able to make difficult decisions without letting emotion cloud their judgement. And, just in case you were under the illusion that all sociopaths are men, research conducted by the Israeli psychologists, Tal Ben Yaacov and Joseph Glickson, found that women with the highest level of general intelligence also scored the highest on measures of psychopathy.

Intuition as emotional intelligence

Whilst many of the emotions we experience are embedded in cognition, involving attentive, conscious reflection, research has shown that intuitive, visceral, reactions help us to instinctively navigate social situations and relationships that are both complex and routine. 'Gut feelings,' for example, assist us in getting a feel for people when we meet them for the first time, and such judgements occur rapidly and instinctively. The American psychologists, Janine Willis and Alexander Todorov, for example, found that it takes no more than a tenth of second to form an opinion about whether we like someone or not, whether or not they are trustworthy and whether we need to exercise caution, and once formed such impressions are quite impervious to change.

These feelings or if you like, unconscious judgements, fall under the rubric of intuition, and whilst intuition was traditionally regarded as subject unworthy of serious study, there has been an increasing level of interest in the role of intuitive decision-making in professional spheres.

In his book the *Power of Intuition*, for example, the American cognitive psychologist, Gary Klein describes how a professional fireman leading a team into a large burning building suddenly felt the hairs on his neck stand on end. He immediately ordered his men to evacuate the area, which saved their lives, and it was not until afterwards, when deconstructing the event, that he realised he had heard a strange sound, which his sub-conscious brain had quite rightly judged to be the sound of the fire about to go into a backdraught - a situation in which oxygen becomes rapidly depleted causing the fire to expand outwards in an explosive manner.

The British psychologist, Guy Claxton explains that intuition may arise in situations such as this, when stimuli present in a person's immediate environment activates their attentional processes at a level that fails to exceed the threshold for stimuli entering consciousness awareness (a process called subthreshold priming). Such reactions have been variously associated with unconscious intelligence, intuition, and of course, emotional intelligence.

Studies have shown that intuition (also referred to as naturalistic decision-making) is associated with instinctive appraisals and insights that flow from many years of experience and expert practice. In her pioneering book, *From Novice to Expert,* for example, the American Nursing Professor, Patricia Benner provided evidence, which showed that expert practitioners acquire an intuitive grasp of clinical situations that allows them to act rapidly without having to consciously rely on protocols, rules or principles to guide their judgement. In a similar vein, the Dutch researcher, Jetske Erisman and his colleagues found that intuition was often employed by child and youth workers in suspected child abuse cases when they instinctively felt that something was wrong despite the absence of concrete cues or evidence. This ability only develops over time with practice and expertise. The Turkish professor of nursing, Nuray Turan and her colleagues, for example, found that nursing students scored low on intuition, whilst the Australian Professor of Occupational Therapy, Lisa Chaffey found that experienced therapists score more highly on the use of intuition than novice therapists.

Similarly, in reviewing the literature around naturalistic decision-making in business-management, the British researchers, Justin Okoli and John Watt found that experts were particularly good at being able to sift out irrelevant cues and focus on the ones that mattered. In addition, they found that the default mode for making complex decisions centred on intuition with conscious redress to cognitive, analytic skills occurring only when a complex problem remained unresolved. Likewise, the Australian neuropsychologist, Luke Downey and his colleagues found that senior managers displaying transformational leadership skill were more likely to score highly on both intuition and emotional intelligence.

Compassion

The British psychologist Paul Gilbert states that compassion is a basic form of kindness, which involves an empathic, interested awareness of suffering in others and oneself.

From a conceptual point of view, compassion differs from empathy in that compassion refers to an act of kindness or benevolence, whilst empathy refers to the ability or capacity to feel someone else's pain, distress, and discomfort. However, in practice the terms are used interchangeably, and compassion occupies a niche in a special class of prosocial behaviours, which include altruism, relating to the giving of help or assistance without expectation of reward or gain.

From a biological-evolutionary perspective, it has been argued that acts of compassion serve to optimise group well-being, cohesion and survival. So it is not surprising to find that compassion has an inherited element. Animal studies, for example, have shown that primates spontaneously engage in compassionate-altruistic acts, which are reinforced at a biological level by the release of the feel-good hormone dopamine. However, human studies suggest that our capacity for compassion is in large part acquired through the transmission of cultural values and attitudes and cognitive-developmental processes during the formative of childhood. As we learnt earlier, for example, culture plays an important role in the transmission of the attitudes and values that support compassion and empathy, with evidence suggesting that collectivist cultures tend to be more compassionate than their individualistic counterparts. Likewise, the American, developmental psychologist Michaela Upshaw and her colleagues propose that our capacity for compassion and empathy develop as we learn the skills of self-reflection and perspective-taking (theory of mind) from our parents.

Gilbert, however, suggests that our capacity to be concerned for the well-being of others is also dependent upon two further factors: Namely, the ability to effectively regulate internal emotion and stress, and the capacity to be present in the here and now.

When we are stressed and anxious, for example, our attentional capacity narrows and shifts to concern about future threats. Likewise if we are depressed, we fret and ruminate about past failures, and our capacity for attending to the immediate world around us is similarly diminished. It's not that people suffering from stress or other mental health problems are selfish per se. It is simply that they don't have the emotional or cognitive 'headroom' to be compassionate and concerned about others. Indeed, Gilbert explains that our capacity to experience empathy and to be compassionate is dependent upon the smooth symbiosis of three affect regulation systems in the brain: Namely, the soothing and contentment system, which promotes 'rest and digest processes', the incentive-resource-seeking system, which stimulates goal-driven behaviour, and the threat-protection system, which elicits the flight-fight response. The soothing and contentment system, as we learnt earlier, develops during early childhood in response to parenting that is sensitively attuned to the infant's needs. This is the system most closely associated with empathy, compassion and caring. When activated it causes the brain to release the soothing hormones oxytocin, which creates sufficient emotional reserve to focus on others and their needs. The incentive-resource-seeking system, on the other hand, is the antithesis of the soothing and contentment system. Whereas the latter promotes rest and regeneration and the capacity for empathy and compassion, the incentive-resource-seeking system stimulates active, goal-driven behaviour that is reinforced by the powerful dopamine-reward system in the brain. As you might imagine, this system is vitally important, as we probably would not get much done without it. However, in this state of activation, we are incentivised to achieve, and our attentional processes are directed towards goal-focussed and egocentric behaviour. It is also worth noting that this system works by creating need and desire, which can, if unconstrained, result in problems such as addiction, which correlate negatively with empathy and compassion.

The last of the three regulatory systems, is the threat-protection system associated with threat detection and response. When this system is engaged, we revert to survival mode. Our attentional processes are diverted towards scanning our environment for potential danger, which if confirmed, triggers the HPA axis into releasing the stress hormone cortisol, which narrows and sharpens attentional processes. Moreover, if this system becomes chronically over-stimulated, the resulting high levels of stress and irritability further erode our emotional stability and capacity for compassion.

Self-compassion

Being compassionate is not only good for others. Recent studies have shown a positive association between *self-compassion* and physical emotional well-being, which is thought to be linked to a reduction in levels of negative self-criticism that perpetuates states like stress and depression and a reduction in brain activity, which is vital for replenishing our cognitive capacities. A recent study for example, conducted by the German neuroscientist, Antonius Wiehler and his colleagues, used imaging techniques to study the effects of prolonged mental activity on cognitive capacity and found that more than six hours of intense activity resulted in excess accumulation of the excitatory neurotransmitter glutamate in the prefrontal cortex, which resulted in cognitive decline *and* physical exhaustion. Clearly we cannot be compassionate towards others or ourselves if we are cognitively exhausted. The authors suggest that the brain rests during sleep (possibly mopping up the surplus glutamate). However, meditative processes also act to quieten the brain and induce a state of calm that promoted compassion and empathy.

Similarly, the Spanish psychotherapist, Miguel Bellosta-Batalla and his colleagues, have shown that regular mindfulness-meditation and self-compassion is associated with a decline in salivary cortisol (which as you may recall is the one body's primary stress hormones). Likewise, in reviewing the literature on the relationship between self-compassion and well-being, the Austrian researchers, Wendy Philips and Donald Hone found that self-compassion was positively associated with global physical health, functional immunity and composite forms of health behaviour. Conversely, the Scottish psychologist, Kate Mackintosh and her colleagues found that low self-compassion was associated with attachment-related avoidance, emotional constriction and an unhealthy over-reliance on the self to solve the problems of the world.

Research has also shown that teaching children about compassion and perspective-taking aids cooperation and learning in school. Moreover, the American educational researchers, Patty Kohler-Evans and Candice Dowd Barnes have proposed that teaching compassion should be an essential part of the educational curriculum, because children are regularly exposed to the worst of humanity by way of persistent exposure to negative images, news headlines and soundbytes, which often glorify individualism, strength and the subjugation of others. For these reasons, Evans and Barnes suggest that taught-curriculums should focus on the importance of being kind to another in order to foster personal awareness, empathy and compassion and to explore ways of taking concrete steps to promote compassion in response to identified issues or problems.

However, in describing compassion, the American educational psychologist, Kirstin Neff makes the point that being compassionate is not synonymous with submissiveness, or acceptance of attitudes and behaviours associated with bullying, selfishness, negligence or subjugation. It does, however, mean that we are better able to accept imperfections in ourselves and others – a theme that I will return to shortly when looking when looking at compassion in the workplace.

Processes that disrupt compassion

According to Gilbert, our capacity for compassion and empathy declines when our brains are overactive and the regulatory systems that promote rest go awry.

Under normal circumstances, the soothing and contentment system, the incentive-resource behaviour and the threat-protection system, work in congenial harmony.

When we go to work, school or college, the incentive-resource-seeking system is active and the threat-protection system sits in stand-by mode, ready to kick in if our attentional processes detect an incoming threat. And when we finally arrive home, the soothing and contentment system swings into operation and we find ourselves able to chill and unwind.

At least that is the theory! In practice, exposure to chronic stress may lock the body's stress response system into a semi-permanent state of alert. Many people find that it is difficult to 'switch off' the incentive-resource-seeking-system, because they remain task-orientated. They may worry about a problem at work, or a swathe of unanswered emails, or there may be concern about one of the children's lack of progress in school, which makes it feel impossible to relax. If scenarios like these become a frequent occurrence – if the demands of family life or work become excessive – they risk becoming chronically stressed and emotionally overloaded, which can impede their ability to be compassionate towards themselves and others.

The explanation that Gilbert offers is situational and stress-based. However, research has shown that people may also have a diminished capacity for compassion and empathy because they are insecurely attached or because they are suffering from trauma, relating to childhood maltreatment or neglect. Compassion and empathy, you may recall, are abilities that are primarily acquired during the developmental years of childhood. Children learn about perspective-taking and they learn to be kind to themselves and forgiving of others thus, it stands to reason that the acquisition of these skills may be severely impaired in the case of parenting that is neglectful or abusive.

Yet the picture is not clear cut. Whilst research carried out by the Israeli neuroscientist, David Greenberg, the Polish psychologists, Malgorzata Gambin and Carla Sharp and the Australian psychologists,

Karen Leith and Roy Baumeister, all showed that individuals with a history of child abuse and co-related mental health problems (such as depression and guilt-proneness) had higher levels of empathy. A meta-analysis of fifty attachment studies conducted by the Chinese psychologist, Xizheng Xu and colleagues, found that on average, the lowest levels of empathy were found in children who had a reactive attachment disorder (disorganised attachment) and the highest levels of empathy in children who were securely attached.

Whilst there is no simple explanation for these seemingly incompatible findings. We should note that Xizheng Xu's findings are entirely compatible with mainstream research, which shows that children who are securely attached tend to have higher levels of empathy and compassion than children who are insecurely attached, whilst children who have a disorganised attachment are typically lacking in compassion for themselves and others. However, these findings, like so much of psychological research, are based on statistical variations around the mean that take little account of individual differences. It is entirely possible (and likely) that some adults survive the horrors of child abuse to emerge with an enhanced awareness and understanding of other people's distress (particularly if they have been able to forge a secure, intimate relationship with a surrogate parent-figure).

Moreover, it is notable that the American psychologist Kenneth Pope and Shirley Feldman-Summers' survey of 500 clinical and counselling psychologists (a profession populated by people who are high in empathy and compassion) revealed that 70% of female therapists and 33% of males had experienced some form of sexual or physical abuse in childhood, with incest reported by 16% of females and 6% of males.

We should also note that chronic guilt was employed as one the key measures employed in the aforementioned studies and not chronic shame. This matters, because individual differences in people's capacity to be compassionate appear to vary depending on whether they emerge from the experience of childhood abuse suffering from chronic guilt or chronic shame. The American psychologist, June Tangney, for example, has noted that people who suffer from chronic, internalised shame tend to be highly self-focused, angry and lacking in compassion, whilst those who suffer from chronic guilt tend to be other-focused and empathic.

Finally, before, I move to explore the relationship between compassion and shame in a little more depth, it is worth noting that the absence of compassion can also affect whole communities. Concern for others may be corrosively eroded when communities are subjected to situational factors, like poverty and chronic deprivation that create powerlessness. Under such conditions, hope and social cohesion can be lost as common values and goals are cast aside in the daily struggle to scrape an existence or when the motivation to escape from stress leads significant numbers of people into alcoholism, drug abuse and criminality, which ultimately strangle empathy and compassion for others.

Self-compassion and shame

Paul Gilbert states that compassion towards the self is more than a luxury. It is an essential part of maintaining ourselves, physically, emotionally, and socially. To be self-compassionate is to avoid undue self-criticism and to create appropriate boundaries around what we can reasonably manage and achieve.

Being self-compassionate also means being kind to ourselves and accepting are that we are human, imperfect, and, thus, prone to errors as well as triumphs. When we do this, it is easier to accept that making mistakes is part of life. Conversely, when we are self-critical, we run the risk of generating unrealistic goals and self-expectations that can lead to an excessive need to prove to ourselves and others that we are OK.

Likewise, excessive self-criticism and unrealistic self-expectations are the hallmarks of internalised shame, which as you may recall, is described by Tangney as a dark emotion that immobilises the self and inhibits personal growth. Indeed, although shame is one a discrete group of self-regulatory emotions that evolved to curb the worst of human excess. It is also associated with events in which individuals are subjugated and debased, and left feeling humiliated, angry, low in self-esteem and powerless.

As a consequence, people who suffer from shame may avoid social interaction and hide themselves away or they may cope by creating a mask or persona that hides the true, authentic self from others. This mask or persona often takes the form of the 'ought-self', which according to the shame-researcher Rene Brown, can result in perfectionism and workaholism in order to relieve deep-rooted feelings of inferiority and low-self-esteem. In a worst-case scenario, this perfectionism leads to self-imposed demands that are so unrealistic as to result in failure, which further reinforces feelings of inferiority in a vicious, negative cycle.

It is generally accepted that the root causes of shame can be traced back to adverse early childhood experiences (the exception being, for example, adults who are exposed to traumatic events involving subjugation and humiliation like rape). Indeed, Kristin Neff states that research shows that people who lack compassion are more likely to have grown up in families that were dysfunctional. Likewise, Tangney and Dearing state that chronic shame and self-criticism is more commonly found in people whose parents were critical and rejecting. They argue that critical parents often selectively value certain characteristics and behaviours in their children and/or set unrealistically high standards that set the stage for the development of chronic feelings of low self-esteem and underachievement and the drive for perfectionism.

In explaining the dynamics of such processes, the eminent psychotherapist Carl Rogers argued that conditional parenting fuels the development of an idealised self (or 'ought self'), that generates unrealistic and perfectionist trait-like tendencies, which invariably resulted in chronic anxiety, guilt and depression. Perfectionism, he proposed occurs when we come to believe that our self-worth is wholly dependent on being perfect at everything we do.

Perfectionists do not allow themselves to make mistakes. They are self-critical of error and fearful of others criticism, all of which is damaging, because perfectionism is associated with a range of complex and serious mental health problems.

Perfectionism, for example, is a known risk factor for anorexia nervosa. The American psychiatrist, Katherine Halmi and her colleagues found perfectionism to be a stable, characteristic trait in women with anorexia, whilst the American psychiatrist, Andrea Bastiani and colleagues reported that perfectionism in anorexia women was self-imposed rather than a response to others' expectations.

Likewise, when examining the causes of depression in British university students, the psychologists, Marianne Etherson and Martin Smith found that perfectionism-generated symptoms of depression were linked to the belief that they were chronically failing to meet other people's expectations. In a similar vein, the British psychologist Christian Jarret noted that women who were praised for their attractiveness and sociability over intelligence in childhood were prone to developing problems with self-validatory problems in adulthood associated with the sense of being measured by their looks rather than their achievements.

In addition, perfectionism has been associated with the development of imposter syndrome, a form of shame in which the 'real self' is perceived to be chronically lacking.

Various studies, for example, have found that academics are prone to experiencing imposter syndrome, which is probably fuelled by the highly competitive and hierarchical nature of academia.

Compassion mindfulness

In echoes of the concept of vulnerability as a *condition humana*, Paul Gilbert argues that to combat compulsive perfectionism relating to shame, we need to be mindfully compassionate towards ourselves and in so doing accept that we all have our strengths and weaknesses.

Mindfulness is a technique that uses breathing to keep attentional processes focused on the present and one's immediate surroundings (as opposed to problem-solving, ruminating about the past or worrying about the future). Mindfulness practitioners learn to manage stress and other uncomfortable, internal states and to be self-compassionate by suspending judgement about the self and one's thoughts, feelings and behaviour.

Viewed from a dynamic perspective, Gilbert states that mindfulness works in three ways: It promotes a focus on the here and now. It helps people to be alongside painful feelings and it promotes self-compassion, by focussing attentional process on present.

By focussing on the present, for example, mindfulness can help to counteract the intrusive attentional processes associated with states of anxiety and depression that keep people captive in their own internal prison. Anxiety states, for example, are frequently associated with future-orientated attentional biases, which cause people to worry incessantly about what might be, whilst depressive states are associated with past-orientated attentional biases, which involve obsessive rumination and replaying of past-failures. Likewise, it is standard practice in mindfulness meditation to use attentional breathing to reduce symptoms of stress and this works in two, interconnected ways. First, by focussing exclusively on the breath, attention is diverted away from the free-flow of consciousness that is associated with worry and concern. Second, by purposively promoting slow, deep breathing, the parasympathetic nervous system and vagal nerve is activated, which induces a natural state of relaxation.

This meditative state stands in marked contrast to the state of anxiety, which is reinforced by short, shallow breathing that keeps the sympathetic nervous system activated. Indeed, in his book *The Body Keeps the Score*, the Dutch psychiatrist, Bessel Van der Kolk states that people who have been traumatised in childhood often unconsciously adopt this as their default pattern of breathing, which has the effect of physically keeping the body locked into a state of chronic alarm. By purposively breathing slowly through the nose, the sympathetic nervous system is deactivated in favour of the parasympathetic nervous system, which lowers cortisol, heart and blood pressure.

A more recent form of mindfulness, called mindfulness-based cognitive therapy or MBCT for short, combines the principles of meditation, which aim to relax the mind and switch attention to the present with cognitive behavioural therapy, which seeks to assuage negative thinking by encouraging those who are plagued by anxiety and depression to challenge the automatic critical assumptions about the self that typically accompany depression and to replace them with deliberative, compassionate thoughts and acts of self-kindness.

MBCT draws on the American psychologist, Aaron Beck's model of depression, which purports that automatic, negative beliefs and arbitrary inferences keep people locked into states of depression. These beliefs and inferences include drawing conclusions about the self, based on selective, false data and the magnification of personal mistakes and the minimisation of successes.

There is now a considerable body of research supporting compassionate mindfulness as technique for reducing psychological distress and bolstering resilience. The American Psychological Association, for example, has reported that multiple studies have shown that mindfulness is an effective treatment for managing stress, anxiety and depression. The Norwegian psychologist, Ragni Haukaas and her colleagues, for instance, showed that guided meditation to improve self-compassion resulted in reduced symptoms and improved flexible attention for students with self-reported depression. Likewise, the American researcher, Yi-Yuan Tang reports in his book, *The Neuroscience of Mindfulness Meditation*, that engaging in regular mindfulness has been shown to alter the activity of several brain regions associated with regulation of affect and self-awareness and to reduce circulating levels of the stress hormone, cortisol.

In addition, positive results have been achieved with relatively with short periods of daily practice. The German research fellow in psychiatry, Britta Hölzel and her colleagues showed that an eight-week mindfulness course results in lowered levels of perceived stress that were mirrored in structural changes in the amygdala. Similarly, the American psychologists, Meagan MacKenzie, Kayleigh Abbot and Nancy Kocovski found a significant reduction in relapse with depressive symptoms, following an eight-week course of MBCT.

Notes

1 We know that the limbic system underpin emotion, because clinical studies of people whose limbic system has been damaged by strokes, tumours, or invasive surgery have shown that individuals without a functioning amygdala cannot feel emotions like fear and, when they make decisions, they are unable to place a value on the choices that they make. Damage to the hippocampus, on the other hand, leads to anterograde amnesia, which is the inability to form new memories and to link memory to experience.
2 The hippocampus also stores information relating to threats and can switch off the primary-fear response.
3 Psychopaths and sociopaths share behavioural traits referred to as the Dark Triad, which centre on high intelligence, low empathy and a Machiavellian a disregard for others. Some authorities use psychopathy to refer to inherited traits, whilst other use sociopathy to describe anti-social traits that arise out of a troubled childhood.

Chapter 8
When compassion fails

Stress and burnout

It is evident that compassion improves resilience and well-being in respect of our personal lives, but what about compassion in the workplace – can compassion improve staff well-being and can it productively coexist alongside managerial systems that are based on internal markets, competition and efficiency-savings, which have reached into just about every part of the public and private sector? These are issues that I will turn to shortly, but first we need to explore the nature of occupational burnout and its prevalence in organisations that exist to provide support and care for vulnerable others.

Whilst the term occupational stress is a catch all-term that is frequently used when an employee is suffering from work-related stress and physical exhaustion, burnout is a discrete form of stress that stems from a chronic and insidious mismatch between occupational demand and the individual's capacity to deliver. The Royal College of Psychiatrists, for example, defines burnout as a serious mental health condition that has three core dimensions: Feelings of physical and emotional exhaustion, increased mental and emotional distance from one's job and reduced professional capacity to act in the interest of clients, patients, and colleagues. Of these factors, emotional exhaustion and emotional distancing (which is also referred to as depersonalisation) are the most common in people working in areas like health, social care and education. Likewise, in carrying out a systematic review of the literature on burnout among physicians, Lisa Rotenstein, from the Harvard Medical, found that emotional exhaustion (72%), depersonalisation (68%) and low personal accomplishment (63%) were the three most commonly reported issues.

When a patient or client is depersonalised, they are treated as an object that is devoid of feelings, and, whilst this may be employed as a way of consciously distancing oneself from others' emotional distress in order to 'objectify' clinical decision-making. Seen in the context of burnout, depersonalisation arises when the person concerned is so emotionally drained that they no longer have the capacity to engage with others on an intimate and compassionate level.

These factors are represented in the *Maslach Burnout Inventory*, which was developed by the American social psychologist Christine Maslach, for the purposes of formally assessing occupational burnout (also known as professional burnout).

The inventory centres on three core domains, personal exhaustion, depersonalisation and negative self-evaluation. Exhaustion takes the form of physical and emotional depletion that results when excessive time and effort is given over to tasks and goals that have poor outcomes. Depersonalisation results from emotional exhaustion and is manifest as emotional distancing, unsympathetic behaviour and cynical attitudes. The third factor, low personal achievement, relates to a perceived loss of role-effectiveness, feelings of low self-esteem, personal powerlessness and insufficiency.

The terms burnout and occupational stress are often used interchangeably and the line that delineates them is a thin one. However, definitions of occupational stress tend to place emphasis on the behavioural symptoms of stress, like physical and emotional exhaustion and sleep disturbance, whilst burnout places additional emphasis on depersonalisation and feelings of personal insufficiency and powerlessness. If these latter factors are not taken into consideration during assessment of work-related stress, an employee may well get signed off with occupational stress without ever being formally diagnosed with burnout (which is problematic, because burnout and its physical and psychological sequelae require specialist help and support, which is unlikely to follow without a proper diagnosis).

The Dutch psychologist Wilmar Schaufeli and his colleagues note that burnout emerged as a concept in its own right in the 1970s as clinicians and researchers sought to understand the causes of exhaustion and fatigue found in people working in areas like health and social work. In showing that burnout went beyond mere exhaustion, researchers discovered that burnout affected not only young, energetic idealists but also seasoned professionals with many years' experience. Moreover, although the condition appeared to be relatively common in the helping professions, it was discovered to be quite rare in professional communities where there was a strong sense of communion, social commitment and shared values (like Montessori schools and religious monasteries). Gradually research revealed that burnout was more likely to occur where there was a dynamic imbalance between resources and demand, a trend which accelerated in the 1990s and beyond as increased working hours and cutbacks to support and finances fuelled a mismatch between role-demands and job expectations. Staff had fewer opportunities to rest and rebuild and there was often incongruity between an organisation's espoused goals, aspirations and values and that which the organisation was actually able to deliver on the ground. This problem, for example, was elucidated in the evidence that Professor Michael West, a British, public health specialist, recently gave to a UK government committee, showing that burnout was being caused by high levels of work-demand coupled with inadequate resources, relating to personnel, training, equipment and technology.

However, burnout is not underpinned by a single theoretical model; rather it is explained by a range of different psycho-social theories.

At its most basic level, burnout is a form of stress that arises when the perceived demands of a given situation outstrips an individual's perceived ability to cope. This is reflected in the Job Demand-Control Model developed by the Danish psychologist, Robert Karasek, which embraces demand factors relating to load, such as workload, time pressures and task complexity, and latitudinal, capacity factors, such as role-freedom, decision-making and job autonomy. In this model, the higher the degree of job strain and the lower the latitude to make autonomous decisions, the higher the risk of burnout. In another model developed by the German psychologist, Johannes Siegrist, burnout is deemed to arise out of a fundamental mismatch between the level of effort required to carry out one's professional role and the level of reward and satisfaction that may be accrued. In this model, burnout occurs when an employee's perceived satisfaction or sense of reward is chronically compromised by working in an environment where high load and demand make it difficult or impossible to carry out one's role effectively.

However, burnout, like all forms of chronic stress, is not a condition that suddenly appears. It often takes years to develop and can be prevented by early detection and treatment.

In describing the chronology of burnout, for example, the psychologist Christine Meinhardt states that burnout typically takes five to ten years to develop.

In the first phase, minor warning signs are present and at this stage the accompanying stress is readily amenable to brief forms of treatment. Such signs include episodic sleep disruption, trouble switching off from work and rumination about work-related events and issues. Treatment commonly involves the teaching of stress management techniques and a focus on achieving a good work-life balance. In the second stage, stress becomes more chronic and entrenched, and as exposure to it continues unabated, the individual begins to experience chronic insomnia with somatic complaints, which may be significant, feelings of exhaustion and deterioration of mental faculties, including memory, decision-making and judgement. In addition, the individual is likely to be very low in self-esteem, anxious and plagued by thoughts of failure. By this stage, the effects of chronic burnout on the sufferer's body and mind may still respond positively to intervention, but treatment has a much more complex and protracted course, which is resource intensive and extremely debilitating for the individuals concerned. The Swiss Professor of Psychiatry, Roland von Kanel, for example, found that chronic burnout characterised by feelings of exhaustion, cynicism and low personal efficacy was a risk factor for chronic somatic disease, high blood pressure and impaired lung function in a sample of 5000 individuals, independent of measures of normal, clinical depression.

The prevalence of occupational burnout

Sadly, occupational burnout in professions that provide support for vulnerable people is depressingly common, and research has shown that over the last decade, burnout has been frequently correlated with high rates of attrition, sickness and problems recruiting and retaining experienced staff, which degrade service-provision and increase levels of jobstrain and role-dissatisfaction. These issues have been found to extend, not only to staff employed in health and social care, but also to those working in education, humanitarian organisations and even frontline, administrative staff, like receptionists, who often bear the brunt of public dissatisfaction with cutbacks and reduced levels of service.

In terms of prevalence data, a General Medical Council's report, published in 2019, found that one in four UK doctors felt burnt out due to a high or chronically excessive workload.

In a similar vein, the Kings Fund reported that National Health Service (NHS) staff were 50% more likely to become burnt out than people in the general population. Likewise Paula McFadden from the Queen's University Belfast Centre of Evidence and Social Innovation found that 33% of UK social workers had symptoms of emotional exhaustion as assessed by the Maslach Burnout Inventory. In a similar vein, the National NHS Survey, published in 2019, showed high levels of staff vacancies with half the work force reporting stress. Elsewhere the UK's Health and Safety Executive reporting in 2021 found that stress, anxiety and depression accounted for 50% of all work-related cases of ill-health with the total number of cases lying at 822,000, giving an equivalent prevalence rate of 2,480 per 100,000 members of staff, making stress, anxiety and depression the most common form of illness followed by skeletomuscular disorders (24%) and all other causes of illness (21%).

Other studies found that the problem of burnout was exacerbated by the SARS-CoV-2 pandemic. Surveying 1,100 health care workers, the charitable organisation, Mental Health America found that 93% of survey participants reported stress, 76% exhaustion and burnout and 52% compassion fatigue, with reasons including job strain, lack of sleep, problems with parenting provision and lack of emotional support. Looking outside of the Western world, Mohammad Jalili and his colleagues, from the Department of Emergency Medicine linked to Tehran university in Iran, found that 53% of staff experienced high level of burnout, in the form of depersonalisation and low self-efficacy.

In terms of social work, the British psychologist, Gail Kinman found that early-career social workers were at particular risk of burnout, which

Chapter 8: **When compassion fails** 131

chimes with a report by the independent social work consultant, Suzy Kitching, which revealed that 59% of social workers left their local authority employer within the first five years and that the average career of a children's social worker was less than eight years.

Similarly, in conducting a survey into a work-related well-being among prison staff, Kinman found relatively high levels of self-reported stress and symptoms of burnout (including emotional exhaustion, desensitisation to prisoner's needs and low job satisfaction) together with a high level of sickness and presenteeism. Likewise, a 2019 report by the UK's Institute for Government looking at the United Kingdom's prison service found a high vacancy rate of around 10% per annum, frequent exposure to harassment and violence and a relatively inexperienced workforce working in a complex and moderately dangerous milieu (only 50% of prison officers had more than five years of service). In a similar vein, in conducting a review of prison staff's mental health, based on 21 reports from nine countries, the Dutch psychologists, Wilma Schaufeli and Maria Peeters found high rates of staff burnout associated with very high staff turnover and attrition, absenteeism, lack of experienced staff and high levels of job dissatisfaction associated with high role demands and low levels of autonomy.

In education a 2021 report published by Gov.UK found relatively high attrition rates associated with high workload demands and negative work-life balance, resulting in one in six teachers leaving the profession within seven years. In a similar vein, a survey of lecturers working in higher education reported in the *Chronicles of Higher Education* in 2021 found that approximately 70% of staff reported stress and fatigue with the burden of emotional distress falling disproportionally on female members of staff.

In terms of humanitarian workers, the Australian psychologist, Colleen McFarlane reported that 10% of a sample of American relief workers had developed post-traumatic stress disorder within three years of returning home, a rate that she states is comparable with levels found in humanitarian peacekeepers. Elsewhere, the occupational health psychologist, Liza Jachens and her colleagues also found that burnout was prevalent in humanitarian work. In a cross-sectional survey of international aid workers, exhaustion was reported by 36% of women and 27% of men, depersonalisation by 9% of women and 10% of men and low personal achievement by 47% of women and 31% of men. Moreover, as in social care and the prison service, research shows that burnout in humanitarian work is commonly associated with the existence of substantive and chronic discrepancies, between core organisational missions, personal ideals and values and the reality of the situation on the ground.

Organisational failings and burnout

As we have just learnt, burnout is associated with work-related stress that characteristically arises when the demands placed on individuals persistently exceed their ability to cope, and whilst coping ability is, in part, determined by individual differences in resilience (i.e., traits, such as openness to change and optimism), evidence shows that burnout occurs more frequently where there is organisational dysfunction that erodes workforce capacity and compassion.

One of the most well-known and infamous examples of dysfunctional management occurred at the UK, Staffordshire NHS, Foundation Trust between 2005 and 2008, when appalling conditions of care continued unabated for several years. According to the findings of the 2013, Francis Enquiry that was established to report on the causes of the failure to provide even the most basic levels of care and dignity, the Trust concerned had created a culture that prioritised fiscal targets over quality of care, which resulted in a lack of organisational compassion and an engrained tolerance of poor-quality care. Clinical staff were found to exhibit symptoms of depersonalisation and the incoming Chief Executive Officer reported that he found a culture of helplessness that was linked to tolerance of poor standards.

However, just a few years later, another independent enquiry, the Ockenden Review, was published in 2022 by GOV.UK, which documented widespread failures of maternity care over several years at the Shrewsbury and Telford Hospital NHS Trust. This report found similar gross, systemic failures of care, associated with poor governance, failure to investigate serious, untoward incidents and evidence of depersonalisation and lack of compassion for grieving parents with brain-dead babies, for example, reportedly being referred to as 'it'.

Chapter 8: **When compassion fails**

Whilst the latter scandals of care rank with some of the most serious failures of care in the NHS, significant, systemic management problems have been found elsewhere in health care in the UK. Professor Michael West, from the UK's King's Fund, for example, who has championed the case for compassion and inclusive leadership, is on record as stating that management systems in health care are often deemed by staff to be punitive, directive and blaming. Moreover, individuals are frequently scapegoated for systemic, organisational failings, whilst legal tools, such as 'gagging orders' (Non-Disclosure Agreements), prevent clinicians from speaking out about professional issues for fear of losing their jobs. Such failings, West states, erode staff autonomy and foster cynicism and burnout that have an insidious, corrosive effect on the delivery of high-quality, compassionate care.

In a similar vein, Professor of Occupational Psychology, Gail Kinman states that the causes of stress and burnout often occur at an organisational level and relate to long hours, the effects of cutbacks and having to cover for absent colleagues who are absent on long-term sick leave. Looking at academia, she points out that a culture of managerialism has led to increased role demands, protocols and systems that exacerbate job stress at a time when support systems for students have been subject to cutbacks. She also found that managers in higher education were perceived as being inadequate and poorly equipped to carry out their roles. In a similar vein, Lord Michael Rose, writing in a 2015 report to the UK Government, entitled *Better Leadership for tomorrow*, noted that NHS management are often viewed with suspicion as dark agents, who are not subject to the same level of scrutiny as clinicians. Indeed, Rose states, rather damningly, that the NHS is 'drowning in bureaucracy' with too many regulatory organisations, making too many reporting requests for information that is not centrally pooled, analysed, disseminated and acted upon. However, this problem is not exclusive to the NHS.

Various studies have shown that staff across public sectors frequently spend more time on paperwork than face to face contact with patient and clients. One study, for example, reported in the UK newspaper *The Guardian*, found that social workers spent 35% time of their time on paper exercises and only 15% of their time in direct contact with clients. Likewise, a survey conducted by the British Association of Social Workers

(BASW) estimated that social workers typically spend twenty-nine hours a week in computer-related administration activities.

The picture in higher education is not dissimilar. American anthropologist, John Zier conducted a time and motion study of North American university professors, which found that they spent just 3% of their working week engaged in direct research activity with a sizeable chunk of their time given over to various administrative duties.

These things matter because high levels of bureaucracy and frequent policy change are major obstacles to high-quality care. Michael West has reported that senior management staff are rotated frequently into differing roles. Many Chief Executive Officers fail to occupy their posts for more than two years resulting in inadequate time to master their briefs and this combined with repeated organisational change and top-down alterations in policy has contributed to a state of generalised change-fatigue and cynicism, which has stifled rather than supported resilient innovation and change. The NHS historian, Chris Ham, for example, notes that the UK's NHS had been subject to major reform roughly every five years. In the period 1990 to the present 2020, the NHS underwent six major reforms governing the structure of the organisation and areas, such as management, commissioning and provision of services: Namely the Health and Community Care Act (1990), the Primary Care Act (1997), the National Health Service Reform and Health Care Professions Act (2002), the Health and Social Care Act (2003), the Health and Social Care Act (2012) and the publication of the blueprint for major structural reform in the NHS 2021 by the, then, Health Secretary Matt Hancock. Similar problems have been documented in teaching. The charity EdPol, for example, writes that stability in teaching in England has been negatively affected by 'policy churn', relating to over eighty major policy implementations in forty years, which they claim a culture of compliance rather than innovation and mastery. In a similar vein, the BASW reports that social work in England has been overseen by three different regulators in less than five years, namely the General Social Care Council, the Health and Care Commission and Social Work for England, leading to similar issues.

The net effect of these changes and the increasing dominance of disengaged and alienating bureaucratic systems has been an apparent diminution of the perceived importance of compassionate care and a corresponding rise in occupational burnout, which fits with the theoretical supposition that burnout occurs when individuals perceive they do not have the capacity or means to fulfil their role effectively.

Compassionate organisations

Although the relationship between resilience and compassionate care may not be immediately obvious, it most certainly exists. In much the same way that nutrients invisible to the naked eye are essential for the well-being and viability of a tree, compassion in the workplace is essential for staff, well-being and role effectiveness.

An employee's ability to excel in their role and to be compassionate (which is of primary importance in organisations that exist to serve vulnerable others) is dependent on their feeling supported and able to meet the demands that are placed upon them. Likewise, an organisation's resilience is reciprocally dependent upon the mental and physical well-being of its employees. When staff feel unable to function in their roles effectively or feel that their values and standards are being compromised by organisational goals that are impossible to meet, they are at high risk of succumbing to burnout, depression and helplessness, which fuel staff attrition, and presenteeism,[1] in a cumulative cycle that further degrades the quality of care.

The British social scientist and psychologist Maria Kordowitz defines a compassionate organisation as one that places concern for staff well-being at the centre of its policies and practices. This involves recognising that staff who support vulnerable others are themselves at heightened risk of stress, depression and vicarious trauma and putting in place strategies that enable the early identification of mental health problems together with practices that actively support staff to develop ways of building resilience.

To enable this, Gail Kinman proposes that organisations need to normalise vulnerability in the workplace so that it is viewed as a *condition humana*, embodied in the principle that we are all inherently susceptible to pressure flowing from demand and overload in the workplace. Without this fundament in place, there is a significant risk that staff who succumb to conditions like stress and burnout are viewed as somehow lacking in the necessary personal qualities (grit, resolve, stiff-upper lip, etc.) that are deemed to render others 'resilient'.

However, as we learnt earlier in this text, nothing could be further from the truth.

Resilience is a multi-dimensional construct that is less a function of an individual's inherited traits and characteristics and more a function of the quality of support that exists in an individual's environment. Organisations that place compassionate at the core of their raison-d'etre are well placed to offer such support, whilst organisations that are characterised by disengaged bureaucratic systems are more likely to regard stress and burnout as weakness and react by scapegoating individuals (or even whole teams) with knee-jerk reactions that include heavy-handed inspections, internal reviews, disciplinary action, demotion and staff dismissal.

Such approaches do little to address the underlying issues and given that stress and burnout are both a cause and a symptom of high rates of staff attrition and sickness, blaming individual members of staff only adds insult to injury. In drawing attention to some of the issues around heavy-handed inspections in UK secondary schools, for example, former headteacher (and author of the book, *Best Job in the World*), Vic Goddard states that new heads can be sacked after two years following a poor Ofsted[2] inspection that may take little account of systemic failures that lie beyond the school, such as the absence of community support for children with special educational needs, learning disabilities and mental health problems and even issues like staff recruitment problems in STEM subjects. In fact, in a recent article published in *Schools Week*, Ofsted was criticised for the somewhat perverse policy of holding individual schools responsible for staff shortages that are a national issue. Moreover, in one of the few pieces of research that has looked at the impact of school inspections on subsequent exam performance, the British education researcher, Leslie Rosenthal reported a small, but persistent drop in exam performance in the year *following* an inspection – a finding he suggests may be due to school inspection focussing teachers' minds on external benchmarks and standards rather than students' integral performance.

Similar problems exist in social work, Sharon Shoesmith, the former director of Haringey children's services in London (an area characterised by multiple indices of deprivation), states that the vilification of

Chapter 8: **When compassion fails**

social workers and the summary sacking of the head of service, following the tragic death of Baby P, hindered efforts to understand and prevent future failures, because staff became anxious, closed and defensive.

Returning to the Mid Staffordshire NHS, Foundation Trust, when the Queen's Council, Sir Robert Francis published his report into the failings at the trust, he emphasised the need to put compassion at the heart of organisations who deliver patient care. Echoing this, the chief executive of Health Education England, Navina Evans, has pointed to three 'compassionate' needs that people have at work: Namely, the need for personal competence, development and personal growth, the need for autonomy and control (the antithesis of helplessness and powerlessness) and the need to perceive that one's efforts and actions make a genuine difference commensurate with one's personal values, goals, professional standards and expectancies.

Additionally, Michael West refers to six key factors that have been shown to characterise organisations that excel in creating environments where staff thrive: These being, having a realistic and attainable vision for high-quality care that is shared by staff at all levels and not just management. Having simplified strategic goals and priorities so that staff are not overloaded with superfluous directives, initiatives and procedures. Creating feedback-rich environments that let individuals and teams know how they are doing (this needs to include positive feedback, as all too often staff complain that they only get information about things that have not gone well). Ensuring staff freedom and autonomy to use their judgement and to make improvements in their areas of work, which West suggests requires high levels of trust and flat-bed, decision-making structures that avoid top-down, heavy handed, management-knows-best edicts. Having a shared commitment to quality improvement and innovation and providing for high levels of staff engagement at all levels, including the promotion of team working and team accountability that creates a sense of shared purpose and affiliation. In addition, West points to the vital importance of creating a no-blame culture that encourages the reporting of errors in a culture free from fear of persecution.

To these points we might reasonably add Kinman's assertion that we need also to recognise that employees, like everyone else, are human and fallible. It is this point that I want to turn to next.

To err is human

Many experts advocate the introduction of a no-blame culture into health and social care along the lines of the model adopted by the aviation industry. In aviation it is accepted that human error often occurs in the context of complex systems, involving multiple operators and dimensions. Errors may arise from a mistake made during aircraft maintenance or aircraft design or when pilots and air crew are subjected to extraordinary levels of stress or when problems arising in complex systems and environments lead to miscommunication or cognitive overload, and errors in perception, attention and decision-making.

In fact, the US Federal Aviation Administration states that the catastrophic accidents are rarely the result of individual failure, but more typically the result of sequences of events that culminate in human error. As a result, the aviation industry *globally* collates and analyses flight data and findings from accident-enquiries to inform aircraft design, pilot training and the science of *human factors*, which focusses on the functional interface between humans and technology. This modus operandi is based on the principle that whilst mistakes, leading to accidents can never be completely eradicated, the likelihood of future error may be reduced by understanding how and why things went wrong.

In addition, pilots (unlike the majority of health and social care professionals) are mandated to take time off to rest and sleep, subjected to random tests for alcohol and rigorously skills-assessed in a flight-simulator every six months. This approach to human error has resulted in a significant drop in aircraft-related mortalities since its introduction and the former NHS Chief Medical Officer, Sir Liam Donaldson, has noted that the odds of dying as a consequence of human error when you board an airplane is now 33,000 times lower than when you enter a hospital. However, having a no-blame system does not mean tolerance of incompetence, negligence or wilful, risky behaviour. It simply means accepting that people are fallible and it is possible to mitigate risk by understanding the root causes of problems and by supporting staff so that the risk of making errors is minimised.

In a recent article in *Health Management*, former UK, Chief Nursing Officer, Marti Moore called for the introduction of a system of analysis and prevention in health care based on the 'no-blame' principles

Chapter 8: **When compassion fails**

employed in the aviation industry. She noted that mistakes are often embedded in system-chains and that the primary barriers to the introduction of a no-blame system in health care are concern about reputational damage affecting prominent individuals, and organisational concern about legal action following admission of error. Moreover, Moore noted that such concerns were circumvented in the aviation industry by the appointment of neutral third parties to oversee reporting procedures, root-cause analyses and recommendations.

In a similar vein, Shreshtha Trivedi, writing in the *Health Services Journal* argues the need for an NHS-wide accountable system of error reporting, analysis and recommendations. In one NHS Hospital Trust, the Wrightington Wigan and Leigh Foundation Trust, for example, the appointment of 'safety champions' drawn from doctors, nurses, administrative staff and hospital porters, together with a systemic approach to the reporting of incidents, including safety surveys, audits, and policies empowering staff to report mistakes, bullying and racism, resulted in higher reporting of errors and incidents, the ousting of ineffectual leaders and a significant drop in overall patient morbidity and mortality during the four years in which the system operated. However, whilst this approach is seemingly commendable, Trivedi notes that to truly benefit from reporting systems, there is a need for a national system, where information about errors and critical incident reporting is pooled and disseminated, as occurs in the global aviation industry.

Nevertheless, improving reporting and analysis of error is not the only route to improving patient and staff well-being. One of the issues that emerges from the literature on human error health and social care is the importance of team accountability.

The former surgeon and current Director of the Institute of Global Health Innovation, Lord Darzi argues that given that multi-disciplinary teams are typically accountable for complex treatments, procedures and decisions about care, it is important that each member of the team is empowered to speak out if they are concerned. In a revealing documentary, for example, entitled *To Err is Human*, first aired on BBC, Radio 4 in 2009, a sequence of events unfolds where a female patient dies from lack of oxygen during routine, minor surgery.

Her husband, an airline pilot, forces the hospital to conduct a root-cause analysis, which reveals that senior operating staff's apparent dismissal of advice from junior (though highly experienced) colleagues had contributed to the tragic sequence of events that culminated in his wife's death. In reflecting on this, Darzi argues that recognition of team accountability is vital in stressful and complex working environments, such as the operating theatre, so that each member of the team feels able and supported to comment and raise clinical concerns. Indeed, team working offers a more flat-bed structure that can avoid some of the flaws inherent in top-down hierarchical structures. As the psychologist Stanley Milgram infamously showed in his experiments conducted in the 1960s, blind obedience to authority can have devastating effects for those at the receiving end.

In his experiment, Milgram recruited people from various walks of life to take part in a series of experiment whose real aims were disguised. In the experiment, the recruits were instructed to play the role of 'teachers', whose task was to administer a painful electric shock to a 'learner' each time he answered a question incorrectly. Present during the experiment was one Milgram's confederates, whose role was to assertively ensure that the participants adhered precisely to the procedures and instructions. Unbeknown to the 'teacher', the electric shocks were fake, and the 'learner' was played by an actor, and whilst some of the participants refused to administer further electric shocks quite early in the procedure, others carried on until the level of shock was ramped up to what they were led to believe approached a near-lethal level. In explaining the outcomes, Milgram reasoned that those involved had followed the instructions of the authority figure, and in doing so, abdicated personal responsibility for their actions, because they were fearful of saying no or because they didn't want to appear awkward and uncooperative.

Sadly, hierarchical structures have been implicated in major health care disasters, such as the avoidable deaths of 35 children undergoing paediatric heart surgery at the Bristol Royal Infirmary during the period 1988 to 1995 and the global failures in care delivery at the North Staffordshire NHS Trust, referred to earlier, which led to an estimated 400 'excess deaths'. In both instances, the resulting public enquiries found evidence that the tragic and avoidable outcomes were attributable to, not only to the absence of robust clinical reporting procedures that enabled mistakes to go unchallenged, but also to the absence of team-accountability that put control in the hands of a few.

Notes

1 Presenteeism is a term that has been coined to describe the practice of habitually turning up for work and going through the motions whilst lacking the physical or psychological capacity (due to sickness) to carry out one's roles effectively.
2 Ofsted stands for Office for Standards in Education, Children's Services and Skills

Chapter 9
Resilience and poverty

Inter-generational poverty

Despite the many negative myths about the causes of poverty and vulnerability, people who live in poverty are resilient in many ways. They manage in trying circumstances with a limited income that is often a fraction of that enjoyed by their wealthy counterparts and they frequently have to cope with multiple, major stressors and chronic health issues.

The UK government's health secretary, Matt Hancock admitted as much in 2020, when he said that he could not survive on statutory sick pay, which amounted to less than a fifth of average weekly earnings. That said, most authorities agree that long-term poverty and social inequality have a corrosive and pervasive effect on resilience that is passed from generation to another like a silent form of DNA.

It is becoming increasingly clear that childhood poverty, and its sequelae, support the transmission and entrenchment of generational vulnerability through complex, and often hidden, bio-psycho-social interactions. As we learnt earlier, there is evidence to suggest that the epigenetic effects of maternal stress may negatively alter stress-reactivity in the developing foetal brain. Likewise, abuse and neglect in infancy has been shown to affect the development of the social brain causing problems with emotional regulation and attentional processes and attachment difficulties that can severely comprise an individual's ability to form intimate, trusting relationships.

The Australian Psychologist, Deirdre Gartland and her colleagues, for example, state that a range of poverty-related factors have been

DOI: 10.4324/9781351035545-11

Chapter 9: **Resilience and poverty**

shown to constrain the normal development of emotional self-regulation, intelligence, optimism, positive self-esteem and social connectedness, which are all regarded as central to the creation and maintenance of lifetime resilience. However, it is only recently that researchers have begun to realise just how pervasive the effects of poverty can be. The American professors of psychology, Clancy Blair and Cybele Raver, for instance, have reported that brain imaging studies of infants living in poverty have identified anomalies in brain structures, which include reduced brain mass in the centres that govern language, executive functions and episodic memory, which were not found in their affluent peers. Blair and Raver point out that these functional deficits are likely to have a significant, negative effect on the normal development of attention, language and recall, which may help to explain why evidence has consistently shown that children living in poverty fair less well in education. Evidence, such as a recent report published by the Institute for Fiscal Studies dated 2022, which revealed that despite intensive efforts to improve educational outcomes for disadvantaged pupils (which include the introduction of results-league tables and rigorous, external school inspections), the marked differences in educational attainment that exists across the class divide have barely changed in twenty years.

However, inter-generational poverty is also associated with socio-economic factors, which include the collapse of community trust and cohesion. Likewise, the loss of material capital associated with corruption in developing countries and the degradation of vital infrastructure in post-industrial communities that exists to support resilient health and education, and the shaming of the poor which has been shown to undermine self-agency, and increase negative stereotyping and victim-blaming, which can contribute to the withholding of funding and resources for people who are disadvantaged.

Moreover, in commenting on the lived-experience of inter-generational poverty, the political activist Darren McGarvey asserts that life in impoverished city communities is characterised by powerlessness, insecurity, addiction and violence. These factors, he argues, together with social stereotyping, spawn apathy and cynicism that lead people to see themselves as pawns rather than playmakers, and the resulting powerlessness is passed down from one generation to the next.

Community resilience

The economic and social costs of poverty and the resulting human vulnerability are huge. According to British Professor of Geographic Information and Cartography, James Cheshire, in the brief ten miles that separates London's prosperous West-end from the socially deprived East-end, there is a ten-year difference in average life expectancy, equating to roughly one year for every mile travelled between the two destinations. Similar differences can be found in the levels of stress, illness and crime and it is a phenomenon that has been documented in many major cities across the world as global inequality has steadily increased. Global wealth and power are now concentrated in the hands of a relatively small number of individuals and multi-national corporations. According to Oxfam, for example, whilst material wealth has doubled in the past two decades, more than half of that wealth has been accrued by less than 5% of the global population, often in the hands of oligarchs and powerful multinational companies who lodge their profits in offshore tax-havens.

The World Bank has charted how these developments have disproportionately affected those living in developing countries, and in the poorest countries, such as Haiti, for example, whole populations have become dependent upon foreign aid to meet the basics of daily living, whilst social instability and spiralling debt have corrosively undermined the country's capacity for resilient growth and regeneration.

Such problems are made worse by political instability and physically precarious environments. The developmental economist, Jasmine Baier and her colleagues from the US Brookings Institution state that more than half of the world's poorest people are destined to live in fragile areas that are prone to natural disasters, such as flooding, earthquakes and drought, and/or live in areas of geo-political instability where war and terror wreak social and economic havoc and create large sub-populations of displaced people and refugees. In the aftermath of major humanitarian disasters, be they natural or man-made, homes are ruined, critical infrastructure is destroyed and the psychological stress, trauma and powerlessness that results from being in an unsafe environment leads to heightened rates of marital breakdown, child abuse, rape, and misuse of alcohol and other illegal substances.

Chapter 9: Resilience and poverty

However, social instability and economic decline also affects communities in the affluent west. The American public policy researchers, Michael Teitz and Karen Chapple note that poverty is common in inner-city areas (often referred to as ghettos) and they suggest that the causes of poverty include major structural shifts in economic capital and infrastructure, leading to low productivity and the inability to be competitive, racial and gender discrimination, the migration of the poor into areas of poverty and social isolation. Indeed, whilst the world's super-rich (the top 5% of the global population, who, according to Oxfam, hold 60% of the world's wealth) can effectively shield themselves from the societal impacts of poverty by building gated communities or relocating to safer climes, the bulk of the world's population cannot.

Yet, according to the political activist and author, Darren McGarvey, we all pay the price for inequality and poverty, because social deprivationis invariably associated with high levels of societal illness and psychological problems, such as stress, depression, child maltreatment, trauma and addiction, which puts an inevitable strain on the public purse via the bill for stretched social services, child-protection systems, educational support for special needs, the court and prison system and, of course, waiting times for access to health services.

Poverty, however, is not an intractable problem. The effects of social deprivation and inequality may be offset by the presence of factors that bolster community resilience and enable community development. Factors which, Anita Chandra, senior policy researcher at the US, RAND Corporation, proposes include strong community engagement stemming from shared culture and values, a history of effective partnership working with statutory agencies, and strong local, leadership and self-preparedness.

Indeed, like personal resilience, community resilience is best described, not as a static phenomenon that reflects a particular community's grit or willpower, but as a dynamic phenomenon that is the product of interaction between the demands and pressures that result from social deprivation (and natural and man-made disasters) and the capacity of a community to respond in terms of resources that economists refer to as economic, social and material capital.

These three types of resource have been shown to play a critical role in determining a community's resilience.

As you may recall, economic capital broadly refers to fiscal factors such as wealth, income and employment. Material capital refers to the provision and availability of goods, services and public infrastructure, such as schools and hospitals, and social capital embraces human factors, such as the presence of cohesive social networks that facilitate support and the sharing of local knowledge and skills.

Expanding on these concepts, the social scientist and economist Professor Paul Spicker writes that economic capital is commonly defined as the basic minimum that people need to survive (AKA absolute poverty), or it may be defined by way of financial indicators, such as per-capita income (the amount of money earned per person in a given area or country) or as access to resources and human assets (including education, health facilities, water and systems of local governance). Economic capital may also be defined with reference to adult literacy rates and mortality ratios, as are employed in the United Nation's Human Development Index. Indeed, using these criteria, research conducted by the United Nations has shown that the world's least developed countries[1] are the most economically vulnerable and susceptible to major 'shocks' caused by major events such as war, famine and epidemics.

With reference to material capital, Spicker explains that there is an inverse, negative relationship between economic development and inequities in the distribution and access of resources, goods and services. Such inequities create and perpetuate social deprivation and cycles of inter-generational poverty, as a consequence, humanitarian aid organisations frequently make specific reference to material inequity when considering the development needs of poor countries across the world.

The third factor, social capital, is defined by the Office for Economic Development as the sum of common, binding relationships and networks that help communities to function effectively and harmoniously. These relationships and networks are collectively referred to as community capacity, a concept first developed by the American public health specialist, Robert Goodman.

According to Goodman and his colleagues, community capacity is characterised by the development and mobilisation of strong local partnerships and leadership, drawn from a representative participant base of grass-root, stakeholders. If done properly this representative base will include participants who are challenged socially and economically.

However, Goodman states that in order to capitalise on such partnerships, those involved must have the skills and ability to understand how environments influence and shape human behaviour, and they must be willing and able to critically challenge existing assumptions and preconceptions about poverty and deprivation.

Michael Bopp and colleagues from the web-based, charitable organisation, CHW Central, state that engaging these networks is one of the most vital steps in the process of resilient community change, and one of the most frequently overlooked. However, McGarvey argues that these engagement processes are frequently fraught with difficulty. People from poor communities, he argues, are often deeply cynical and mistrusting of experts who are 'parachuted in' with grand ideas about how to achieve reform. This mistrust may also extend to the assumption that offers of support from government bodies and external support agencies invariably come with 'strings attached', such as implicit change-agendas that may lie at odds with the wishes of the grass-root community.

Whilst it is possible for vulnerable communities to edge their way out of poverty, Wayne Feiden, who is a director of public planning at the US, German Marshall Fund, states that progress typically requires significant investment in social and material capital, to support the revitalisation of run-down city centres, and vital infra-structure, high-speed internet access, high-quality schools and health centres and the creation and funding of facilities that support and showcase local culture. There is, he says, no silver bullet. Change requires political commitment to long-term, sustainable policies bound to a vision that flows from the aspirations and desires of the communities involved. Moreover, as McGarvey suggests, change cannot be successfully imposed on communities. It needs to be driven from within, and it is incumbent upon impoverished peoples to take responsibility and proactively engage in sculpting policies and agendas for change.

Corruption and stigmatisation

For poor communities that are lacking in material capital, the problem is often made worse by corruption and exploitation, which leaches vital resources away from those who need them most. The International Monetary Fund, for example, has reported that corruption and poor governance directly increases material inequality and reduces social capital and economic growth. Similarly, the World Economic Forum, which is a not-for-profit organisation that aims to bring together communities, business leaders and politicians, has estimated that the global cost of corruption to developing countries is $1.26 trillion dollars per annum and often takes the form of the expropriation of state assets in off-shore tax havens (as highlighted by the Publication of the Pandora Papers in 2021), bribes handed to high-ranking officials to secure lucrative multi-million-dollar contracts and inducements given to lower ranking officials to secure a place in medical school or employment as a policeman.

However, inequity in the distribution of wealth and resources is not confined to corruption in developing countries. The UK's Institute for Fiscal Studies, for example, found a 25% difference in pay for workers in the affluent southeast versus the poorer, post-industrial northeast. Similarly, the UK, think-tank, the Institute for Public Policy Research reported that the amount spent on transport-infrastructure in London was four times that per-person compared to the North of England. Such differences have also been documented in the United States. In tracking the distribution of community development funding, the Urban Institute found that funding was only weakly correlated with levels of distress and need with urban, low-population areas often losing out to larger and more densely populated towns and cities.

Whilst these latter findings may be partly explained by the fact that major cities across the globe generally receive more in state funding, because they are viewed as centres of national wealth creation, the flip side is that outlying regions, areas and communities are often deprived of fiscal resources or, worse still, are viewed as a net, negative drain on national wealth. The British sociologist, Tom Slater for example, writes that in the 1990s, the UK prime minister Tony Blair proposed that there would be economic and social benefits accrued from the demolition of 'sink-estates', defined by high levels of social housing stock, unemployment, crime and anti-social behaviour. A decade later, the policy was revamped by prime minister David Cameron whilst, more recently, the coalition government in Denmark has set in motion a programme to demolish problematic 'social ghettos', referred to as 'Udsatte Boligområder', as determined by high rates of unemployment, low levels of educational attainment and a high proportion of first- or second-generation inhabitants of non-western background.

Critics of these forms of social engineering point out that whilst the rationale behind these policies are generally well-intentioned, there is little concrete evidence (no pun intended) to demonstrate that they are fiscally or socially advantageous. In addition, they have pointed to the risks to people's health and well-being associated with forcible eviction, the dissolution of established social networks that aid community resilience and the risk that the residents involved are tarred by association for problems of poverty that are largely systemic, structural and beyond their control. The United Nation's High Commissioner for Human Rights, for example, has been critical of Denmark's use of criteria to identify social ghettos, which singles out communities with a high proportion of inhabitants of non-western backgrounds, because it renders them vulnerable to marginalisation, stigmatisation and social exclusion.

There is, perhaps, a balance to be struck here. Whilst heavy-handed social engineering of this nature risks feeding into the common narrative that those who live in social deprivation are responsible for their own misfortune and incapable of engaging in positive change, we also need to take note of the Wayne Feiden's earlier observation that lifting people out of poverty often requires significant investment in social and material capital.

Yet, the danger remains that in dismantling communities, social capital is lost, and existent systemic problems are simply relocated to another locality.

The problem of motivation

Lifting communities out of poverty is synonymous with changing people's beliefs, attitudes and behaviour and it is a process that typically requires patience, understanding, persistence and strategies for creating internal or intrinsic motivation for change.

Intrinsic motivation refers to behaviour and actions that are driven primarily by processes of internal reward, which may be physical or psychological. The physical sense of pleasure that we associated with internal motivation is primarily derived from activation of the brain's innate, dopamine-reward centre and the psychological sense of pleasure is derived from cognitive-affective processes that are associated with states, such as pride and self-efficacy.

Extrinsic motivation, on the other hand, is associated with behaviour that occurs in order to gain a reward or (as is often the case) to avoid something unpleasant, such as coercion, punishment, scolding or sanctions.

Behaviours associated with intrinsic (internal) motivation are typically self-sustaining and do not need to be continually reinforced by external rewards, whilst behaviours associated with extrinsic (external) forms of motivation tend to cease as soon as the reward or punishment is withdrawn. This difference is crucial and professionals who work in fields whose explicit goal is to facilitate behaviour change will typically elect to employ techniques that promote internally driven behaviours, for the simple reason that they are more likely to result in lasting, meaningful change.

There is nothing inherently wrong with extrinsic methods of behaviour-change (though there is an important caveat that I will return to shortly) and there are circumstances where their use can be effective in changing people's behaviour. In public health, for example, successive governments across the globe have employed coercive health warnings on cigarette packets to warn people of the dangers of smoking. These warnings initially took the form of text-based messages and, more laterally, pictorial images of diseased lungs and necrotic limbs that are designed to elicit discomfort, anxiety and cognitive dissonance. According to the American public health specialist, Seth Noar and his colleagues, these methods have been moderately effective in promoting smoking cessation and saving lives. The prevalence of smoking in young people and adults has remained significantly lower in countries that employ warnings on packets of cigarettes versus those which do not. Likewise, smoking cessation rates are higher in countries that employ graphic, pictorial warnings versus those that employ only text-based warnings.

There is, however, an important ethical and moral issue here, and extrinsic modes of behaviour-change should only be used when combined with the provision of viable alternatives that afford a sense of control and self-efficacy. In the case of smoking-cessation, this may be achieved through provision of access to support groups or counselling or the provision of nicotine replacement products.

Chapter 9: **Resilience and poverty**

Not only is this ethically sound it is also clinically effective. Methods that seek to create fear and cognitive dissonance without enhancing personal control risk driving people in the direction of avoidance and denial, which can paradoxically increase risk behaviour. At the start of the AIDS epidemic back in the 1980s, for example, the UK was engaged in a public health campaign that centred on a widely distributed poster campaign, which utilised large, graphic images of multiple, black coffins and the message 'Dying to Know'. In Australia, a similar campaign employed images of the Grim Reaper, and whilst these fear-based approaches were found to be highly successful in raising the public's awareness of the risk of contracting AIDS, they did little to promote a change in risky sexual behaviour in the target group, which was the gay community. Moreover, the American public health researcher, Amy Fairchild and her colleagues noted that the campaign led to the public shaming and stigmatisation of a community that was already marginalised. Likewise, in reviewing the literature on the role of stigmatisation in HIV/AIDS, the American public health specialist, Anish Mahajan and his colleagues concluded that stigmatisation had the undesirable effect of limiting uptake to critical support services.

Elsewhere, the American psychologist, Melanie Tannenbaum and her colleagues conducted a meta-analysis of the use of fear in promoting behaviour-change, which revealed that whilst the use of fear did have a positive effect in promoting behaviour change, the overall effect size was low.[2] In addition, a subsequent meta-analysis conducted by the American professor of communication, Elisabeth Bigsby, found that the use of fear had a greater impact on behaviour-change when combined with methods that increased self-efficacy, which as you may recall is psychological construct that refers to an individual's sense of control and mastery.

That said, extrinsic methods of changing behaviour are commonly used in many spheres of life, not least because they offer up the illusory promise of rapid behaviour change based on various form of punishment and sanctions, whose intuitive appeal does not reflect the complexities involved in eliciting change processes that result in enduring and self-sustaining changes in people's beliefs, attitudes and behaviours.

To illustrate this important point, I want to look at three behaviour-change methods that rely almost exclusively on extrinsic methods of reinforcement and which are widely employed in the public sphere: Namely, welfare sanction, punitive judicial sanctions and school-exclusion.

Welfare sanctions

As we have learnt, poverty and social deprivation are associated with higher-than-average rates of unemployment. In response (and some cynics might say to appease the sections of the electorate who regard the poor as inherently lazy and undeserving), many western governments have opted to make the receipt of welfare conditional upon active job-seeking.

A common strategy involves employing Benefit Sanctions (AKA Welfare Conditionality in the United States and elsewhere), which result in the withdrawal of all or a part of a claimant's benefits if he or she is deemed to have broken their contract to seek employment.

Viewed from a psychological perspective, this strategy relies on the principle of conditionality, which is a form of extrinsic motivation, defined as the motivation of behaviour via external pressure, threats and sanctions or the withholding of benefits.

Duncan McVicar, from Queen's University in Northern Ireland, states that the majority of developed countries apply some form of benefit sanctions in respect of welfare claimants who have been deemed to persistently infringe the rules governing the seeking of employment. In terms of efficacy, the Danish professor of Economics, Michael Svarer from Aarhus University has provided evidence demonstrating that moderate to high levels of benefit sanctions are effective in getting people off welfare and back into the labour market. However, whilst McVicar agrees that the threat of benefit sanctions has generally been shown to increase rates of job-seeking in the ranks of the unemployed, he also notes that recipients are often forced into inferior forms of employment associated with poor pay and conditions, whilst other studies have pointed to serious problems inherent in the efficacy, formulation and application of the rules that are applied to job-seekers.

Professor, Sharon Wright and her colleagues, for example, at Glasgow University, conducted a study involving policy stakeholders, practitioners and benefit recipients, which found that welfare sanction rules often lacked legitimacy and were applied arbitrarily, leading to considerable distress and life-altering consequences, whilst other studies have shown that the stress associated with welfare sanctions is strongly associated with illness, family breakup, homelessness and even suicide. A five-year study of benefit recipients, for example, carried out by the Welfare Conditionality Project, a group comprised of academics from six UK universities, found that for a substantial minority of benefit recipients, the impact of sanctions led to a range of serious, unintended outcomes including exacerbation of pre-existing mental and physical health problems, counterproductive job-compliance, and complete withdrawal from the welfare system, leading to social destitution and 'survival crime'.

As with Wright's study, the Welfare Conditionality Project was also highly critical of the treatment of vulnerable people, noting that the ethical and moral legitimacy of benefit sanctions was highly questionable, particularly given the system's general ineffectiveness in helping vulnerable recipients secure appropriate employment. In a similar vein, the British newspaper, *The Guardian,* recently ran an article, which provided evidence alleging that the UK's Department of Work and Pensions (which administers benefits and sanctions) had refused to publish a report that its own department had commissioned to examine the effects of welfare reforms, including conditionality on recipients' mental health and well-being.

Tough on crime

Since the 1990s, politicians in the United Kingdom (and elsewhere in the USA) have been fond of declaring that they will be tough on crime. Courts have been encouraged or instructed to mete out harsher, longer sentences with the result that the prison population in the UK has quadrupled in the period 1900 to 2108, with most of that growth occurring since the 1990s. The picture in the USA is very similar. The American not-for-profit organisation, The Sentencing Project, states that during the past forty years there has been a staggering, 500% increase in the prison population, and people of colour and ethnic origin are substantially more likely than their white counterparts to be handed custodial sentences.

Indeed, in keeping with the tough on crime mantra, and in order to ensure that would-be criminals are dissuaded from committing crimes, the UK's prison regime is widely regarded as being punitive, deeply unpleasant, unsafe and designed to dissuade would-be criminals from engaging in illegal activities.

A report based on an unannounced inspection of Belmarsh prison in 2021, by HM Chief Inspector of Prisons, for example, found that 1:4 prisoners felt unsafe. There was inadequate support and protection for victims of violence and poor governance and a paucity of recording of violent incidents involving staff and prisoners. In a similar vein, the government agency GOV.UK, reported that in the year ending 2021–2022 there were 318 deaths in prison custody across England and Wales (many of which were suicides), 59,000 self-harming incidents and 25,000 assaults on prisoners and staff.

The criminal justice systems in the UK and USA are based largely on the principle of deterrent (extrinsic motivation). Custodial sentences in harsh conditions are designed to make would-be criminals think twice before committing a crime. However, evidence suggests that this principle is fundamentally flawed. In conducting a meta-analysis of 116 studies, for example, the American criminologist Damon Petrich, found that custodial sentences had no meaningful effect in preventing reoffending.

Petrich's findings chime with the literature in general and, despite the general increase in the frequency and severity of jail sentences, deterrents have done little to reduce overall levels of crime or the frequency of reoffending. If we look at prison populations and reoffending rates, across different parts of the world, we find that the USA has the highest rates of incarnation and rates of reoffending per head of population. For every 100,000 head of population, there are 700 people in prison and the national, two-year re-conviction rate lies at 60%. The UK has a prison population that is markedly lower than that of the USA at 167 per 100,000 (which is the highest in Europe), but retains a similarly high, two-year reoffending rate which lies as 48%.

Moreover, the flaw in the premise that wielding a bigger stick deters people from engaging in crime becomes even more obvious when the data from the UK and USA are compared with those from Scandinavian countries whose criminal justice systems are grounded, not in punitive, deterrent-based systems of justice, but in the principles of restorative justice that seek to minimise the severity and length of sentences. In Norway, for example, there are only 49 people incarcerated for every 100,000 population and the two-year reoffending rate stands at 20%. In Finland the prisoner-population ratio is 59 people per 100,000 head of population and the two-year reoffending rate is 36%.

These differences have been explained by fundamental differences in the philosophies and modus operandi of the different penal systems. In the USA there is a basic focus on punishment, security and retribution rather than restoration and rehabilitation, whilst in Scandinavian countries the opposite is true. In Norway, the court system automatically applies the shortest possible sentences in the lowest, possible levels of security with open prison widely used for non-violent offenders. In Denmark, levels of violence and suicide in prison are low and many inmates can cohabit with their wives and children at weekends. Moreover, there is a strong focus on rehabilitation and building self-esteem, based on the principle that those convicted of crime are less likely to resort to crime on their release if they have reasonable prospects of getting employment and being successfully reintegrated back into society.

Of relevance here, is Maruna Shadd's research involving prison inmates in the UK. In interviews, he found that 'persistent offenders', lacked self-agency and felt powerless to change their life circumstances. Inmates were resigned to a life of crime, which they attributed to poverty, stigma and association with criminal-peers, and they tended to be focused almost exclusively on material goals rather than personal relationships.

These offenders reported feeling 'doomed' to a life of deviance, because their prospects of a normal life outside of prison was curtailed by the stigma of association with crime.

Shadd referred to this as a 'condemnation script', which he suggests fits with evidence that, for many persistent offenders, the likelihood of changing one's life-course without external support and encouragement is low.

A depressingly similar picture emerges from research that has examined the relationship between childhood problems and persistent adult offending. The British Emeritus Professor of criminology, David Farrington, for example, highlights the strong association between adult criminality and low verbal IQ and low peer-popularity in childhood. In a similar vein, Lea Pulkinnen, a Finish professor of human development, points to the negative relationship that exists between developmental deficits, such as delayed cognitive-emotional maturity, low self-regulation, impulsivity[3] and hyperactivity, and severely constrained educational attainment and employment prospects in adult life. Moreover, whilst some children 'mature', and overcome these deficits (often with the support of a coach or mentor), others drift haphazardly into a life of crime, that is often reinforced by drug and alcohol dependency (in the UK, for example, about 60% of those sent to prison for short sentences have a drug or alcohol-related problem).

The community psychologist Rhiannon Cobner and her colleagues state that if we want to understand and alleviate criminality, we need to dig deep and consider the context in which criminal behaviour develops and occurs. Simply applying punitive measures, they suggest, does little to address place-based factors that are associated with criminality.

When we look at the characteristics of communities blighted by high levels of crime, for example, we typically find low levels of social cohesion and trust, high level of violence and drug dependency and inadequate access to high-quality education and employment opportunities.

In such circumstances, simply wielding a stick in the form of punitive custodial sentences does little to solve the problems that underlie persistent offending. Likewise, punitive systems do little to help persistent offenders develop the motivation and capacity to change their behaviour and life-circumstances. Indeed, when we contrast punitive criminal justice systems with restorative ones, the facts seem speak for themselves and fit with the psychological reality that lasting and meaningful behavioural change is associated not with external coercion, but with the internal desire and support for change.

School exclusion

In the UK' school exclusion is defined as the removal of a child from school for a temporary or permanent period. It is described by GOV.UK

Chapter 9: **Resilience and poverty**

as a disciplinary procedure that occurs when children misbehave, and it is often employed in cases where children as disruptive in class or when they are involved in bullying, verbal or physical aggression towards other pupils or members of staff.

Exclusion rates from school vary markedly across the globe. Data from the Norwegian Centre for Educational Measurement show that in 2018, Sweden had the highest rates of school exclusion in the world at 11.09%, Korea had the lowest at 0.56%, whilst the UK sat slightly over the median with 5.47%. However, these data sets are not directly comparable because the UK data, for example, refer exclusively to exclusion occurring outside of the school premises (which may be temporary defined as, up to forty-five days, or permanent), whilst the data from Sweden refer to exclusion occurring both within and outside of the school.[4]

There are many problems associated with school exclusion in the UK. Whilst it is designed to modify a child's abhorrent behaviour in a positive direction, data show that the measures are often employed in a discriminative manner. In addition, information from the Department of Education, dated 2019, shows that children from ethnic groups are significantly overrepresented in school exclusions, as are children with special educational needs (which include serious mental health issues, such as autistic spectrum disorder and attention deficit hyperactivity disorder). Moreover, rates of exclusion are highest in primary school children aged 4–11 years who have special education needs. The Royal Society of Arts, for example, a charitable organisation that supports children with special educational needs, reported that during the period 2017/2018, 83% of all exclusions from primary schools involved children with a registered special need. Whilst UK law explicitly states that it is unlawful to exclude children from school that have special educational needs, various caveats permit headteachers to exclude a pupil if they are not able to manage his or her needs in school.

This problem is exacerbated by a general lack of support for children with complex social and behavioural problems that are frequently associated with social deprivation and chaotic home environments where there may be domestic violence and abuse.

These points are important, because school exclusion is a disciplinary measure that falls into the category of extrinsic methods of behaviour-change and coercive measures should only be used to modify behaviour when there are safeguards in place to ensure that the recipient of such coercion is afforded opportunities and help to change their behaviour by developing self-efficacy and achieving greater self-regulatory control. However, such support is frequently lacking.

Using requested data from 48 National Health Service Trusts, the British newspaper *The Independent* recently reported that children with serious mental health needs are waiting up to three years for an initial assessment and even longer for treatment. Likewise, Educational Welfare Officers (AKA attendance officers) who are tasked with enforcing the rules relating to school exclusion have limited statutory scope for ensuring that specialist support is actually put in place to help excluded children and their families. Moreover, the ratio of Educational Welfare Officers per pupil is eye-wateringly low. According to GOVUK, there is only one Educational Welfare Officer per 5,600 pupils. In a similar vein, the British Psychological Society recently reported in that in England there are only 3,000 educational psychologists to provide expert support for children who have special needs, which works out at one per every 3,500 school children. Perhaps then, it is not surprising that Morag Henderson, a senior researcher at University College London, found that pupils who had contact with an Educational Welfare Officer had significantly lower odds of exiting school at sixteen with good examination results (GCSEs) and a place at university.

In addition, whilst the law advises that children who are excluded should be sent to specialist Pupil Referral Units, research shows that these units frequently lack sufficient numbers of qualified staff to manage the education of children with complex needs.

As a consequence, some children are simply left to their own devices, and they 'drop of the radar'. The UK's All-Party Parliamentary Group on knife-crime, for example, recently noted that children who are excluded from school frequently fall victim to gang exploitation, particularly with regards to 'county-lines' drug trafficking, and, as the National Children's Society has documented, the sexual exploitation of excluded girls by pimps.

The government response to this impasse has predictably been to wield yet another stick. Parents of excluded children can be fined up to 5,000 pounds if their child is caught on the street during school hours, a tactic that has had no demonstrable impact on reducing the significant problems that are associated with school exclusion.

Breaking the cycle of inter-generational poverty

Many of the vulnerabilities that we have encountered in this book have their roots in impoverished communities and problems in childhood.

You may recall, for example, the findings of the Troubled Families Report, highlighted earlier in this book, which painted a picture of families living in social deprivation, typically headed by lone parents, who were found to be grappling with multiple stressors relating to poor physical and mental health, offspring with special education needs, child school-refusal and school exclusion, family involvement in crime and antisocial behaviour and high levels of unemployment and domestic abuse. The associated programme was, like the Family Nurse Partnership initiative, designed to target families where there was cyclical link between child maltreatment and social deprivation.

Evidence presented earlier in this book shows that the mechanisms involved range across the social, psychological and biological spectrum of development and well-being.

Not only does social and economic deprivation cause personal stress and hardship. The resulting stress also affects the developing structures and systems in the immature brain that biologically determine the children's ability to emotionally contain stress. The aversive effects also extend to the development of the structures that support cognition and, in particular, the systems that govern attention and executive processing, with far-reaching implications for how a child will fair in school and elsewhere in life. In a similar vein, epigenetic studies have shown that maternal stress, can affect the development of the infant's stress response architecture in utero, so that they are born with an abnormal sensitivity to stress.

In addition, attachment research has shown that parental maltreatment and neglect can, in the absence of an appropriate caregiving substitute, lead to the development of a disorganised attachment style, which is, in turn, associated with emotional dysregulation, poor educational and employment outcomes and the increased risk of early entry into a life of crime, which evidence shows is difficult to escape.

Sociological studies have also documented the cyclical relationship between maltreatment in childhood and poverty in adulthood and there is one study commissioned by the UK Charity, the Joseph Rowntree Foundation in 2016, that I want to draw particular attention to.

In this study, the lead investigator Paul Bywaters and his colleagues posed two key questions: Is there evidence to support the widely held assertion that poverty increases the likelihood of child maltreatment, neglect and abuse and does child maltreatment, neglect and abuse increase the likelihood of lifetime poverty in adulthood.

In answering the first of these questions, the report found that child maltreatment occurs across all layers of society, regardless of factors, such as class and ethnicity. However, rates of abuse in the lower social classes D and E were found to be nearly double that found in the relatively affluent social classes A-C.[5] Expanding on this, the report found that there was a cyclical relationship between a neighbourhood's economic status (as assessed by factors, such as housing stress, the availability of drugs and alcohol and relative property value) and child maltreatment. In one of the reported studies, the percentage of children registered on a child protection plan in the most deprived areas was nearly ten times higher than that found in the most affluent. In addressing the second question, the report found 'overwhelming evidence' that poverty and low income are related to early child abuse, neglect and maltreatment across all parts of the globe. Whilst the report explains that the mechanisms involved are complex and difficult to untangle, they draw attention to the proven relationship between child maltreatment and early entry into juvenile crime, which limits adult life opportunities, and the strong association between child maltreatment and adult mental health issues, which impact negatively on protective factors, such as self-efficacy beliefs and optimism.

These are factors that have been liberally evidenced in this book and its stands to reason that given the complex, entrenched and systemic nature of deprivation, careful consideration needs to be given to the issues that precipitate and maintain inter-generational neglect and abuse at a societal level. Yet, Urie Bronfenbrenner (whose Bioecological model of development we encountered earlier) states that unfortunately, it is not uncommon to find that authorities reflexively attempt to manage many of the common problems associated with poverty and problematic child development, such as school refusal and exclusion, and later crime, unemployment, through reflexive, coercive methods

Chapter 9: **Resilience and poverty**

that only serve to undermine self-efficacy and increase powerlessness. Indeed, as we have learnt, harsh penal regimes, the frequent use of school exclusion and the application of conditional sanctions that affect welfare benefits, actually create more problems than they solve and have the unintended effect of increasing vulnerability and cementing inter-generational poverty through powerlessness.

So, we need to ask what works – how can the negative cycle of child maltreatment and adult poverty be broken? Well, we have already encountered evidence-based programmes, such as the Family Nurse Partnership and Sure Start and their American equivalents, which seek to provide support for the development of parenting skills and the many psycho-social problems that are associated with raising children in poverty. In addition, we have Bowlby's attachment theory and Bronfenbrenner's Bioecological model, which both provide mature, conceptual frameworks and reference points, for understanding normative development and the causes and consequences of abuse and neglect. Bowlby's theory, for example, informs us that healthy development of the self is dependent upon the formation of early emotional bonds that facilitate self-confidence and sufficient trust in others to enable balanced, intimate relationships with significant others in later life. Similarly, Bronfenbrenner's Bioecological model tells us that if we want to understand the cyclical nature of adverse child development and the problems associated with poverty and abuse, we need to look at how distal and proximal factors shape parenting and the wider social environment.

In addition, I would like to draw attention to an evidenced-based, technical report published in 2016, by the American, Centers for Disease Control and Prevention (CDC), which was developed by the behavioural scientist Beverly Fortson and her colleagues.

The report provides information to professionals that are involved in supporting families and communities where there is a history of deprivation and abuse, including child maltreatment and domestic violence. It documents resilient interventions that are intended to strengthen economic support for families to reduce stress, the provision of high-quality preschool care and education, the enhancement of parenting skills, therapeutic treatment for the effects of abuse and neglect and sectorial involvement in the development and coordination and strategies, each of which I will look at in turn.

One of the key strategies suggested by Fortson is the strengthening of economic support to families in order to reduce stress. In this context you may remember Wayne Feiden's assertion that in order to lift families out of poverty, it is often necessary to improve social and material capital. Raising a child in poverty is a stressful experience and the CDC states that families can be supported through fiscal means, such as child support payments and tax credits, the introduction of a minimum or living wage, subsidised childcare, paid sick leave and maternity pay and practical policies that encourage employers to offer family-friendly, working practices that are flexible and consistent and which take account of inevitable problems that arise when rearing a child such as the need to be home because of child-sickness. The aim of these policies is to reduce stress within families, which is known to contribute to child abuse and neglect and domestic violence, and from a psychological perspective, they are aimed at enhancing perceived control and minimising perceived powerlessness.

The second, key strategy relates to improving and enhancing parenting skills, by supporting positive-parenting interventions that target complex behavioural problems, such as the management of anger and violence and the appropriate use of disciplining techniques that avoid the use of physical punishment and restraint. The CDC report also refers to the *Parent-Child Interaction Therapy programme*, which utilises coaching techniques to improve parenting skills and parental self-efficacy, the *Incredible Years Programme,* which provides on-line resources for parents and professionals, such as teachers and coaches, and the *SafeCare* programme, developed by the National Safe Care Training and Research Centre at Georgia University in the USA, which aims to reduce child abuse and neglect in high-risk families by focussing on parent-child interactions, child safety and child health.

A further key strategy involves the provision of high-quality preschool care and education.

research has shown, for example, that childhood abuse and neglect may be mediated through the provision of high-quality pre-school care and education, which reduces parental stress and provides the best possible opportunities for children to develop socially and educationally so that the families don't get locked into a poverty cycle of poor education and employment opportunities (which are known to increase abuse).

Examples of these types of intervention include the previously mentioned Sure Start programme and its American equivalent, Early Head Start, which aims to encourage the development of social skills and language through play and interaction with other children, to promote the local participation of families and to encourage positive parenting skills and the early identification of emotional and developmental problems and learning difficulties that might be associated with problems at home or underlying conditions, such as attention deficit hyperactivity disorder and autistic spectrum disorder.

In addition, initiatives may be targeted at improving the quality of pre-school education through formal accreditation and licencing which is designed to set appropriate minimum standards.

The CDC report also recommends strategies that provide therapeutic treatments for the insidious effects of abuse and trauma. Trauma-informed interventions, for example, that seek to reduce the impact of complex trauma, shame and sexualised behaviours, which can otherwise be carried forward as next generation abuse in parenthood. An example, being the previously encountered Keiser-ACE programme(s), which is designed to help young people who have been subject to early abuse and those who care for them, such as foster-parents. In addition, treatment programmes may be designed to tackle domestic violence and anger-management.

The final strategy identified by the CDC report encompasses sectorial involvement, which refers to the active participation of public health and legislative bodies in the development of programme and strategies. Such initiatives may look to improve coordination for the development and roll-out of population-based strategies and interventions or to alter societal attitudes and norms towards tolerance of violence and neglect of children (i.e., with regards to the use corporal punishment and other forms of discipline) or to shift ideas about responsibility for childcare and development away from the individual and towards shared responsibility, which may then be reflected in policies and changing attitudes (i.e., employers who are prepared to offer flexible working or schools that offer extended drop off and collect times to accommodate parents' working commitments).

Sectorial involvement may also relate to legislative changes that are designed to improve the lot of children and parents (again, such as the banning of corporal punishment).

In addition, public health involvement may look to enhance the training of primary care professionals, such as nurses in early identification of problems relating to post-natal depression and signs of physical and emotional abuse and the training of youth workers and coaches who have the potential to act as important role models for young people who are experiencing difficulties.

Social support and resilience

In the literature on resilience, one factor stands out in being singularly important in preventing and mediating stress and that is social support.

Social support takes two basic forms, namely practical support (also referred to as instrumental support), which commonly takes the form of advice, signposting and direct, hands-on assistance, and emotional support, which relates to compassionate empathy and help for relief from pain and isolation.

To fully grasp the importance of social support, we need to remember that it works by altering peoples' perceptions of seemingly difficult and challenging situations and circumstances, so that they come to see them as manageable. This basic tenet applies, not only to individuals, but also to groups and communities, and the flip side, as we have learnt, related perceptions of powerlessness and helplessness.

Viewed from a broader, conceptual perspective, social support is seen to operate in two basic ways, which are referred to as the main effect of social support and the buffering effect of social support.

The main effect of social support refers to the idea that the quality of the distal and proximal environments that people inhabit has a direct effect in mitigating potential stress. You may recall from Bronfenbrenner's Bioecological model, for example, that proximal support factors include immediate family, friends and neighbours, whilst distal support factors refer to the wider socio-economic milieu and the quality of infrastructure to support health, education and employment. If you have a kind, supportive family with nice neighbours and friends and live in a nice environment that is free of excessive crime and other social problems, fewer demands are likely to be placed on you and you will be less likely to experience stress, than someone who lives in a family where this is frequent discord, conflict or violence or are socially isolated and lacking confidants to share your problems with or inhabit an environment where there is high socio-economic deprivation and low levels of social cohesion.

The second way that social support works is by buffering individuals from the worst effects of significant events like unemployment, sickness, divorce and life-transitions that often crave major personal adjustment, such as adolescence, parenthood and serious illness and attachment losses, such as forced retirement and bereavement. In such situations, the supportive presence of significant others bolsters our resilience by helping to give us a sense of control and by warding off feelings of isolation, alienation, anxiety and depression. This is the principle behind common sayings like a 'problem shared is a problem halved' or expressions like 'I just needed a shoulder to cry on'.

In a similar vein, the psychologists, Albar Marin and Garcia Ramirez from the University of Seville, have shown that we may also get important emotional support from people in our work environment, particularly where these is a good degree of intimacy and kinship.

In a literature review of resilience in the workplace, for example, the British organisational psychologist, Angelique Hartwig and her colleagues found that team resilience is characterised by strong relational bonds and strong sense of team cohesion and identity that facilitate a sense of psychological safety, and which encourage cooperation and sharing. Resilient teams, she argues, foster collective and individual self-efficacy and are an important source of support when problems and issues arise. However, Marin and Ramirez note that teams can also be a source of stress. Team working, for example, can exacerbate stress where there is a culture of workaholism, long working hours and neglect of self-care. Indeed, a study conducted by the Harvard Business School, published in 2015, found that work-related anxiety was a major source of stress and ill-health with one of the contributing factors being conflict between work and family commitments, conflated by a culture of long working hours.

Teams can also create stress when social and cognitive dynamics lead to dysfunctional patterns of behaviour and decision-making. Groupthink, for example, which was first identified by the American psychologist, Irving Janis back in the 1970s, occurs when members uncritically accept the values and decisions of the group for fear of rocking the boat. In his book *Problem Solving in Teams and Groups*, the American professor of communication, Cameron Piercy notes that four factors have been shown to contribute to groupthink. Cohesion, referring to our basic need to feel that we belong and are valued. Isolation occurring when decisions are made by a group behind closed doors without consideration of alternative perspectives. Biased leadership, as when a group's leader holds too much authority and stifles individual contributions, and decisional stress, which occurs when a group feels under time-pressure to make decisions and choices (again without redress to alternative points of view). The British, Professor of Patient Safety, Brian Toft argues that groupthink was one of the contributing factors to excess death rates associated with the Bristol heart surgery scandal mentioned earlier in this text and it can cause significant levels of individual stress for those whose dissenting voices are ignored or ridiculed.

On balance, however, groups tend to function as important stress mediators rather than stress generators and one of the additional ways that group or team working can alleviate stress is the use of humour, which gives vent to tension by allowing emotional expression in situations that are highly stressful, frightening or emotionally taboo.

Many years ago, for example, I was taking part in ward-round on what was called a 'continued care' ward for patients that had long-term, psychiatric problems. During the ward-round a patient knocked on the door and entered to tell us that a patient called Mary was in the process of strangling another patient called Angela.[6] We looked at each other and did not immediately move. Angela was in the later stages of Huntington's chorea, a progressive, degenerative illness, and in her younger days (when she was still active and mobile) had made several, serious attempts to commit suicide. Mary, on the other hand, had a chronic compulsive disorder, which led her to act in random, sometimes bizarre ways, including occasional, mock attempts at strangling other in-patients. As we looked at each other, we silently shared the irony of the situation, and, without a word, the ward's Charge Nurse got up and left the room to calmly resolve the situation. That event has stuck in my mind, not least, because I remember it brought us closer together as team and reinforced a shared sense of purpose.

Chapter 9: **Resilience and poverty**

The British lecturer in emergency medicine, Sarah Christopher states that Black Humour, or Gallows Humour, as it sometimes called, is frequently used by emergency service personnel as a way of distancing themselves from events that are emotionally or visually disturbing. In such situations, humour acts as a safety valve for feelings that might otherwise be suppressed. (Suppression of feelings, such as fear, anxiety and powerlessness can fuel stress.) Likewise, writing in the *Journal of Organisational Behaviour*, the American psychologist, Michael Sliter and his colleagues found that humour provided a sense of bonding in firefighters exposed to traumatic events, whilst acting as a buffer for conditions, such as trauma, absenteeism and burnout.

Notes

1 This includes most of the countries in Sub-Saharan Africa and countries in Asia and the Far East, such as Afghanistan, Bangladesh, Yemen, Myanmar and Nepal.
2 The stated effect reported using Cohen's D statistic was .29. As rule of thumb, a large effect would give an effect size in the region of .80, whilst a low effect would give an effect size in the region of .20. The conclusion being that the reported impact of fear on behaviour change was marginal, though statistically significant.
3 As I was editing this book prior to publication, a study was published by researchers at Imperial College's Centre for Mental Health, which estimated that 25.5% of the UK youth, prison population have ADHD.
4 In the UK exclusion from the classroom, but within the confines of school is commonly referred to as 'time-out', a temporary measure, which is very different from school exclusion which involves removal (temporary or permanent) from the school's premises.
5 A useful link to the standard categories of social class employed in the UK can be found at: https://en.wikipedia.org/wiki/NRS_social_grade.
6 The patients' names have been changed for reasons of confidentiality.

Chapter 10
Behaviour change and resilience

The principles of change

Change is a natural and essential precursor to the development of resilience.

When we change tact because things are not going to plan, we are acting in a way that is resilient. Likewise, when we admit mistakes or recognise that we are fallible, it is the first step in a process of change that will ultimately make us stronger and more personally robust. Similarly, when an organisation in health, social care or education conducts a detailed investigation into an untoward incident that it then openly shares with all interested parties, it is acting in a way that improves the resilience of the organisation and all those who benefit from it.

In short, change is inextricably bound to resilient development and in this final chapter I want to set out what psychology has taught us about the factors and processes that promote (and inhibit) change, starting with the British and American psychologists, Stephen Rollnick and Williams Millers' assertion that when someone makes a commitment to change, they do so because they believe that change is both important, achievable and desirable.

This is an important statement, and it tells us a lot about the beliefs systems and appraisals that underpin behaviour change. To be motivated to engage in change, an individual needs to believe that change is important and in their interest, and that doing nothing will be disadvantageous or harmful. They also need to believe that change is achievable, meaning that they judge they have the personal capacity

Chapter 10: **Behaviour change and resilience**

and/or external support to ensure a satisfactory outcome. In addition, the individual must believe that change is desirable, and something that they genuinely want, rather than something that someone else thinks is a good idea.

These principles may be applied *to both* individuals and to communities and are encapsulated in the psychological constructs that we met earlier, referred to as internal or intrinsic motivation. When someone believes that change is in their interest, we say they are intrinsically motivated to engage in behaviour change and when they act as a consequence of some external stimulus or coercion, we say they are extrinsically motivated to engage in change. Of the two types of motivation, Rollnick and Miller assert that research and practice has shown that lasting and meaningful change is unequivocally associated with the former and not the latter, not least because behaviours which occur in response to external pressure have a habit of reverting back to the status quo as soon as that pressure is withdrawn.

In addition, I also want to reinforce the significance of the idea that individual perceptions are paramount with regards to behaviour change. This is reflected, for example, in common reference to the phrase the *perceived importance of change*, which is employed to draw attention to the idea that the process of change is a highly subjective thing that hinges on personal beliefs, judgements and perceptions. In practice, this means that failure to engage in change can, viewed from an outsider's perspective, sometimes appear illogical or even detrimental. To take an example, I like to think that my behaviours are health-orientated and rationale, I don't smoke cigarettes, I'm careful about my diet and I generally make sure I get plenty of daily exercise. However, my consumption of alcohol regularly exceeds the recommended government guidelines and I justify this fact, by reassuring myself that a glass or two of wine lowers my levels of stress and is, therefore, in fact, healthy. Of course, this is jiggery-pokery and whilst I am aware of the discrepancy between my health-beliefs and my behaviour, it does not bother me sufficiently to exchange my glass of chianti for an evening cup of tea.

Indeed, the irrational nature of human behaviour is something that therapists and counsellors learn about early on and is encapsulated in the old saying that you can take a horse to the well, but you can't force it to drink the water. In metaphorical terms, the horse needs to be convinced that drinking is in its own best interests and pushing and shoving will do little to help. Interestingly enough, this level of awareness is not reflected in general medical practice. The French pharmaceutical researchers, Vincent Zaugg and his colleagues, for example, recently conducted a Cochrane literature review,[1] which showed that medical practitioners systematically overestimate patient compliance with medical advice, which in terms of long-term treatment regimens hovers around a meagre 50%. As a consequence, instances of non-compliance with treatment advice or medication are often missed.

Health beliefs

The issue of non-compliance, or non-adherence as it sometimes referred to, is not a new phenomenon. It was first identified by psychologists way back in the 1960s, when interest in this issue, together with the problem of drug and alcohol addiction, led to the development of a small number of conceptual models and frameworks that are still widely used today.

The first of these is the Health Belief Model that was developed back in the 1960s by the American psychologists, Marshall Becker and Irwin Rosenstock. It is widely regarded as one of the best theoretical models of health-behaviour change and has an excellent evidence base. According to this model, the decision to engage in behaviour change is heavily influenced by four factors: Namely, perceived severity of symptoms, perceived susceptibility, perceived costs versus benefits of engaging in change, and perceived cues versus barriers to support.

Perceived severity relates to physical medical symptoms or mental health symptoms that can range from severe to benign. In general terms, research has shown that severe symptoms (like acute pain) and highly unusual symptoms (like blood in one's urine) are perceived as serious and act as important 'help-seeking cues' that motivate people to comply with medical instructions and/or seek timely medical advice. Conversely, mild symptoms and common symptoms tend to be ignored. Treatment compliance for asymptomatic conditions like essential hypertension, for example, tends to be poor. Likewise, people are less likely to seek medical advice for symptoms that are associated with common illness. Perceived severity, however, may have little or nothing to do with physical symptomatology. People who have been chronically misusing alcohol, for example, are often driven to seek professional help, not because of symptoms like physical pain, but because some social or domestic crisis has brought home the pressing need to address their addiction. Similarly, people are sometimes motivated to change their behaviour, because some transitional life event has created a strong desire for change. A first-time mother may decide to engage with the Family Nurse Partnership Programme, for example, because she wants to do all she can to minimise the chances of her baby being exposed to the type of traumatic experiences that she experienced as a young child.

In addition, the appraisal processes that normally influence treatment compliance and help-seeking behaviour, may be distorted by psychological defence mechanisms like denial and repression, particularly where fear is involved. A smoker with a persistent cough may avoid approaching their general practitioner, because they are worried that the cough is a symptom of lung cancer. In a similar vein, back in the 1970s, when treatment-outcomes for breast cancer were much poorer then than they are today, delay in seeking treatment advice for common symptoms, such as a lump in breast tissue, lay in in the order of months rather than days or weeks.

The second factor, perceived susceptibility, relates to individual perceptions of vulnerability and susceptibility, which are affected by factors, such as age, gender and familial vulnerability. A family history of disease, for example, may act as a prompt for help-seeking or for making lifestyle changes relating to diet, smoking, drinking and levels of activity – as can age,because we know that certain types of disease, like cancer, become more prevalent as we get older.

Likewise gender can play a role in individual perceptions of vulnerability. Male breast cancer often goes undetected and is diagnosed late, because males generally do not regard themselves as susceptible to the disease.

The third factor in the Health Belief Model relates to the perceived benefits and costs of change, and the perceived cues or barriers. The basic idea being that if the benefits appear to outweigh the costs, people will engage in change and vice-versa.

Some barriers have been shown to be particularly important. The financial cost of seeking help, for example, is a known, major barrier and deterrent. Data from the American Centers for Disease Control and Prevention have shown that people who do not have ready access to free or low-cost universal health care are sometimes dissuaded from seeking help or adhering with treatment advice, simply because they cannot afford it, or because competing priorities place demands on their limited financial resources. Similarly, help-seeking behaviour may be hindered by practical constraints, which include excessive travel-distance to sources of support, poor accessibility in terms of transport and/or opening times that are incompatible with work or home-related responsibilities and commitments.

Indeed, in a ten-year review of the Health Belief Model, Nancy Janz and Marshall Becker found that that perceived barriers to change was the most influential, behaviour-change factor, followed by perceived susceptibility. The weakest factor was perceived severity, which at first site may appear counter-intuitive. After all, if you had a potentially serious condition, would you not be motivated to seek expert help at the earliest possible opportunity?

The answer to this apparent conundrum lies in the wisdom offered by Miller and Rollnick.

For people to engage in change (which includes seeking help and engaging in treatment for a wide range of serious conditions like cancer and alcohol addiction) they have to believe that there is viable treatment option (i.e. something that works) and they have to believe that they have the personal capacity and resources to follow through. If these conditions are not met, they may bury their head in denial like the proverbial ostrich, because the fear is impossible to live with.

In a similar vein, the motivation to engage in behaviour-change has also been linked to the self-efficacy and optimism. Ralf Schwarzer, who is a German professor of psychology, for example, states that research shows that people who are high in self-efficacy and optimism are generally more willing and able to engage in behaviour change than people who are low in self-efficacy and high in the trait of pessimism.

Attitudes, intentions and change

The Theory of Reasoned Action was developed by the American psychologists, Icek Azjen and Martin Fishbein to explain the complex relationship that exists between attitudes and behaviour. According to the model, our behaviour is not only shaped by our personal beliefs and attitudes, but also by the prevailing beliefs, norms and attitudes that exist in the community and wider society in which we reside. The British psychologist, Vivien Swanson, for example, showed that prima gravida mothers' decision to breast- or bottle-feed was strongly influenced by social attitudes and norms. Mothers that initiated breastfeeding and continued after six weeks were more likely to have had close, social referents who held positive attitudes about breastfeeding, whilst those who discontinued reported experiencing social pressure to bottle-feed.

Of course, taking account of social norms and expectations before we engage in change has the adaptive function of ensuring that any new behaviour sits within the bounds of what is socially and morally acceptable. Whilst this is often socially adaptive it can also be personally problematic. Jim White, a Scottish clinical psychologist, for example, has shown that men in inner-city areas blighted by social deprivation are generally reluctant to seek help for prevalent mental health conditions like stress, anxiety, depression and alcohol misuse, because the prevailing macho-culture, and its norms and attitudes, portray help-seeking as a sign of weakness (real men don't cry). Whilst such attitudes have mellowed somewhat following the recent spate of candid disclosures about mental health problems from high-profile figures, such as Paul Scholes, the former Manchester United footballer, the actor and author Stephen Fry and the British Royal, Prince Harry, they still exist and remain a major barrier to improving men's mental health.

The Theory of Reasoned Action also draws attention to the important differences that exist between attitudes and intentions. The attitudes that we hold are, as noted, greatly influenced by prevailing social norms and attitudes and, as a result, we have tendency to say what we think others want to hear. For this reason experienced professionals working in the field of behaviour-change prefer to elicit a person's intentions rather than attitudes, because research has shown they are a more reliable indicator of what people are actually likely to do.

Stages of change

The final model in the field of behaviour-change that I want to draw attention to is the Stages of Change Model, developed by the American psychologists, James Prochaska and Carlo DiClemente, which is commonly used by psychologists, counsellors and therapists to determine where clients find themselves in the process of change.

The model has five stages that run the gauntlet of behaviour change.

In the first, pre-contemplation stage, the client has no real intention of taking any action to engage in change. They may be in denial or ignorant of the problem or it may be that the issue is not sufficiently important as to be a priority.

In the second, contemplation stage, the client is actively thinking about change, but is not engaged in affirmative action. They may be conflicted about the benefits of change and ambivalent, because the costs appear to outweigh the benefits. Indeed, with conditions like addiction, it is not uncommon for people to remain locked in a state of ambivalence for months or years and one of the key treatment targets is often to move people into a position where they believe the pros of change outweigh the cons.

In the third, preparation stage, there is a deliberative intention to act, associated with preparative plans of action. This may involve collecting information and learning about change or taking small steps to prepare for change.

In the fourth, action stage, a strategy for change has been set in motion and maintained for a short period of time. It is common during this stage for people to experience a relapse and one of the preparatory goals for change is to anticipate and contextualise potential relapses and to develop strategies for doubling down and moving forward without undue self-chastisement.

In the fifth, maintenance stage, the change in behaviour has been maintained for a considerable period of time that may be measured in months or years. During this stage coping strategies may still be actively employed to cope with temptation and relapse.

In the six and final, termination stage, the person is so far into the change-process that there is no desire to re-engage with old patterns of behaviour and methods of coping.

Chapter 10: **Behaviour change and resilience**

These three models, the Health Belief Model, the Theory of Reasoned Action and the Stages of Change Model form the bedrock of behaviour change theory and practice. However, there are other theories that are worthy of note. Albert Bandura's social learning theory, for example, emphasises the importance of role-modelling and imitation in shaping our behaviour. As we learnt earlier, for example, coaches and mentors can act positive role models that children and youth desire to imitate and they have been shown to play an important role in turning troubled lives around, particularly in respect of youth crime and substance abuse.

In a similar vein, seeing other people being successful tends to breed a sense of optimism and a positive mind-set that reinforces the idea that change is possible. In his book *Positive Psychology*, for example, the Irish psychologist, Alan Carr notes that optimistic parents act as good role models for their children by using a positive explanatory style and by attributing success to personal effort rather than chance factors and by teaching their children how to deal with setbacks in a constructive way. Conversely, pessimistic parents are more likely to attribute success to external factors, such as luck or other the input of others, and to externalise frustration as anger and irritation by seeking to blame others when things do not go to plan. Hence, optimistic parents give their children a sense of 'can do' which puts them in good stead to change and adapt whenever the need arises.

However, it is important to note that such processes can yield the opposite effect, particularly in people who are clinically depressed or very low in self-esteem and self-efficacy, because seeing other people being effective can amplify personal perceptions of helplessness and inadequacy. To help with this type of issue, and when working with people that are low in self-efficacy, it is common to discourage the setting of grand goals that may ultimately prove to be unachievable and to focus instead on small incremental goals that allow people to experience success and a sense of mastery. If we broaden these ideas to the level of communities, we find that small community projects can serve a useful function in helping residents gain a sense of control and confidence that may not be immediately forthcoming in long-term projects that may take years to reach fruition.

Achieving change through dialogue

As has just been noted, many of the concepts and ideas contained in the psychological models of behaviour change can be usefully applied to community settings. Community action to engage in change, for example, is usually prompted by recognition that there is a pressing problem or issue that needs to be addressed. Likewise, communities need to believe that there is a viable solution that is within their power to achieve, and that the cues (support for change) outnumber the barriers.

However, if you are looking to engage a community in process of change, it is worth remembering Darren McGarvey's observation that communities often view expert outsiders with cynicism and scepticism, particularly if they try to engage them with ideas and vocabulary that are perceived as being foreign, intimidating or even offensive. Hence, in adopting the role of facilitator or change-agent, it is important to remember that how one is perceived is crucial, and particularly so when working with peoples and communities that in some way feel devalued, impotent ostracised.

In a similar vein, the British psychologist, Rhiannon Cobner and her colleagues emphasise the importance of meaning-making, in respect of the need to provide a compelling narrative for change that makes sense at a grass roots level. Without taking these basic steps, efforts to facilitate change may never get much further than the starting block. This is a lesson I learnt the hard way, when, a number of years ago, I went to a conference organised by the UK's National Farmers' Union about farmers' mental health and well-being.

As you may know, modern farming is a solitary undertaking that exposes workers to long, isolated working hours, lashings of bureaucratic red-tape and financial hardship that can result in serious mental health issues like depression, for which farmers are reluctant to seek help. During the course of the day, we listened to a number of interesting presentations from farmers taking part in the conference and by early afternoon I was convinced that I could clearly see the issues *and* the solutions. So, I clumsily jumped in with suggestions to improve the farmer's lot. It went down like a ton of bricks. I had entered the scene, to all intents and purposes, as an 'Ivory-Tower academic', a 'do-gooder' and outsider who knew little or nothing about farming, and I had crucially failed to consider (as Cobner suggests) the need for careful,

Chapter 10: **Behaviour change and resilience** 177

preparatory work, which would have involved taking the time to get to know those concerned and to listen to their stories and perspectives. I should have known better.

As previously mentioned, the public health specialist, Goodman recognised the importance of these processes in espousing his principles for how to effectively engage individuals and communities in projects and listening and authentic engagement stand at the top of the list. Reflecting this, the literature is full of important concepts like stakeholder-involvement, user-empowerment, and community partnerships, which collectively pay homage to the principle that inclusion and participation are both necessary and desirable for projects that involve change.

In a similar vein, the British psychologists, Andrew Robson and John Hart have presented evidence that community support is more palatable to those at the receiving end, when it is couched in terms that frame it, not as acts of charity, but as initiatives aimed at building a community's resilience and control. Such approaches, they suggest, pay due regard to people's dignity, and they point to an example of research conducted in Nairobi, which investigated how participants from low-income backgrounds found the use of the Community-Empowerment more palatable than the phrase Poverty-Alleviation. Moreover, Robson and Hart found that framing aid in terms of community empowerment rather than poverty-relief did not change donor-perceptions of the worthiness of charitable giving as some quarters had feared.

In summary, whilst engaging people in change can be a challenging endeavour, we know a lot about the factors and circumstances that facilitate change, as well as the factors that inhibit it. Moreover, there are plenty of robust, practical guidelines to aid those who seek to engage individuals and communities in actions and behaviours that enhance resilience and well-being, and on a final note, I would like to draw attention to Rollick and Miller's observation that the most important factor in any process of change is the development of an authentic relationship between the actors that is built on trust, mutual respect and understanding.

Note

1 A Cochrane systematic review of the literature is regarded by many as the gold standard in research evaluation. The Cochrane library of reviews can be access at: https://www.cochranelibrary.com/cdsr/about-cdsr.

Epilogue

For a long time, I could not make up my mind about whether to include an epilogue or not. However, on reflection I came to conclusion that although writing the book had been a voyage of academic discovery, it has also been a vehicle for personal discovery and I felt the need to end the book on a slightly more personal level.

I must confess that I started the book believing that I knew quite a lot about vulnerability and resilience, and have been humbled to discover how little I actually understood.

Likewise, I have been fascinated and intrigued by advances in unfamiliar disciplines like bio-genetics and the neurosciences, and how they have begun to unravel the intricate and often delicate interplay between our genes, environment and life experiences that shape who we become.

I was gratified too, to learn that many of the conclusions that I had reached independently through my research, were born out by experts in the field and particularly with regard to the idea that vulnerability and resilience are dynamic phenomena rather than trait-like entities.

However, I also wanted to say that although I have tried to be diligent and accurate in selecting research for the book, all academic works, no matter how well researched, end up painting a selective picture of reality that to a greater or lesser degree reflects the author's preferences and interests.

Whilst on balance, I believe the evidence I have presented is salient, relevant and contemporary, I sometimes felt that I was at the mercy of Google's search algorithms and although they appeared to work superbly well, I could never be completely sure that I was 'hitting' on the most salient piece of research. Likewise, although the internet has proved to be a boon for independent academics like myself, the marked proliferation of pay-to-view research sites for those with non-institutional access meant that I had to find inventive ways of legally accessing the pieces of research that were not freely available on the web.

Anyway in concluding, I hope that you have found reading this book as interesting as I have writing it, and that you are able to further pursue some or all of the topics that are salient for your area of work and personal interest.

Bibliography resilience

Ainsworth, M.D., Blehar, M., Walters, E., and Wall, S.N. (2015). *Patterns of attachment: A psychological study of the strange situation*. Routledge Publishers.
Ajzen, I. and Fishbein, M. (1980). *Understanding attitudes and predicting social behavior*. Englewood Cliffs, NJ: Prentice-Hall.
Albar Marin, M.J. and Garcia-Ramirez, M. (2005). Social support and emotional exhaustion among hospital staff. *European Journal of Psychiatry*. 19(2). https://scielo.isciii.es/scielo.php?pid=S0213-61632005000200004&script=sci_arttext&tlng=en
All-Party Parliamentary Group on Knife Crime (2019). *Back to school? Breaking the link between school exclusions and knife crime*. Report accessed online 15.3.2022. http://www.preventknifecrime.co.uk/wp-content/uploads/2019/10/APPG-on-Knife-Crime-Back-to-School-exclusions-report-FINAL.pdf
American Psychological Association-female doctoral candidates. As cited in Fowler, G.F., Cope, M.A., Michalski, D., Luona, L., and Conroy, J. (2018). Women outnumber men in psychology graduate programmes. *Monitor on Psychology*. 49(11). Accessed online 3.4.2022. https://www.apa.org/monitor/2018/12/datapoint
Asmussen, K., Feinstein, L., Martin, J., and Chowdry, H. (2016, July). *Foundations for life: What works to support parent–child interactions in the early years*. Early Intervention Foundation. https://www.eif.org.uk/report/foundations-for-life-what-works-to-support-parent-child-interaction-in-the-early-years
Attachment, Regulation and Competency. Online website. Accessed 31.3.2022. https://arcframework.org/what-is-arc/
Aursand, L. and Rutkowski, D. (2021). Exemption or exclusion? A study of student exclusion in PISA in Norway. *Nordic Journal of Studies in Educational Policy*. 7(1): 16–29. https://doi.org/10.1080/20020317.2020.1856314
Baier, J., Kristensen, M.B., and Davidson, S. (2021) *Poverty and fragility: Where will the poor live in 2030*. Online report published in Future Development. The Brooking Institution. Accessed online May 16.5.2022. https://www.brookings.

edu/blog/future-development/2021/04/19/poverty-and-fragility-where-will-the-poor-live-in-2030/
Bandura, A. (1986). *Social foundations of thought and action.* Upper Saddle River, NJ: Prentice Hall.
Barlow, J. (2016). Questioning the outcome of the building blocks trial. *The Lancet.* 387(10028): 1615–1616. https://doi.org/10.1016/S0140-6736(16)30201-X
Bastiani, A.M., Roa, R., Weltzin, T., and Kaye, W.H. (1995). Perfectionism in anorexia nervosa. *International Journal of Eating Disorders.* 17(2): 147–152. https://doi.org/10.1002/1098-108X(199503)17:2<147::AID-EAT2260170207>3.0.CO;2-X
BASW (2018a). *Social workers spend 80% of their time on administration.* Online report accessed 24.4.2022. https://www.basw.co.uk/media/news/2018/may/basw-england-80-20-campaigns-latest-news-and-resources
BASW (2018b). *Regulation of social work and social workers in the United Kingdom.* Online report accessed 18.4.2022. https://www.basw.co.uk/system/files/resources/Social%20Work%20Regulation%20-%20Contexts%20and%20Questions.pdf
Beck, A. (2009). *Depression: Causes and treatment.* University of Pennsylvania Publishing.
Bellosta-Batalla, M., Ruiz-Robledillo, N., Sarinana-Gonalez, P., Capella-Solano, T., et al. (2018). Increased salivary IgA response as an indicator of immunocompetence after a mindfulness and self-compassion-based intervention. *Mindfullness.* 9: 905–913. https://doi.org/10.1007/s12671-017-0830-y
Benner, P. (1984). *From novice to expert.* Addison-Wesley Publishers.
Benoit, D. (2004). Infant–parent attachment: Definition, types, antecedents, measurement and outcome. *Paediatrics & Child Health.* 9(8): 541–545. https://doi.org/10.1093/pch/9.8.541
Berkley Center (2012). *The Danish prison system.* Article published online. Accessed 22.3.2022. https://berkleycenter.georgetown.edu/posts/the-danish-prison-system
Berkowitz, L (1993). *Aggression: Its causes, consequences and control.* Temple University Press.
Bernard, K. and Dozier, M. (2010). Examining infant's cortisol responses to laboratory tasks among children varying in attachment disorganisation: Stress reactivity or return to baseline? *Developmental Psychology.* 46(6): 1771–1778. https://doi.org/10.1037/a0020660
Bigbsy, E. and Albarracin, D. (2022). Self and response efficacy information in fear appeals: A meta-analysis. *Journal of Communication.* 72: 241–263. https://doi.org/10.1093/joc/jqab048
Bitsika, V. and Sharpley, C. (2004). Stress, anxiety and depression among parents of children with autism spectrum disorder. *Journal of Psychologists and Counsellors in Schools.* 14(2): 151–161.

Blair, C. and Cybele Raver, C. (2016). Poverty, stress and brain development: New directions for prevention and intervention. *Academy of Paediatrics*. 16(3 Suppl): S30–S36. https://doi.org/10.1016/j.acap.2016.01.010

Bopp, M., Germann, K., Bopp, J., Smith, N., et al. (2000). *Assessing community capacity for change*. Report published online. Accessed 29.3.2022. https://chwcentral.org/wp-content/uploads/2013/07/Assessing-Community-Capacity-for-Change.pdf

Bowlby, J. (1990). *A secure base: Parent child attachment and healthy human development*. Basic Books publishers.

Briquet, P. As cited in Mai, F.M. and Merskey, H. (1980). Briquets treatise on hysteria. A synopsis and commentary. *Archives of General Psychiatry*. 37(12): 1401–1405. https://doi.org/10.1001/archpsyc.1980.01780250087010

British Psychological Society (2022). *BPS renews calls to priorities children's mental health and well-being following Education Committee's catch up report*. Online report accessed online 28.3.2022. https://www.bps.org.uk/news-and-policy/bps-renews-calls-prioritise-children's-mental-health-and-wellbeing-schools-following

Bronfenbrenner's Bioecological Model. Accessed online 13.3.2022 and cited in: Godwin, S.A. and O'Neal, K.K. (2015). Child social development in context: An examination of some propositions in Bronfenbrenner's Bioecological Theory. *Sage Open*. Accessed online 11.5.2022. https://doi.org/10.1177/2158244015590840

Brooks, N. and Fritzon, K. (2016). Psychopathic personality characteristics amongst high functioning populations. *Crime Psychology Review*. 2(1). https://doi.org/10.1080/23744006.2016.1232537. Authors' note: This article has now been retracted.

Brown, R. (2015). *Daring greatly: How the courage to be vulnerable transforms the way we live, love, parent and lead*. Penguin Books.

Bruce, J., Gunnar, M.R., Pears, K.C., and Fisher, P.A. (2013). Early adverse care, stress neurobiology, and prevention science: Lessons learned. *Prevention Science*. 14(3): 247–256.

Bywaters, P., Bunting, L., Davidsob, G., Hanratty, J., et al. (2016). *The relationship between poverty, child abuse and neglect: An evidence review*. The Joseph Rowntree Foundation. Report accessed online 16.4.2022. https://www.jrf.org.uk/report/relationship-between-poverty-child-abuse-and-neglect-evidence-review

Campbell, K.L., Samu, D., Davis, S.W., Geerlings, L., Mustafa, A., and Tyler, L.K. (2016). Robust resilience of the frontal syntax system to aging. *Journal of Neuroscience*. 36(19): 5214–5227. https://doi.org/10.1523/JNEUROSCI.4561-15.2016

Carr, A. (2011). *Positive psychology: The science of happiness and human strengths*. Routledge Publishers.

Cattell, R. (n.d.). *Fluid and crystallised intelligence.* As cited in online Wikipedia article. Accessed online 28.3.2022. https://en.wikipedia.org/wiki/Fluid_and_crystallized_intelligence

CDC-Kaiser Ace Study (n.d.). Report published by the Centres for Disease Control and Prevention. Accessed online 5.5.2022. https://www.cdc.gov/violenceprevention/aces/about.html?CDC_AA_refVal=https%3A%2F%2

Centers for Disease Control and Prevention (2016). *Preventing child abuse and neglect: A technical package for policy, norm and programmatic activities.* Report compiled by Fortson, B.L., Klevens, J., and Merrick, M.T. Accessed online 29.4.2022. https://doi.org/10.15620/cdc.38864

Centers for Disease Control and Prevention (2020). Cited in online article published by kff.org. *Disparities in health and health care: 5 key questions and answers.* Accessed online 1.5.2022. https://www.kff.org/racial-equity-and-health-policy/issue-brief/disparities-in-health-and-health-care-5-key-question-and-answers/

Chaffey, L., Unsworth, C.A., and Fossey, E. (2012). Relationship between intuition and emotional intelligence in occupational therapists in mental health practice. *The American Journal of Occupational Therapy.* 66(1): 88–96. https://doi.org/10.5014/ajot.2012.001693

Chandra, A., Acosta, J.D., Howard, S., Uscher-Pines, L., Williams, M.V., et al. (2011). *Building community resilience to disasters: A way forward to enhance national health security.* Santa Monica, CA: RAND Corporation. https://www.rand.org/pubs/technical_reports/TR915.html

Cheshire, J. (n.d.). *Lives on the line: Expectancy and child poverty as a tube map.* Online blog accessed 23.4.2022. https://jcheshire.com/featured-maps/lives-on-the-line/

Christ, G., Bonnano, G., Malkinson, R., & Shimson Rubin, S. (2003). *Bereavement experiences after the death of a child.* Article accessed online 12.12.2021. https://www.researchgate.net/publication/253725159_Bereavement_Experiences_after_the_Death_of_a_Child

Christopher, S. (2015). An introduction to black humour as a coping mechanism for student paramedics. *Journal of Paramedic Practice.* 7(12). https://doi.org/10.12968/jpar.2015.7.12.610

Chronicles of Higher Education (2021). *Burned out and overburdened.* As cited in an online article in businesswire.com. Accessed online 27.3.2022. https://www.businesswire.com/news/home/20210225005616/en/Fidelity-Investments-The-Chronicle-of-Higher-Education-Study-More-Than-Half-of-College-and-University-Faculty-Considering-Leaving-Teaching-Citing-Burnout-Caused-by-Pandemic

Claxton, G. (n.d.). Investigating human intuition: Knowing without knowing. *The Psychologist.* Accessed online 31.3.2022. https://thepsychologist.bps.org.uk/

volume-11/edition-5/investigating-human-intuition-knowing-without-knowing-why

Cobner, R., Daffin, J., and Brown, S. (2021). The landscape of poverty. *The Psychologist*. 34: 22–25. Accessed online 21.3.2022. https://thepsychologist.bps.org.uk/volume-34/summer-edition/landscape-poverty

Costa, P. and McCrae, R.R. (1999). Chapter 5: A five-factor theory of personality. In L.A. Pervin & O.O. John (Eds.), *Handbook of personality theory and research* (2nd ed.). New York: Guildford Press.

Danish Ghettos (n.d.). *How Denmark's 'ghetto list' is ripping apart migrant communities*. Article published in *The Guardian* newspaper. Accessed online 26.3.2022. https://www.theguardian.com/world/2020/mar/11/how-denmarks-ghetto-list-is-ripping-apart-migrant-communities

Darzi, A. and Donaldson, L. (n.d.) *To err is human*. BBC Radio documentary. Published 29.5.2009. Accessed 14.4.2022. https://www.bbc.co.uk/programmes/b00cxkrp

Decety, J. and Meyer, M. (2008). From emotion resonance to empathic understanding: a social developmental neuroscience account. *Developmental Psychopathology*. 20(4): 1053–1080. https://doi.org/10.1017/S0954579408000503

Department for Work and Pensions Departmental Report 2006 (2006). *Report on tackling poverty and worklessness*. https://assets.publishing.service.gov.uk/government/uploads/system/uploads/attachment_data/file/272288/6829.pdf

Diagnostic and statistical manual of mental disorders (DSM-5-TR). As cited by American Psychiatric Association. Accessed online 15.3.2022.

Donaldson, L. *Medical error risk 1 in 300*. Online article, published in *The Guardian* 7.11.2006. Accessed 7.5.2022. https://www.theguardian.com/society/2006/nov/07/health.lifeandhealth

Douglas, C., Bateson, M., Walsh, C., and Bedue, A. (2012). Environmental enrichment induces optimistic biases in pigs. *Applied Animal Behaviour Science*. 139(1–2): 6573. https://doi.org/10.1016/j.applanim.2012.02.018

Downey, L.A., Papgeorgiou, V., and Stough, C.K.K. (2006). Examining the relationship between leadership, emotional intelligence and intuition in senior female managers. *Leadership and Organization Development Journal*. 27(4): 250–264. https://doi.org/10.1108/01437730610666019

Dozier, M. and Bernard, K. (2017). Attachment and biobehavioural catchup: Addressing the needs of infants and toddlers exposed to inadequate or problematic parenting. *Current Opinion in Psychology*. 15: 111–117. https://doi.org/10.1016/j.copsyc.2017.03.003

Drigas, A.S. and Papoutsi, C. (2018). A new layered model on emotional intelligence. *Behavioural Science (Basel)*. 8(5): 45. https://doi.org/10.3390/bs8050045

Dyer, L. (2001). Bristol enquiry. *The British Medical Journal*. 323(7306): 181. https://doi.org/10.1136/bmj.323.7306.181

EdPol (2021). *Education policy churn*. Online article accessed 26.3.2022. https://www.edpol.net/problems/

Employment Research Institute (2013). *Lone parents, employment and wellbeing – What does the evidence tell us?* Report accessed online 16.5.2022. https://www.gcph.co.uk/assets/0000/4123/Helen_Graham_-_GCPH_presentation_181013.pdf

Etherson, M.E., Smith, M.M., Hill, A.P., and Berry, S.B. (2022). Perfectionism, mattering, depressive symptoms and suicidal ideation in students: A test of the perfectionism social disconnection model. *Personality and Individual Differences*. 191. https://doi.org/10.1016/j.paid.2022.111559

Evans, N. (n.d.). *Compassionate and inclusive leadership*. Video posted online 8.6.2019. Accessed 12.5.2022. https://www.youtube.com/watch?v=8GE8u9Qi4II

Fairchild, A.L., Bayer, R., Green, S.H., Colgrove, J., et al. (2018). The two faces of fear: A history of hard-hitting public health campaigns against tobacco and AIDS. *American Journal of Public Health*. 108(9): 1180–1186. https://doi.org/10.2105/AJPH.2018.304516

Family Nurse Partnership (n.d.). *Online NHS website*. Accessed 2.2.2021. https://fnp.nhs.uk

Family Nurse Partnership (2021). *Report on building-blocks 2-6*. Accessed online 8.5.2022. https://www.fnp.nhs.uk/news/publication-of-building-blocks-2-6-study/

Farrington, D.P. (1989). Early predictors of adolescent aggression and adult violence. *Violence and Victims*. 4(2). https://doi.org/10.1891/0886-6708.4.2.79

Federal Aviation Administration (n.d.). *Human factors*. Online resource. Accessed 30.4.2022. https://www.faasafety.gov/files/gslac/courses/content/258/1097/AMT_Handbook_Addendum_Human_Factors.pdf

Feiden, W. (2016). *Small opportunity cities: Transforming small post-industrial cities into resilient communities*. Online report. Accessed 26.3.2022. https://www.gmfus.org/sites/default/files/Feiden_SmallOpportunityCities_Apr16_web.pdf

Fitzgerald, M. (2020). *Criticism of attachment theory*. https://doi.org/10.13140/RG.2.2.24012.77445

Francis Enquiry (2013). Calkin, S. *Analysis: Francis Report to life on lid on how poor care could persist*. Report in Nursing Times (Re 'culture of learned helplessness'). Accessed online 5.4.2022. https://www.nursingtimes.net/news/reviews-and-reports/analysis-francis-report-to-lift-lid-on-how-poor-care-could-persist-04-02-2013/

Francis Report (2013). *Report of the Mid Staffordshire, NHS foundation trust public enquiry. Executive summary.* Accessed online 6.4.2022. https://assets.publishing.service.gov.uk/government/uploads/system/uploads/attachment_data/file/279124/0947.pdf

Frankenhuis, W.E. (2010). Did insecure attachment styles evolve for the benefit of the group? *Frontiers in Psychology.* 1: 172. https://doi.org/10.3389/fpsyg.2010.00172

Franz, M., Lensche, H., and Schmitz, N. (2003). Psychological distress and socioeconomic status in single mothers and their children in a German city. *Social Psychiatry and Psychiatric Epidemiology.* 38(2): 59–68. https://doi.org/10.1007/s00127-003-0605-8

Fry, P.S. and Keyes C.L.M. (2010). *New frontiers in resilient aging: Life-strengths and well-being in late life.* Cambridge University Press.

Gartland, D., Riggs, E., Muyeen, S., Giallo, R., Afifi, T.O., MacMillan, H., Herrman, H., Bulford, E., and Brown, S.J. (2019). What factors are associated with resilient outcomes in children exposed to social adversity? A systematic review. *BMJ Open.* 9(4): e024870. https://doi.org/10.1136/bmjopen-2018-024870

George, C. and Solomon, J. (1999). The caregiving behavioural system. In J. Cassidy & P. Shaver (Eds.), *Handbook of attachment: Theory, research, and clinical application* (pp. 649–670). New York: Guilford Press.

General Medical Council (2019). *Wellbeing and retention of doctors.* Online report. Accessed 10.5.2022. https://www.gmc-uk.org/-/media/documents/somep-2019---chapter-2_pdf-81119428.pdf

Gilbert, P. (2010). *The compassionate mind.* Little Brown Book Group.

Goddard, V. (2014). *The best job in the world.* Crown House Publishing.

Goddard, V. (2014, March 11) *A poor Oftsed report could lead to headteachers being disappeared.* Article published in the *The Guardian.* Accessed online 5.5.2022. https://www.theguardian.com/education/2014/mar/11/heads-poor-ofsted-report-dismissal-shortages

Goleman, D. (2017). *Empathy.* Harvard Business School Publishing.

Goodman, R.M., Speers, M.A., and Mclerory, K. (1998). Identifying and defining the dimensions of community capacity to provide a basis for measurement. *Health Education and Behavior.* 25(3). https://doi.org/10.1177/109019819802500303

Gov.UK (2017, September). *Exclusion from maintained schools, academies and pupil referral units: Statutory guidance for those with legal responsibilities in relation to exclusion.* Department of Education. Accessed online 3.4.2022. https://www.gov.uk/government/publications/school-exclusion

Gov.UK (2021). *School workforce in England.* Online report accessed 22.2.2022. https://explore-education-statistics.service.gov.uk/find-statistics/school-workforce-in-england

Gov.UK (n.d.). *Safety in custody statistics, England and Wales: Deaths in prison custody to March 2002, assaults and self-harm to December 2021.* Report accessed online 23.3.2022. https://www.gov.uk/government/statistics/safety-in-custody-quarterly-update-to-december-2021/safety-in-custody-statistics-england-and-wales-deaths-in-prison-custody-to-march-2022-assaults-and-self-harm-to-december-2021

Gov.UK (2002, March). *Ockenden review: Summary of findings, conclusions and essential action.* Department of Health and Social Care. https://www.gov.uk/government/publications/final-report-of-the-ockenden-review/ockenden-review-summary-of-findings-conclusions-and-essential-actions

GOV.UK (2022). *School attendance: Improving the consistency of support: New burdens assessment.* Online report. Accessed 26.4.2022. https://www.gov.uk/government/publications/school-attendance-improving-the-consistency-of-support-new-burdens-assessment/school-attendance-improving-the-consistency-of-support-new-burdens-assessment

Greenberg, D.M. (2018, October 3). Elevated empathy in adults following childhood trauma. *PLoS ONE*, open-access journal. https://doi.org/10.1371/journal.pone.0203886

Gunderson, G.G., Herpetz, S.C., Skodol, A.E., Torgesen, S., and Zanarini, M.C. (2018). Borderline personality disorder. *Nature Reviews Disease Primers*. 4: 18029. https://doi.org/10.1038/nrdp.2018.29

Halmi, K.A., Sinday, S.R., Stober, M., Kaplan, A., et al. Perfectionism in anorexia nervosa: Variation by clinical subtype, obsessionality, and pathological eating behavior. *The American Journal of Psychiatry*. 157(11): 1799–1805. https://doi.org/10.1176/appi.ajp.157.11.1799

Ham, C., Baird, B., Gregory, S., Jabbal, J., and Alderwick, H. (2015). *The NHS under the coalition government.* Published by the Kings Fund. https://www.kingsfund.org.uk/publications/nhs-under-coalition-government

Hancock, M. (2020). Corona virus: Matt Hancock admits her couldn't live on statutory sick pay. Reported in the *Independent Newspaper.* Accessed online 18.5.2022. https://www.independent.co.uk/news/health/coronavirus-uk-statutory-sick-pay-matt-hancock-question-time-covid-19-a9413821.html

Harlow, E. (2019). Attachment theory: Developments, debates and recent applications in social work, social care and education. *Journal of Social Work Practice.* 35(1). https://doi.org/10.1080/02650533.2019.1700493

Harvard Business School (2015). *National health costs could decrease if managers reduce work stress.* Online article accessed 4.4.2022. https://hbswk.hbs.edu/item/national-health-costs-could-decrease-if-managers-reduce-work-stress

Harvard study of IQ and career success. Cited in Stephen, A.F., Sampson, J., Elrod, C. (2009). *Applied social intelligence: A skills-based primer.* Published by Human Resource development.

Hartwig, A., Clarke, S., Johnson, S., and Willis, S. (2020). Workplace team resilience: A systematic review and conceptual development. *Organizational Psychology Review*. 10(3–4): 169–200. https://doi.org/10.1177/2041386 620919476

Haukus, R.B., Gjerde, I.B., Varting, G., Hallan, H., and Solem, S. (2018). A randomized control trial comparing attention training technique and mindful self-compassion for students with depression and anxiety. *Frontiers of Psychology*. 9: 827. https://doi.org/10.3389/fpsyg.2018.00827

Heinke, M.S. and Louis, W.R. (2009). Cultural background and individualistic, collectivistic values in relation to similarity, perspective taking, and empathy. *Journal of Applied Social Psychology*. 39(11): 2570–2590. https://doi.org/10.1111/j.1559-1816.2009.00538.x

Henderson, M., Yi Cheung, S., Sharland, E., and Scourfield, C. (2015). The outcome of educational welfare officer contact. *British Educational Research Journal*. 42(3). https://doi.org/10.1002/berj.3212

Herman, J.L. (1997). *Trauma and recovery: The aftermath of violence-from domestic abuse to political terror.* Perseus Books Group.

HM Chief Inspector of Prisons. (26–27 July and 2–6 August 2021). *Report of unannounced inspection of HMP Belmarsh*. Report accessed online 23.3.2022. https://www.justiceinspectorates.gov.uk/hmiprisons/wp-content/uploads/sites/4/2021/11/Belmarsh-web-2021-2.pdf

Hodgdon, H., Kinniburgh, K., Gabowitz, D., and Blaustein, M.E. (2013). Development and implementation of trauma-informed programming in youth residential treatment centers using the ARC framework. *Journal of Family Violence*. 28(7): 679–692. https://doi.org/10.1007/s10896-013-9531-z

Holzel, B.K., Carmody, J., Vangel, M., Congleton, C., et al. (2011). Mindfulness practice leads to increases in regional brain grey matter density. *Psychiatric Research*. 191(1): 36–43. https://doi.org/10.1016/j.pscychresns.2010.08.006

Institute for Fiscal Studies (2020). *Levelling up: What it might it mean for public spending?* Online article accessed 29.3.2022. https://ifs.org.uk/publications/14747

Institute for Fiscal Studies (2022). *Lack of progress on closing educational inequalities disadvantaging millions through out life*. Report compiled by Farquharson, C., McNally, S., and Tahir, I. Accessed online 16.8.2022. https://ifs.org.uk/publications/16152

Institute for Public Policy Research (2019). *Revealed: North set to receive £2,389 less per person than London on transport*. Online report. Accessed 30.3.2022.

International Consortium of Investigative Journalists (n.d.). *Pandora papers*. Online report. Accessed 30.3.2022. https://www.icij.org/investigations/pandora-papers/

International Monetary Fund (1997). *Good governance: The IMF's role*. Report publishes online. Accessed 26.3.2022. https://www.imf.org/external/pubs/ft/exrp/govern/govern.pdf

Jachens, L., Houdmont, J., and Thomas, R. (2018). Effort-reward imbalance and burnout among humanitarian aid workers. *Disasters*. 43(1): 67–68. https://doi.org/10.1111/disa.12288

Jalili, M., Nirooman, M., Hadavand, F., Zeina, K., and Fotouhi, A. (2021). Burnout among healthcare professionals during Covid-19 pandemic: A cross-sectional study. *International Archives of Occupational and Environmental Health*. 94: 1345–1352. https://doi.org/10.1007/s00420-021-01695-x

Janis, I. (1991). *Groupthink*. In E. Griffin (Ed.), *A first look at communication theory* (pp. 235–246). New York: McGrawHill.

Janz, N.K. and Becker, M.H. (1984). The health belied model: A decade later. *Health Education Quarterly*. 11(1): 1–47. https://doi.org/10.1177/109019818401100101

Jarrett, C. (2010). Feeling like a fraud. *The Psychologist*. 23: 380–383. Accessed online 4.4.2022. https://thepsychologist.bps.org.uk/volume-23/edition-5/feeling-fraud

Karasek, R. (2008). Low social control and physiological deregulation: The stress disequilibrium theory, towards a new demand control model. *Scandinavian Journal of Work, Environment and Health*. (6): 117–135.

Kholer-Evans, P. and Dowd-Barnes, C. (2015). *Civility, compassion and courage in schools today*. Rowan and Little Field Publishers.

Kings Fund Report into NHS staff burnout. Cited in *Workforce burnout and resilience in the NHS and social care* (2021). Evidence presented to the House of Commons Health and Social Care Committee. Accessed online 30.4.2022. https://committees.parliament.uk/publications/6158/documents/68766/default/

Kinman, G. (1998). *Pressure points: A survey into the causes and consequences of occupational stress in UK academic and related staff*. A report accessed online 15.4.2022. https://www.researchgate.net/profile/Gail-Kinman/publication/266473393_A_Survey_into_the_Causes_and_Consequences_of_Occupational_Stress_in_UK_Academic_and_Related_Staff/links/551be18a0cf2fe6cbf75f764/A-Survey-into-the-Causes-and-Consequences-of-Occupational-Stress-in-UK-Academic-and-Related-Staff.pdf

Kinman, G. (2018). People need a period of stability, otherwise they may actively resist change. *The Psychologist*. 31: 42–45.

Kinman, G. and Clements, A. (2020). *Survey of work-related wellbeing*. Report commissioned by the Prison Officers' Association. Accessed online 17.3.2022. https://www.poauk.org.uk/media/1888/poa-survey-of-work-related-wellbeing-1.pdf

Kinman, G. and Grant, L. (2017). Building resilience in early career social workers: Evaluating a multi-modal intervention. *British Journal of Social Work*. 47(7): 1979–1998. https://doi.org/10.1093/bjsw/bcw164

Kitchin, S. (2020). *Recruitment and retention of social workers*. Middlesbrough. gov.cuk. Presentation accessed online 27.2.2022. https://moderngov.middlesbrough.gov.uk/Data/Children%20and%20Young%20People%27s%20Social%20Care%20and%20Services%20Scrutiny%20Panel/202001061600/Agenda/$att1017784.pptx.pdf

Klein, F.A. (2017). *Sources of power: How people make decisions*. MIT Press.

Kordowicz, M. (2019). Creating compassionate organisations. *The Psychologist*. 32: 34–35.

Leith, K.P. and Baumeister, R. (2008). Empathy, shame, guilt and narratives of inter-personal conflicts: Guilt-prone people are better at perspective taking. *Journal of Personality*. 66(1): 1–37. https://doi.org/10.1111/1467-6494.00001

Lewin, K. Cited in Ehrlich, C. and Fasbender, U. (2017). Approach-avoidance conflict. In V. Zeigler-Hill (Ed.), *Encyclopedia of personality and individual differences* (pp. 1–7). Springer.

Lewis, M., Sullivan, M.W., Stranger, C., and Weiss, M. (1989). Self-development and self-conscious emotions. *Child Development*. 6(1): 146–156. https://doi.org/10.2307/1131080

Liotti, G. (1999). Disorganization of attachment as a model for understanding dissociative psychopathology. In J. Solomon & C. George (Eds.), *Attachment disorganization* (pp. 291–317). The Guilford Press.

MacKenzie, M.B., Abbott, K.A., and Kocovski, N.L. (2018). Mindfulness-based cognitive therapy in patients with depression: Current perspectives. *Neuropsychiatric Disease and Treatment*. 14: 1599–1605. https://doi.org/10.2147/NDT.S160761

Mackintosh, K., Power, K., Schwannauer, M., and Chan, S.W.Y. (2018). The relationship between self-compassion, attachment and interpersonal problems in clinical patients with mixed anxiety and depression and emotional distress. *Mindfulness (NY)*. 9(3): 961–971. https://doi.org/10.1007/s12671-017-0835-6

Maclean, P. Cited in Yale Medicine Magazine. (2008). *A theory abandoned but still compelling*. https://medicine.yale.edu/news/yale-medicine-magazine/article/a-theory-abandoned-but-still-compelling/

Mahajan, A.P., Sayles, J.S., Patel, V.A., Remien, R.H., et al. (2008). Stigma in the AIDS/HIV epidemic: A review of the literature and recommendations on the way forward. *AIDS*. 22(Suppl 2): S67–S69. https://doi.org/10.1097/01.aids.0000327438.13291.62

Maslach, C., Jackson, S.E., and Leiter, M.P. (1997). Malsach burnout inventory. In C.P. Zalaquett & R.J. Wood (Eds.), *Evaluating stress: A book of resources* (3rd ed., pp. 191–218). Scarecrow Education.

Bibliography resilience

Maslow, A. (n.d.). As cited in Wikipedia article. *Maslow's hierarchy of needs.* Accessed online 16.4.2022. https://en.wikipedia.org/wiki/Maslow%27s_hierarchy_of_needs

McDonald, K., Sciolla, A.F., Folsom, D., Bazzo, D., et al. (2015). Individual risk factors for physician boundary violations: The role of attachment style, childhood trauma and maladaptive beliefs. *General Hospital Psychiatry.* 37(5): 489–496. https://doi.org/10.1016/j.genhosppsych.2015.06.002

McFadden, P. (2015) *Measuring burnout amongst UK social workers: A commissioned study.* Report accessed online 29.3.2022. https://www.qub.ac.uk/sites/media/Media%2C514081%2Cen.pdf

McFarlane, C.A. (2004). Risks associated with the psychological adjustment of humanitarian aid workers. *The Australasian Journal of Disaster and Trauma Studies.* 2004(1).

McGarvey, D. (2018). *Poverty safari: Understanding the anger of Britain's underclass.* Pan Macmillan.

McVicar, D. (2020). The impact of monitoring and sanctioning on unemployment rates and job-finding rates. *IZA World of Labour.* Accessed online 23.5.2022. https://wol.iza.org/uploads/articles/540/pdfs/impact-of-monitoring-and-sanctioning-on-unemployment-exit-and-job-finding-rates.pdf

Meinhardt, C. (2009). *Social support, institutional support: A key element in the prevention of burnout and PTSD.* Institute ODEF. Article accessed online 2.5.2022. https://www.odef.ch/wp-content/uploads/2017/03/CMsocsupport-preventionburnout.pdf

Mental Health America (2020). *The mental health of healthcare workers in Covid-19.* Report accessed online 27.3.2022. https://mhanational.org/mental-health-healthcare-workers-covid-19

Merriam Webster Dictionary (n.d.). *Resilience quotation re P.G. Wodehouse.* Accessed online 1.4.2022. https://www.merriam-webster.com/dictionary/resilience

Miccoli, A., Song, J., Romanowicz, M., Howie, F., Simar, S., and Lynch, B.A. (2022). Impact of parental adverse childhood experiences on offspring development in Early Head Start: Parental adversity and offspring development. *Journal of Primary Care & Community Health.* 13: 21501319221084165. https://doi.org/10.1177/21501319221084165

Milgram, S. (n.d.). Obedience to authority. In Wikipedia article *Milgram experiment.* Accessed online 12.4.2022. https://en.wikipedia.org/wiki/Milgram_experiment

Miller, W.R. and Rollnick, S. (2013). *Motivational interviewing: Helping people change* (3rd ed.). Guilford Press.

Moore, M. (2020). Going from a culture of blame and denial to a culture of safety. *Health Management.* 20(2). https://healthmanagement.org/c/hospital/issuearticle/going-from-a-culture-of-blame-and-denial-to-a-culture-of-safety

Morris, D. (1977). *Manwatching: A field guide to human behaviour*. New York: Abrams.

National State Conference of State Legislatures (2018, August). *Preventing and mitigating the effects of adverse childhood experiences*. Report accessed online 16.5.2022. https://www.ncsl.org/Portals/1/HTML_LargeReports/ACEs_2018_32691.pdf

Neff, K.D. and Vonk.R. (2009). Compassion versus global self-esteem: Two different ways of relating to oneself. *Journal of Personality*. 77: 1. https://doi.org/10.1111/j.1467-6494.2008.00537.x

Nelson, C.A., Fox, N.A., and Zeanah, C.H. (2014). *Romania's abandoned children: Deprivation, brain development, and the struggle for recovery*. Cambridge, MA, and London, England: Harvard University Press.

NHS Staff Survey (2019). *Report of results published by NHS Providers*. Accessed online 30.3.2022. https://nhsproviders.org/media/689188/nhs-staff-survey-results-2019-nhs-providers-otdb.pdf

Nielsen, S.S., Norredam, M., Christiansen, K.L., Obel, C., Hilden, J.H., and Krasnik, A. (2008). Mental health among children seeking asylum in Denmark – The effect of length of stay and number of relocations: A cross-sectional study. *BMC Public Health*. Open Access article. Accessed online 16.5.2022. https://bmcpublichealth.biomedcentral.com/articles/10.1186/1471-2458-8-293

Noar, S.M., Hall, M.G., Francis, D.B., et al. (2016). Pictorial cigarette pack warnings: A meta-analysis of experimental studies. *Tobacco Control*. 25: 341–354.

Nuffield Trust (2017, November 27). *New report reveals stark difference in dental health between the north and south of England*. Report accessed online 31.1.2022. https://www.nuffieldtrust.org.uk/news-item/new-report-reveals-stark-difference-in-dental-health-between-north-and-south-of-england

OECD (2021). *The well-being of nations: The role of human and social capital*. Executive Summary. OECD Report. Accessed online 12.4.2022. https://www.oecd.org/education/innovation-education/1870573.pdf

Office for National Statistics (n.d.). *Families and households in the UK: 2019*. Report accessed online 20.4.2022. https://www.ons.gov.uk/peoplepopulationandcommunity/birthsdeathsandmarriages/families/bulletins/familiesandhouseholds/2019

Ofsted (2019). *Teacher well-being at work in schools and further education providers*. Report accessed online 4.4.2022. https://assets.publishing.service.gov.uk/government/uploads/system/uploads/attachment_data/file/936253/Teacher_well-being_report_110719F.pdf

Okoli, J. and Watt, J. (2018). Crisis decision-making: The overlap between intuitive and analytical strategies. *Management Decision*. 56(5). https://doi.org/10.1108/MD-04-2017-0333

Oxfam (2016). *62 People own the same as half the world, reveals Oxfam Davos report.* Press release. Accessed online 14.3.2022. https://www.oxfam.org/en/press-releases/62-people-own-same-half-world-reveals-oxfam-davos-report

Petrich, D.M., Pratt, T.C., Jonson, C.L., and Cullen, F.T. (2021). Custodial sanctions and reoffending: A meta-analytic review. *Crime and Justice.* 50(1). https://doi.org/10.1086/715100

Phillips, W.J. and Hine, D.W. (2021). Self-compassion, physical health and behaviour: A meta-analysis. *Health Psychology Review.* 15(1): 113–139. https://doi.org/10.1080/17437199.2019.1705872

Piercy, C.W. (2019). *Problem solving in teams and groups.* University of Kansas Libraries.

Pika, S. (2022, February 8). Chimpanzees regularly capture insects and apply them onto wounds. Reported in online report. *SCI NEWS.* http://www.sci-news.com/biology/chimpanzee-self-medication-10529.html. Accessed online 15.4 2022.

Pope, K.S. and Feldman-Summers, S. (1992). National survey of psychologists' sexual and physical abuse history and their evaluation of training and competence in these areas. *Professional Psychology: Research and Practice.* 23(5): 353–361. https://doi.org/10.1037/0735-7028.23.5.353

Positive Psychology Centre (n.d.). Website assessed online 5.5.2022. https://ppc.sas.upenn.edu/people/martin-ep-seligman

Price, D. (2021). *Laziness does not exist.* Atria Books.

Prochaska, J.O. and Diclemente, C.C. (1983). Stages and processes in self-change of smoking- toward an integrative model of change. *Journal of Counselling and Clinical Psychology.* 51(3): 390–395. https://doi.org/10.1037//0022-006X.51.3.390

Pulkkinen, L. and Hamalainen, M. (1995). Low self-control as a precursor to crime and accidents in a Finnish longitudinal study. *Criminal and Mental Health Behaviour.* 5(4): 424–438. https://doi.org/10.1002/cbm.1995.5.4.424

Rippon, G. (2020). *The gendered brain: The new neuroscience that shatters the myth of the female brain.* Vintage Publishing.

Roberts, H. (2000). What is sure start? *Archives of Disease in Childhood.* 82(6): 435–437. https://doi.org/10.1136/adc.82.6.435

Robling, M.R., Bekkers, M.-J., Bell, K.B., Butler, C.C., Cannings-John, R., and Channon, S.C. (2016). Effectiveness of a nurse-led intensive home visitation programme for first-time teenage mothers (building blocks): A pragmatic randomized control trial. *The Lancet.* 387(10014): 146–155. https://doi.org/10.1016/S0140-6736(15)00392-X

Robson, D. (2020). Understanding the correlates of donor intention: A comparison of local, national and international charity destinations. *Nonprofit and Voluntary Sector Quarterly.* 50(12). https://doi.org/10.1177/0899764020927097

Rogers, C.R. (1951). *Client-centered therapy: Its current practice, implications and theory.* Boston, MA: Houghton Mifflin.

Rogers, C.R. (1957). The necessary and sufficient conditions of therapeutic personality change. *Journal of Consulting Psychology.* 21(2): 95–103. https://doi.org/10.1037/h0045357

Rose, M. (2015). *Better leadership for tomorrow.* NHS Leadership Review. Report accessed online 15.4.2022. https://assets.publishing.service.gov.uk/government/uploads/system/uploads/attachment_data/file/445738/Lord_Rose_NHS_Report_acc.pdf

Rosenthal, L. (2004). Do school inspections improve school quality? Ofsted inspections and school examination results in the UL. *Economics of Education Review.* 23: 143–151. http://citeseerx.ist.psu.edu/viewdoc/download?doi=10.1.1.602.6908&rep=rep1&type=pdf

Rotenstein, L.S., Torre, M., Ramos, M.A., Rosales, R.C., et al. (2018). Prevalence of burnout among physicians: A systematic review. *Journal of the American Medical Association.* 320(11): 1131–1150. https://doi.org/10.1001/jama.2018.12777

Royal Society of Arts (2020, January 17). *Exclusions of students with special educational need and disabilities show we are falling short of social inclusion.* Online blog. Accessed 14.4.2022. https://www.thersa.org/blog/2020/01/inclusive-education-send

Safe Care Model (n.d.). *National SafeCare Training and Research Centre.* Online article accessed 12.4.2022. https://safecare.publichealth.gsu.edu/safecare-curriculum/

Salovey, P. and Mayer, J.D. (1990, March 1). Emotional intelligence. *Imagination, Cognition and Personality.* 9(3). https://doi.org/10.2190/DUGG-P24E-52WK-6CDG

Sameroff, A. (2009). The transactional model. In A. Sameroff (Ed.), *The transactional model of development: How children and contexts shape each other* (pp. 3–21). American Psychological Association. https://doi.org/10.1037/11877-001

Samulowitz, A., Gremyr, I., Erikson, E., and Hensing, G. (2018). Brave men and emotional women: A theory-guided literature review on gender-bias in health care and norms towards patients with chronic pain. *Pain and Research Management.* https://doi.org/10.1155/2018/6358624

Schachter, S. and Singer, J. (1962). Cognitive, social and physiological determinants of emotional state. *Psychological Review.* 69(5): 379–399.

Schaufeli, W.B., Leiter, M.P., and Maslach, C. (2008). *Burnout: 35 years of research and practice.* Accessed online 15.5.2002. https://www.academia.edu/14961130/Burnout_35_years_of_research_and_practice?from=cover_page

Schaufeli, W.B. and Peeters, M.C.W. (2000). Job stress and burnout: A literature review. *International Journal of Stress Management.* 7(1). https://doi.org/10.1023/A:1009514731657

Schools Week (2022, July 10). *Ofsted judging schools negatively for staff shortages.* Accessed online 6.5.2022. https://schoolsweek.co.uk/ofsted-judging-schools-negatively-for-teacher-shortages/

Schroeder, S., Tan, C.M., and Urlacher, B. (2021). The role of rural and urban geography and gender in community stigma around mental illness. *Heath Education and Behavior.* 48(1): 6373. https://doi.org/10.1177/1090198120974963

Schwarzer, R. (1994). Optimism, vulnerability and self-beliefs as health-related cognitions: A systematic overview. *Psychology and Health.* 9(3): 161–180. https://doi.org/10.1080/08870449408407475

Shadd, M. (2001). *Making good: How ex-convicts reform and rebuild their lives.* American Psychological Association.

Sheffield Morris, A., Havs-Grudo, J., Zapata, M.I., Treat, A., and Kerr, L. (2021). Adverse and protective childhood experiences and parenting attitudes: The role of cumulative protection in understanding resilience. *Adversity and Resilience Science.* 2(3): 181–192. https://doi.org/10.1007/s42844-021-00036-8

Shoesmith, S. (2016). Stop scapegoating social workers to better protect children. Article published in *The Guardian*, 19.8.2016. Accessed online 12.5.2022. https://www.theguardian.com/society/2016/aug/19/stop-scapegoating-social-workers-to-better-protect-children-shoesmith-says

Siegrist, J. (2002). Effort-reward imbalance at work and health. In P.L. Perrewé & D.C. Ganster (Eds.), *Historical and current perspectives on stress and health* (Vol. 2, pp. 261–291). Elsevier Science/JAI Press. https://doi.org/10.1016/S1479-3555(02)02007-3

Simpson, J.A., Kim, J.S., Fillo, J., Ickes, W., Rholes, W.S., et al. (2018). Attachment and empathic accuracy in relationship-threatening situations. *Perspectives in Social Psychology Bulletin.* 37(2): 242–254. DOI: 10.1177/0146167210394368

Skinner, B.F. As cited in Pritchard, M.S. (1976). On taking emotions seriously: A critique of B.F. Skinner. *Journal for the Theory of Social Behaviour.* 6(2): 211–232. https://doi.org/10.1111/j.1468-5914.1976.tb00366.x

Slater, T. (2018, June 12). The invention of the 'sink-estate': Consequential categorisation and the UK housing crisis. *The Sociological Review.* https://doi.org/10.1177/0038026118777451

Sliter, M., Kale, A., and Yuan, Z. (2014). Is humor the best medicine? The buffering impact of coping humor on traumatic stressors in firefighters. *Journal of Organizational Behavior.* 35(2). https://doi.org/10.1002/job.1868

Sonuga-Barke, E.J.S., Mistry, M., and Qureshi, S. (1998). The mental health of Muslim mothers in extended families living in Britain: The impact of intergenerational disagreement on anxiety and depression. *British Journal of Clinical Psychology*. 37(4). https://doi.org/10.1111/j.2044-8260.1998.tb01397.x

Soukup, T., Lamb, B.W., Arora, S., Darzi, A., et al. (2018). Successful strategies implementing multidisciplinary working in care of patients with cancer: An overview and synthesis of the available literature. *Multidisciplinary Health Care*. 11: 49–61. https://doi.org/10.2147/JMDH.S117945

Sourander, A. (2003). Refugee families during asylum seeking. *Nordic Journal of Psychiatry*. 57(3). https://doi.org/10.1080/08039480310001364

Southwick, S.M., Bonnano, G.A., Masten, A., Panter-Brick, C., et al. (2014). Resilience definitions, theory and challenges: Interdisciplinary perspectives. *European Journal of Psychotraumatology*. 5. https://doi.org/10.3402/ejpt.v5.25338

Spicker, P. (2007). *Poverty: An international glossary*. Zed Books Ltd.

Sternberg, R. (n.d.). As cited in Triarchic theory of intelligence. Wikipedia. Accessed online 28.3.2022. https://en.wikipedia.org/wiki/Triarchic_theory_of_intelligence

Svarer, M. (2007). *The effects of sanctions on job finding rate: Evidence from Denmark*. IZA Discussion Paper No. 3015, University of Aarhus Economics Working Paper No. 2007-10. https://doi.org/10.2139/ssrn.1012805

Swanson, V. and Power, K.G. (2005). Initiation and continuation of breastfeeding: Theory of planned behaviour. *Journal of Advanced Nursing*. 50(3): 272–282. https://doi.org/10.1111/j.1365-2648.2005.03390.x

Tang, Y. (2017). *The neuroscience of mindfulness meditation*. Palgrave MacMillan publishing.

Tangney, J.P. and Dearing, R.L. (2002) *Shame and guilt*. Guilford Publications. IZA discussion paper No 3015. Accessed online 25.5.2022.

Tannenbaum, M.B., Hepler, J., Zimmerman, R.S., Saul, L., Jacobs, S., Wilson, K., and Albarracín, D. (2015). Appealing to fear: A meta-analysis of fear appeal effectiveness and theories. *Psychological Bulletin*. 141(6): 1178–1204. https://doi.org/10.1037/a0039729

Teitz, M.B. and Chapple, K. (1998). The causes of inner-city poverty: Eight hypotheses in search of reality. *Cityscape: A Journal of Policy Development and Research*. 3(3): 33–70.

The Children's Society (2021). *Excluded or missing from education and child exploitation: Literature review and stakeholder views on safeguarding practice*. Report accessed online 26.3.2022. https://tce.researchinpractice.org.uk/wp-content/uploads/2022/02/2757_TCE_Education__Exploitation_briefing_v2.pdf

The Guardian (2022). *British minister accused of trying to hide report on impact of Tory welfare reforms*. Online article accessed 16.8.2022. https://

www.theguardian.com/society/2022/aug/14/british-minister-accused-of-trying-to-hide-reports-on-impact-of-tory-welfare-reforms

The Incredible years programme. As cited in online article. *Incredible Years Parenting Programme. Study Review*, What works for Children's Social Care. Accessed 16.4.2022. https://whatworks-csc.org.uk/evidence/evidence-store/intervention/incredible-years-parenting-programme/

The Independent (2022). *Vulnerable children wait almost three years to access mental health care, whilst others seen in just a week.* Newspaper article. Accessed online 16.4.2022. https://www.independent.co.uk/news/health/child-mental-health-waiting-times-b1972830.html

The Urban Institute (2019). *Tracking the uneven distribution of community development funding in the US.* Report accessed online 29.3.2021. https://www.urban.org/sites/default/files/publication/99704/tracking_the_unequal_distribution_of_community_development_funding_in_the_us_1.pdf

The World Bank (2022). *Greater transparency on hidden and distressed debt can reduce global financial risk and support recovery.* Online report 2.12.2022. Accessed 30.3.2022. https://www.worldbank.org/en/news/press-release/2022/02/15/greater-transparency-on-hidden-and-distressed-debt-can-reduce-global-financial-risks-and-support-recovery

Thomaes, K., Doorepaal, E., Draijer, N., and Jansma, E.P. (2013). Can pharmacological and psychological treatment change brain structure in PTSD: A systematic review. *Journal of Psychiatric Research*. 50(1). https://doi.org/10.1016/j.jpsychires.2013.11.002

Thurstone, L. and Gardener, H. As cited in *WikiBooks*, Applied history of psychology/Theories on intelligence/Gardener's theory about multiple intelligences. Accessed online 28.3.2022. https://en.wikibooks.org/wiki/Applied_History_of_Psychology/Theories_on_Intelligence/Gardner%27s_theory_about_multiple_intelligence

Toft, B. (2009). *Memorandum by Professor Brian Toft.* Presented to UK Parliament Patient Safety - Health Committee. Accessed online 15.4.2022. https://publications.parliament.uk/pa/cm200809/cmselect/cmhealth/151/151we26.htm

Tonry, M. (2006). The prospects for institutionalization of restorative justice in western countries. In I. Aetersen, T. Daems, & L. Robert (Eds.), *Institutionalization restorative justice*. Routledge Publishers.

Trivedi, S. (2015). Patient safety: Errors need to be minimised. *Health Services Journal*. Accessed online 14.4.2022. https://www.hsj.co.uk/supplement-archive/patient-safety-errors-need-to-be-minimised-/5087223.article

Troubled Families Programme: Improving Families' Lives (2019–2020). Report published by the UK's *Ministry of housing communities and local government*. Accessed 17.4.2021. https://assets.publishing.service.gov.uk/

government/uploads/system/uploads/attachment_data/file/889452/Improving_families__lives_-_Annual_report_of_the_Troubled_Families_Programme_2019-2020.pdf

Turan, N., Aydin, G.O., Ozsbazan, A., Kaya, H., Aksel, G., Yilmaz, A., et al. (2019). Intuition and emotional intelligence: A study in Nursing Students. *Cogent Psychology*. 6(1). https://doi.org/10.1080/23311908.2019.1633077

UK Office for National Statistics (2021). *Families*. Report accessed online 11.3.2022. https://www.ons.gov.uk/peoplepopulationandcommunity/birthsdeathsandmarriages/families

United Nations High Commissioner for Human Rights (2019). Report recommending the dissolution of the Danish Government's "Ghetto Package". Accessed online 22.3.2022. https://www.ohchr.org/sites/default/files/documents/issues/racism/sr/amicus/2022-06-28/AmicusBrieftoDenmark-Intervention-SRs-Achiume-Rajagopal-EN.pdf

Upshaw, M.B., Kaiser, C.R., and Sommerville, J.A. (2015). Parents' empathic perspective-taking and altruistic behavior predicts infant's arousal to others' emotions. *Frontiers in Psychology*. https://doi.org/10.3389/fpsyg.2015.00360

US Department for Health and Human Service (n.d.). *Attachment and biobehavioral catch-up (ABC): Infant model effectiveness research report updated: 2020*. https://homvee.acf.hhs.gov/effectiveness/Attachment%20and%20Biobehavioral%20Catch-Up%20%28ABC%29%20-Infant/In%20Brief

Vaillant, G.E., McArthur, C.C., and Bock, A. (2022). *Grant study of adult development 1938–2000*. Accessed online 14.4.2022. https://doi.org/10.7910/DVN/48WRX9

Van Der Kolk, B. (2014). *The body keeps the score: Brain mind and body in the healing of trauma*. Viking Books.

Ventola, P., Lei, J., Paisley, C., Lebowitz, E., and Silverman, W. (2017). Parenting a child with ASD: Comparison of parenting style between ASD, anxiety and typical development. *Journal of Autism and Developmental disorders*. 47(9): 2873–2884. https://doi.org/10.1007/s10803-017-3210-5

Von Kanel, R., Princip, M., Holzgang, S.A., Fuchs, W.J., et al. (2020). Relationship between job burnout and somatic diseases: A network analysis. *Scientific Report*. 10, Article number 18438. https://doi.org/10.1038/s41598-020-75611-7

Walsh, F. (2012a). Facilitating family resilience: Relational resources for positive youth development in conditions of adversity. In M. Ungar (Ed.), *The social ecology of resilience*. New York, NY: Springer. https://doi.org/10.1007/978-1-4614-0586-3_15

Walsh, F. (2012b). Family resilience: Strengths forged through adversity. In F. Walsh (Ed.), *Normal family processes* (pp. 399–427). New York: Guildford Press.

Warrier, V. (n.d.). As cited in *Study finds that genes play a role in empathy*. Online article published by University of Cambridge. Accessed online 12.4.2022. https://www.cam.ac.uk/research/news/study-finds-that-genes-play-a-role-in-empathy

Welfare Conditionality Project (2018). *Final findings report. Welfare conditionality project 2013–2018*. Accessed online 24.5.2022. https://eprints.whiterose.ac.uk/154305/1/1._FINAL_Welfare_Conditionality_Report_complete.pdf

Wellons, S. (2012). *The devil in the boardroom. Corporate psychopaths and their impact on business*. Accessed online 15.4.2022. https://digitalcommons.wou.edu/cgi/viewcontent.cgi?article=1005&context=pure

Werner, E. E. and Smith, R.S. (n.d.). *An epidemiologic perspective on some antecedents and consequences of childhood mental health problems and learning disabilities: A report from the Kauai Longitudinal Study*. Report accessed online 13.4.2022. https://www.jaacap.org/article/S0002-7138(09)61044-X/pdf

West, M. (2022). *Compassionate leadership: Sustaining wisdom, humanity and presence in health and social care*. The Swirling Leaf Press.

West, M. (n.d.). *What does compassionate and inclusive leadership mean to us?* England NHS.UK. Report accessed only 23.3.2022. https://www.england.nhs.uk/culture/what-does-compassionate-and-inclusive-leadership-mean-to-us/

West, M. (2019). It doesn't have to be this way. *The Psychologist*. 32: 30–33. Accessed online 12.4.2022. https://thepsychologist.bps.org.uk/volume-32/august-2019/it-doesnt-have-be-way

West, M. (2021). *Workforce burnout and resilience in the NHS and social care*. Evidence tabled to UK government committee looking at workplace culture. Accessed online 23.3.2022. https://publications.parliament.uk/pa/cm5802/cmselect/cmhealth/22/2206.htm

White, J. (2008). CBT and the challenge of primary care: Developing effective, efficient, equitable, acceptable and accessible services for common mental health problems. *Journal of Public Mental Health*. 7(1): 32–41. https://doi.org/10.1108/17465729200800006

White, S., Gibson, M., and Wastell, D. (2019). Child protection and disorganized attachment: A critical commentary. *Children and Youth Services Review*. 105. https://doi.org/10.1016/j.childyouth.2019.104415

Wiehler, A., Branzoli, F., Adanyeguh, I., Mochel, F., and Pessiglione, M. (2022). A neuro-metabolic account of why daylong cognitive work alters the control of economic decisions. *Current Biology*. 2(16): 3564–3575. https://doi.org/10.1016/j.cub.2022.07.010

Willis, J. and Todorov, A. (2006). First impressions: Make your mind up after 110 ms exposure to a face. *Psychological Science*. https://doi.org/10.1111/j.1467-9280.2006.01750.x

Wodehouse, P.G. (1922). *The adventures of sally.* Chapter 15. Penguin Publishers.

World Economic Forum (2019). *Corruption costs developing countries $1.26 trillion every year-yet half of EMEA think it's acceptable.* Online article. Accessed 30.3.2022. https://www.weforum.org/agenda/2019/12/corruption-global-problem-statistics-cost/

Wright, S., Fletcher, D.R., and Stewart, A.B.R. (2020). Punitive benefit sanctions, welfare conditionality, and the social abuse of unemployed people in Britain: Transforming claimants into offenders? *Social Policy and Administration.* 54(2). https://doi.org/10.1111/spol.12577

Wrightington, W. and Leigh Teaching Hospitals NHS Foundation Trust (n.d.). *Safety champions.* Article accessed online 12.4.2022. https://www.wwl.nhs.uk/research-champions

Xizheng, X., Liu, Z., Gong, S., and Wu, Y. (2022). The relationship between empathy and attachment in children and adolescents: Three-level meta-analyses. *International Journal of Environmental Research and Public Health.* 19(3): 1391. https://doi.org/10.3390/ijerph19031391

Yaacov, T.B. and Glickson, J. (2018). Intelligence and psychopathy: A study on non-incarcerated females from the normal population. *Cogent Psychology.* 5(1). https://doi.org/10.1080/23311908.2018.1429519

Yukihiro, H. (2015). Brain plasticity and rehabilitation in stroke patients. *Journal of Nippon Medical School.* 82(1): 4–13. https://doi.org/10.1272/jnms.82.4

Zaugg, V., Korb-Savoldelli, V., Durieux, P., and Sabatier, B. (2018). Providing physicians with feedback on medication adherence with chronic diseases taking long-term medication. *Cochrane Library.* https://doi.org/10.1002/14651858.CD012042.pub2

Ziker, J. (2014). *The long, lonely job of homo academicus.* Online report published via Boise State University, Blue Review. Accessed online 12.4.2022. https://www.boisestate.edu/bluereview/faculty-time-allocation/

Zilberstein, K. and Messer, E.I. (2007). Building a secure base: Treatment of a child with disorganised attachment. *Clinical Social Work Journal.* 38(1): 85–97. https://doi.org/10.1007/s10615-007-0097-1

Bibliography vulnerability

Abbot, P. and Chase, D.M. (2008). Culture and substance abuse: Impact of culture affects approach to treatment. *Psychiatric Times.* 25(1): 43.

Aboriginal Healing Foundation (n.d.). *Addictive behaviours among aboriginal people in Canada.* Report accessed online 6.7.2021. https://www.ahf.ca/downloads/addictive-behaviours.pdf

Agnieszka, B., Langstrom, N., Larsson, H., and Lundstrom, S. (2017). Increased risk of substance use-related problems for autistic spectrum disorders: A population-based cohort study. *Journal of Autism and Developmental Disorders.* 47(1). https://doi.org/10.1007/s10803-016-2914-2

Agrawal, A. and Lynseky, M. (2008). Are there genetic influences on addiction: Evidence from family, adoption and twin studies. *Addiction.* 103(7): 1069–1081. https://doi.org/10.1111/j.1360-0443.2088.02213.x

Ainsworth, M. (n.d.). As cited in *Strange Situation* published online by Wikipedia. Accessed 23.3.2021. https://en.wikipedia.org/wiki/Strange_situation

Alloy, L.B. and Abramson, L.Y. (1979). Judgment of contingency in depressed and nondepressed students: Sadder but wiser? *Journal of Experimental Psychology: General.* 108(4): 441–485. https://doi.org/10.1037/0096-3445.108.4.441

APA task force on socioeconomic status (n.d.). Report published by the American Psychological Association. Accessed 14.5.2022. http://www.apa.org/pi

Avshalom, C. and Silva, P. (1995). Temperamental qualities at age three predict personality traits in young adulthood: Longitudinal evidence from a birth cohort. *Child Development* 66(2): 486–498. https://doi.org/10.2307/1131592

Bacigalupe, A. and Martin, A. (2020). Gender inequalities in depression/anxiety and the consumption of psychotropic drugs. *Scandinavian Journal of Public Health.* https://doi.org/10.1177/1403494820944736

Bandura, A. (1997). *Self efficacy: The exercise of control.* W.H. Freeman Publishers.

Belcher, A.M., Volkow, N.D., Moeller, F.G., and Ferre, S. (2014). Personality traits and vulnerability or resilience to substance use disorders. *Trends in Cognitive Science.* 18(4): 211–217. https://doi.org/10.1016/j.tics.2014.01.010

Berkowitz, L. (1993). *Aggression: Its causes, consequences and control.* Temple University Press.

Biblical Famine in Ethiopia (n.d.). Ethiopian famine: How landmark BBC report influenced modern coverage. Article published in the Guardian Newspaper. Accessed 2.20.2022. https://www.theguardian.com/global-development/poverty-matters/2014/oct/22/ethiopian-famine-report-influence-modern-coverage

Bowlby, J. (1990). *A secure base: Parent child attachment and healthy human development*. Basic Books publishers.

Bremner, D.J. (2006). Traumatic stress effects on the brain. *Dialogues in Clinical Neuroscience*. 8(4). https://doi.org/10.31887/DCNS.2006.8.4/jbremner

Briere, B., Weathers, F.W., and Runtz, M. (2005). Is dissociation a multidimensional construct? Data from the Multiscale Dissociation Inventory. *Journal of Traumatic Stress*. 18(3): 221–231.

Brooks, A.W., Schroeder, J., Risen, J., Gino, F., Galinsky, A.D., Norton, M.J., and Schweitzer, M.E. (2016). Don't stop believing: Rituals improve performance by decreasing anxiety. *Organizational Behavior and Human Decision Processes*. 137: 71–85. https://doi.org/10.1016/j.obhdp.2016.07.004

Brown, R. (2015). *Daring greatly: How the courage to be vulnerable transforms the way we live, love, parent and lead*. Penguin Books.

Chess, S. and Thomas, A. (1991). Temperament and the concept of goodness of fit. In J. Strelau & A. Angleitner (Eds.), *Explorations in temperament: International perspectives on theory and measurement* (pp. 15–28). Plenum Press. https://doi.org/10.1007/978-1-4899-0643-4_2

Christiansen, S.G., Reneflot, A., Stene-Larsen, K., and Haige, L.J. (2020). Alcohol-related mortality following the loss of a child: A register-based follow-up study from Norway. *BMJ Open*. 10(6): 1–9. https://bmjopen.bmj.com/content/bmjopen/10/6/e038826.full.pdf

Cohen, F.S. and Densen-Gerber, J. (1982). A study of the relationship between child abuse and drug addiction in 178 patients: Preliminary results. *Child Abuse and Neglect: The International Journal*. 6(4): 383–387.

Connolly, C.G., Bell, R.P., Foxe, J.J., and Garavan, H. (2013). Dissociated grey matter changes with prolonged addiction and extended abstinence in cocaine users. *PLoS One*. 8(3): e59645. https://doi.org/10.1371/journal.pone.0059645

Cooley, C.H. (1902). *The looking glass self*. As cited online in Wikipedia. https://en.wikipedia.org/wiki/Looking-glass_self

Danese, A., Pariante, C.M., and Caspi, A. (2007). Childhood maltreatment predicts adult inflammation in a life-course study. *Proceedings of the National Academy of Science*. 104(4): 1319–1324. https://doi.org/10.1073/pnas.0610362104

Diagnostic and statistical manual of mental disorders (DSM-5-TR) (n.d.). As cited by American Psychiatric Association. Accessed online 15.3.2022. https://psychiatry.org/psychiatrists/practice/dsm

Doku, D.T., Neupane, S., Dobewall, H., and Rimpela, A. (2020). Alcohol related mortality and all-cause mortality following bereavement in two successive generations. *PLoS One*. Published December 10, 2020. https://doi.org/10.1371/journal.pone.0243290

Dorey, P. (2010). A poverty of imagination: Blaming the poor for inequality. *The Political Quarterly*. 81(3):333–343. https://doi.org/10.1111/j.1467-922020.02095.x

Durkheim, E.A. (n.d.). *From Wikipedia*. Accessed 3.9.2021. https://en.wikipedia.org/wiki/Anomie

Dweck, C.S., Chiu, C.Y., and Hong, Y.Y. (1995). Implicit theories and their role in judgments and reactions: A word from two perspectives. *Psychological Inquiry*. 6(4): 267–285.

Elinor, A., Fraser, S., and Burnaby, B.C. (1997). The development of Romanian children adopted to Canada: Final report. Accessed online 4.9.2021. https://www.researchgate.net/profile/Lianne-Fisher/publication/238341349_The_Development_of_Romanian_Orphanage_Children_Adopted_to_Canada/links/548e18610cf214269f24381c/The-Development-of-Romanian-Orphanage-Children-Adopted-to-Canada.pdf

Family Nurse Partnership (n.d.). *Online NHS website*. Accessed 2.2.2021. https://fnp.nhs.uk

Fernando, S. and Perera, H. (2012). School refusal: behavioural and diagnostic profiles of a clinical sample. *Sri Lanka Journal of Psychiatry*. 3(1): 10–13. https://doi.org/10.4038/SLJPSYC.V3I1.4453

Fonzo, G.A., Goodkind, M.S., Oathes, D.J., Zaiko, Y.V., et al. (2017). Brain activation during emotional reactivity and regulation predicts psychotherapy outcome in posttraumatic stress disorder. *American Journal of Psychiatry*. 174(12): 1163–1174. https://doi.org/10.1176/appi.ajp.2017.16091072

Fraser, A. (n.d.). *The dark side of resilience*. Article accessed online April 7, 2022. https://dradamfraser.com/blog-content/2017/12/7/the-dark-side-of-resilience

Gilbert, P. (2019). Distinguishing shame, humiliation and guilt: An evolutionary functional analysis and compassion focused interventions. In C.H. Mayer & E. Vanderheiden (Eds.), *The bright side of shame*. Cham: Springer. https://doi.org/10.1007/978-3-030-13409-9_27

Glaser, D. (2000). Child abuse and neglect and the brain: A review. *The Journal of Child Psychology and Allied Disciplines*. 41(1): 97–116. https://doi.org/10.1017/S0021963099004990

Hall, W., Carter, A., and Forlini, C. (2015). The brain disease model of addiction: Is it supported by the evidence and has it delivered on its promises? *Lancet Psychiatry*. 2: 105–110. https://doi.org/10.1016/S2215-0366(14)00126-6

Hawkley. L.C. and Cacioppo, J.T. (2010). Loneliness matters: A theoretical and empirical review of consequences and mechanisms. *Annals of Behavioural Medicine*. 40(2): 218–27. https://doi.org/10.1007/s12160-010-9210-8

Herman, J.L. (1994). *Trauma and recovery*. River Orams Press.

Hobson, N., Schroeder, J., Risen, J., Xygalatas, D., and Inzlicht, M. (2017). The psychology of rituals: An integrative review and process-based framework. *SSRN*. https://doi.org/10.2139/ssrn.2944235

Hoffman Report (2015). *Report to the Special Committee of the Board of Directors of the American Psychological Association*. Accessed online 16.4.2022. https://www.apa.org/independent-review/revised-report.pdf

Holmes and Rahe Life Events Scale (n.d.). *Wikipedia*. Accessed online 15.3.2022. https://en.wikipedia.org/wiki/Holmes_and_Rahe_stress_scale

Hutchinson, P., Abrams, D., and Christian, J. (2004). Chapter 3: The social psychology of exclusion. In D. Abrams, M.A. Hogg, & J.M. Marques (Eds.), *The social psychology of inclusion and exclusion* (pp. 29–50). Psychology Press Publishers.

Insel, T.R. and Wang, P.S. (2010). Rethinking mental illness. *JAMA*. 303(19): 1970–1971. https://doi.org/10.1001/jama.2010.555

James, O. (2007). *Affluenza*. Ebury Publishing.

Janet, P. As cited in Van der Kolk, B., Brown, P., and Van der Hart, O. (1989). Pierre Janet on post-traumatic stress. *Journal of Traumatic Stress*. 2(4): 365–378. https://doi.org/10.1002/jts.2490020403

Jones, E.E. and Harris, V.A. (1967). The attribution of attitudes. *Journal of Experimental Social Psychology*. 3(1): 1–24.

Joseph Rowntree Foundation (2022). *The essential guide to understanding poverty in the UK*. Accessed online 14.3.2022. https://www.jrf.org.uk/report/uk-poverty-2022

Kagan, J. (1991). Temperamental factors in human development. Reprint of an article published in *American Psychologist*. Accessed online 17.12 2021. https://www.researchgate.net/profile/Jerome-Kagan/publication/21226928_Temperamental_Factors_in_Human_Development/links/00b495266d8d3a839a000000/Temperamental-Factors-in-Human-Development.pdf

Kahneman, D. and Deaton. A. (2010). High income improves evaluation of life but not emotional well-being. *Proceedings of the National Academy of Science*. 107(38): 16489–16493. https://doi.org/10.1073/pnas.1011492107

Kaminsky, Z., Wilcox, H.C., Eaton, W.W., Van Eck, K., et al. (2015). Epigenetic and genetic variation at *SKA2* predict suicidal behavior and post-traumatic stress disorder. *Translational Psychiatry*. 5: e627.

Kelly, G. As cited in George Kelly (psychologist). *Wikipedia*. Accessed online 18.7.2021. https://en.wikipedia.org/wiki/George_Kelly_(psychologist)

Keysers, C. (2011). *The empathic brain*. CreateSpace Independent Publishing Platform.

Keyser Family Foundation (2001, April 29). *National survey on poverty in America*. https://www.kff.org/medicaid/poll-finding/national-survey-on-poverty-in-america/. Accessed 21.3.2021.

Kings College London (2021). *Unequal Britain: Attitudes to inequalities after COVID-19*. Report. Accessed online 2.4.2022. https://www.kcl.ac.uk/policy-institute/assets/unequal-britain.pdf

Layard, R. (2008). *Happiness: Lessons for a new science* (2nd ed.). Penguin Books.

Lepianka, D. (2007). *Are the poor to be blamed or pitied? A comparative study of popular poverty attributions in Europe*. Doctoral Thesis. University of Tilburg. Accessed 17.2 2022. https://www.researchgate.net/publication/259581451_Are_the_Poor_to_Be_Blamed_or_Pitied_A_comparative_Study_of_Popular_Poverty_Attributions_in_Europe

Lerner, M.J. (1980). The belief in a just world. In *Perspectives in social psychology*. Boston, MA: Springer. https://doi.org/10.1007/978-1-4899-0448-5_2

Luna. F. (2018). Identifying and evaluating layers of vulnerability—A way forward. *Developing World Bioethics*. 19(2): 86–95. https://doi.org/10.1111/dewb.12206

Maayan, A., Saar, A., and Araten-Bergman, T. (2016). The person in the disabled body: A perspective on culture and personhood form the margins. *International Journal of Equity in Health*. 15(1): 147. https://doi.org/10.1186/s12939-016-0437-2

Manstead, A. (2018). The psychology of social class: How socioeconomic status impacts thought, feelings, and behaviour. *British Journal of Social Psychology*. 57(2): 267–291. https://doi.org/10.1111/bjso.12251

Matte, G. (2018). *In the realm of hungry ghosts*. Ebury Publishing.

Matthew T.T., Kiel, E.J., McDermott, M.J., and Gratz, K.L. (2013). The effect of trauma cue exposure on cocaine cravings among cocaine dependent inpatients with and without posttraumatic stress disorder: Exploring the mediating role of negative affect and discrete negative emotional states. *Journal of Experimental Psychopathology*. 4(5): 485–501.

Marcel, G. (n.d.). *Existential angst*, as cited in Wikipedia. Date of access, June 5, 2021. https://en.wikipedia.org/wiki/Gabriel_Marcel#Existential_themes

Mason, S.M., Flint, A.J., Field, A.E., Austin, S.B., and Rich-Edwards, J.W. (2013). Abuse victimisation in childhood or adolescence and risk of food addiction in adult women. *Obesity (Silver Spring)*. 21(12): E775–E871. https://doi.org/10.1002/oby.20500

McCoy, M.B. (2014). *Wounded heroes: Vulnerability as a virtue in ancient greek literature and philosophy*. Oxford Scholarship Online: January 2014. https://doi.org/10.1093/acprof:oso/9780199672783.001.0001

McCrory, E., De Brito, S.A., and Viding, E. (2011). The impact of childhood maltreatment: A review of neurobiological and genetic factors. *Frontiers of Psychiatry*. 2: 48. https://doi.org/10.3389/fpsyt.2011.00048

McGarvey, D. (2018). *Poverty safari: Understanding the anger of Britain's underclass*. Pan Macmillan.

McKenzie, S., Oliffe, J.L., Black, A., and Collings, S. (2022). Men's experience of mental illness across the lifespan: A scoping review. *American Journal of Men s Health*. 16(1). https://doi.org/10.1177/15579883221074789

Meaney, M.J. and Szyf, M. (2005). Environmental programming of stress responses through DNA methylation: Life at the interface between a dynamic environment and a fixed genome. *Dialogues in Clinical Neuroscience*. 7(2): 103–123. https://doi.org/10.31887/DCNS.2005.7.2/mmeaney

MIND (n.d.). *Christmas and mental health*. Online resource. Accessed 17.1.2022. https://www.mind.org.uk/information-support/tips-for-everyday-living/christmas-and-mental-health/why-christmas-is-hard/

Ministry of Housing Communities and Local Government (2020). *Improving families' lives: Annual report of the troubled families programme 2019–2020*. Accessed 17.4.2021. https://assets.publishing.service.gov.uk/government/uploads/system/uploads/attachment_data/file/889452/Improving_families_lives_-_Annual_report_of_the_Troubled_Families_Programme_2019-2020.pdf

Morina, N., Stangier, U., and Risch, A.K. (2008). Experiential avoidance in civilian war survivors with current versus recovered posttraumatic stress disorder: A pilot study. *Behaviour Change*. 25(1): 15–22. https://doi.org/10.1375/bech.25.1.15

Mosteller, F. (1995). The Tennessee Study of class size in the early school grades. *The Future of Children*. 5(2), Critical Issues for Children and Youths (Summer–Autumn, 1995), pp. 113–127. https://www.jstor.org/stable/i273896

Mowat, J.G. (2015). Towards a new conceptualization of marginalisation. *European Educational Research Journal*. 14(5): 454–476. https://doi.org/10.1177/1474904115589864

Mueller, M. and Peterson, Z.D. (2012). The relationship between childhood maltreatment, emotion regulation and sexual risk taking in men from urban STD clinics. *Journal of Aggression, Maltreatment and Trauma*. 21(3): 277–299. https://doi.org/10.1080/10926771.2012.659802

Murray-Parkes, C. (2010). *Bereavement: Studies of grief in adult life* (4th ed.). Routledge.

Nadal, R. (n.d.). *Tug. Tuck. Wipe. Repeat: Nadal's rituals help defy his breaking body*. Article published in *The Guardian*. Accessed 4.4.2022. https://www.theguardian.com/sport/2022/jan/28/tug-tuck-wipe-repeat-nadals-rituals-help-defy-his-breaking-body

Nadar, M.A. and Czoty. P. (2005). PET imaging of dopamine D_2 receivers in monkey models of cocaine abuse: Genetic predisposition versus environmental modulation. *American Journal of Psychiatry*. 162(8): 1473–1482. https://doi.org/10.1176/appi.ajp.162.8.1473

Natarajan, S. and Jackson, P. (n.d.). *Lhakpa Sherpa: Woman climbs Everest for record tenth time.* News article published by BBC online. Accessed 12.05.2022. https://www.bbc.com/news/world-asia-61424866

Neilsen, M. and Andersen, M.M. (2014). Should we hold the obese responsible? *Cambridge Quarterly of Healthcare Ethics.* 23(4): 443–451. https://doi.org/10.1017/S0963180114000115

Ohlmeier, M., Peters, K., Buddensiek, N., and Seifert, J. (2005). *ADHD and addiction.* Accessed online. https://www.researchgate.net/publication/286864978_ADHD_and_addiction

Patton, G.S. (n.d.). Cited online in *Wikipedia.* Accessed 13.3.2021. https://en.wikipedia.org/wiki/George_S._Patton

Pheonix, O. (n.d.). *Painful truths about vicarious trauma: Statistics from the field.* Media Blog. Accessed online 11.11.2021. https://olgaphoenix.com/blog/painful-truths-about-vicarious-trauma-statistics-from-the-field/

Piff, P.K. and Moskowitz, J.P. (2018). Wealth, poverty, and happiness: Social class is differentially associated with positive emotions. *Emotion.* 18(6): 902–905. https://doi.org/10.1037/emo0000387

Pilling, J., Konoly, T., Demetrovics, Z., and Kopp, M.S. (2012). Alcohol use in the first three years of bereavement: A national representative study. *Substance Abuse Treatment, Prevention and Policy.* 7: Article number 3. https://link.springer.com/content/pdf/10.1186/1747-597X-7-3.pdf

Population Reference Bureau (2002). *American attitudes about poverty and the poor.* Report. Accessed 20.2.2022. https://www.prb.org/resources/american-attitudes-about-poverty-and-the-poor/

Premak, D. and Woodruff, G. (1978). Does the chimpanzee have a theory of mind? *The Behavioral and Brain Sciences.* 4: 515–526.

Rajkumar, P.R. (2021). *The relationship between measures of individualism and collectivism and the impact of COVID-19 across nations. Public Health in Practice (Oxford, England).* 2: 100143. https://doi.org/10.1016/j.puhip.2021.100143

Razer, M. and Friedman, V.J. (2017). *The cycle of exclusion: From exclusion to excellence.* Brill Publishers. https://doi.org/10.1163/9789463004886_002

Rohmer, O. and Louvet, A. (2016). Implicit stereotyping against people with disability. *Group Processes and Intergroup Relations.* 21(1). https://doi.org/10.1177%2F1368430216638536

Rust, T. (n.d.). *Helping Alzheimer's patients stay independent.* Online article in PsyPost. Accessed 12.12.2021. https://www.psypost.org/2012/07/helping-alzheimers-patients-stay-independent-12920

Sapolsky, R.M. (2004). *Why zebras don't get ulcers* (3rd ed.). New York. Henry Holt.

Schimmel, J. (2009). Development as happiness: The subjective perception of happiness and UNDP's analysis of poverty, wealth and development. *Jour-*

nal of Happiness Studies. 10(1): 93–111. https://doi.org/10.1007/s10902-007-9063-4

Schneier, F.R., Foose, T.E., Hasin, D.S., Heimberg, R.G., et al. (2010). Social anxiety disorder and alcohol use disorder comorbidity in the national epidemiologic survey on alcohol and related conditions. *Psychological Medicine.* 40(6): 977–988. https://doi.org/10.1017/S0033291709991231

Seligman, M.E.P. and Maier, S.F. (1976). Learned helplessness: Theory and evidence. *Journal of Experimental Psychology.* 105(1): 3–46.

Selye, H. (1950). Stress and the general adaption syndrome. *British Medical Journal.* 1(4667): 1383–1392. https://doi.org/10.1136/bmj.1.4667.1383

Shackman, A.J., Stockbridge, M.D., Tillman, R.M., et al. (2016). The neurobiology of dispositional negativity and attentional biases to threat: Implications for understanding anxiety disorders in adults and youth. *Journal of Experimental Psychopathology.* 7(3): 311–342. https://doi.org/10.5127/jep.054015

Social Metrics Commission Report. *Middle-class consume more drugs and alcohol than the poorest.* In the Guardian Newspaper. Accessed online 14.6.2021. https://www.theguardian.com/society/2018/sep/16/middle-class-consume-more-drugs-and-alcohol-than-poorer-people

Spangler, G. (2015). Chapter 13: Individual dispositions as precursors of differences in attachment quality: Why maternal sensitivity is nevertheless important. In K. Grossman, I. Bretherton, E. Waters, & K. Grossman (Eds.), *Maternal sensitivity.* Routledge Publishers. https://doi.org/10.1080/14616734.2013.842065

Spence, R., Kagan, L., and Bifulco, A. (2019). Why are life events troubling? *The Psychologist.* 32: 48–51.

Stand Together (n.d.). *Shifting perceptions of low-income families is key to getting them out of poverty.* Online Article. Accessed March 10, 2022. https://standtogether.org/news/shifting-perceptions-of-low-income-families-is-key-to-getting-them-out-of-poverty/

Stanton, P. (2019). Cited in *Vietnam vets proved that addiction is a product of life circumstances.* Published in Media Blog. Filtermag.org. Accessed online 18.10 2021. https://filtermag.org/vietnam-vets-proved-that-addiction-is-a-product-of-life-circumstances/

Stock, K. (2010). Wall street drug use: Employees giving up cocaine for pot and pills. *The Wall Street Journal.* Accessed online 6.6.2021. https://www.wsj.com/articles/BL-DLB-26074

Strohmeier, H. and Scholte, W.F. (2015). Trauma-related mental health problems among national humanitarian staff: A systematic review of the literature. *European Journal of Psychotraumatology.* 6: 28541. https://doi.org/10.3402/ejpt.v6.28541

Sussman, S., Lisha, N., and Griffiths, M. (2011). Prevalence of addictions: A problem of the majority or the minority? *Health Promotion and Evaluation.* 34(1): 3–56. https://doi.org/10.1177/0163278710380124

Szymanski, D.M. and Stewart-Richardson, D.N. (2014). Psychological, relational and sexual correlates of pornography use on young adult heterosexual men. *The Journal of Men's Studies.* 22(1): 64–82. https://doi.org/10.3149/jms.2201.64

Tangney, J.P. and Dearing, R.L. (2002). *Shame and guilt.* Guilford Publications.

Tangney, J.P., Youman, K., and Stuewig, J. (2009). Proneness to shame and proneness to guilt. In M.R. Leary & R.H. Hoyle (Eds.), *Handbook of individual differences in social behaviour.* Guilford Press.

Taylor, S.E. and Brown, J.D. (1988). Illusion and well-being: A social psychological perspective on mental health. *Psychological Bulletin.* 103(2): 193–210. https://doi.org/10.1037/0033-2909.103.2.193

Tobi, E. (2009). DNA methylation differences after exposure to prenatal famine are common and timing- and sex-specific. *Human Molecular Genetics.* 18(21): 4046–4053. https://doi.org/10.1093/hmg/ddp353

Toussaint, L. (n.d.). *What other cultures can teach us about forgiveness.* BBC Futures. Accessed 7.12.2021. https://www.bbc.com/future/article/20201109-what-other-cultures-can-teach-us-about-forgiveness.

Uher, R. (2014). Gene–environment interactions in severe mental illness. *Frontiers of Psychiatry.* https://doi.org/10.3389/fpsyt.2014.00048

United Nations Department of Economic and Social Affairs (n.d.). *Social inclusion.* Online resource accessed 6.6.2022. https://www.un.org/development/desa/socialperspectiveondevelopment/issues/social-integration.html

United Nations Educational, Scientific and Cultural Organisation (n.d.). *The principle of respect for human vulnerability and personal integrity: Report of the international bioethics committee of UNESCO (IBC).* https://unesdoc.unesco.org/search/6f3e2a04-850e-402e-b6bd-8f222d89fd42

Van der Kolk, B.A. (2000). Posttraumatic stress disorder and the nature of trauma. *Dialogues in Neuroscience.* 2(1): 7–22. https://doi.org/10.31887/DCNS.2000.2.1/bvdkolk

Van der Kolk, B.A. (2015). *The body keeps the score: Brain, mind, and body in the healing of trauma.* Penguin Publishers.

Vollm, B.A., Taylor, A.N.W., Richardson, P., Corcoran, R., et al. (2006). Neuronal correlates of theory of mind and empathy: A functional magnetic resonance imaging study in a nonverbal task. *Neuroimage.* 29(1): 90–98. https://doi.org/10.1016/j.neuroimage.2005.07.022

Warshaw, M.D., Fierman, E., Pratt, B.S., Hunt, M., et al. (1993). Quality of life and dissociation in anxiety disorder patients with histories of trauma or PTSD. *American Journal of Psychiatry.* 150: 1512–1516.

Washington Post (n.d.). *'Learned helplessness': The chilling psychological concept behind the CIA's interrogation methods.* Accessed online. 26.2.2022. https://www.washingtonpost.com/news/morning-mix/wp/2014/12/11/the-chilling-psychological-principle-behind-the-cias-interrogation-methods/

Weiss, J.M. (1972). Psychological factors in stress and disease. *Scientific American.* J226(6): 104–113. https://doi.org/10.1038/scientificamerican0672-104

Wikipedia (n.d.). *Transtheoretical model of stress.* Accessed 7.1.2022. https://en.wikipedia.org/wiki/Transtheoretical_model

Wilson, J.J. (2016). *Joblessness and poor neighbourhoods.* Video published by the Stanford Centre for Inequality. Accessed online 12.12.2021. https://inequality.stanford.edu/publications/media/details/joblessness-and-poor-neighborhoods-william-julius-wilson

World Bank's Baseline for Poverty (n.d.). Online publication. Accessed 23.2.2022. https://www.worldbank.org/en/topic/poverty

World Bank Group (2000). *Voices of the poor: Crying out for change.* Report published by Oxford University Press for the World Bank. https://openknowledge.worldbank.org/handle/10986/13848

World Health Organisation (n.d.). *International statistical classification of diseases and related health problems (ICD).* Accessed online 12.12.2021. https://www.who.int/standards/classifications/classification-of-diseases

Yehuda, R., Daskalaksis, N.P., Bierer, L.M., Bader, H.N., et al. (2016). Holocaust exposure induced intergenerational effects on FKBP5 methylation. *Biological Psychiatry.* 80(5): 372–380. https://doi.org/10.1016/j.biopsych.2015.08.005

Zappe, P.W. (n.d.). *The last Messiah.* Accessed 4.3.2021. https://en.wikipedia.org/wiki/The_Last_Messiah

Zentner, M. and Shiner, R.L. (2012). Chapter 32: Fifty years of progress in temperament research: A synthesis of major themes, findings, and challenges and a look ahead. In M. Zentner & R.L. Shiner (Eds.), *Handbook of temperament* (p. 673). Guilford.

Zhang, E.Y. (2014). Vulnerability, compassion, and ethical responsibility: A Buddhist perspective on the phenomenology of illness and health. In J. Tham, A. Garcia, & G. Miranda (Eds.), *Religious perspectives on human vulnerability in bioethics* (pp. 41–54). Springer Publishers.

Zuckerman, M. (1999). Diathesis-stress models. In M. Zuckerman (Ed.), *Vulnerability to psychopathology: A biosocial model* (pp. 3–23). American Psychological Association. https://doi.org/10.1037/10316-001

Index

Note: Page numbers followed by "n" denote endnotes.

Abbot, K. 125
Abbott, P. 66
Abrams, D. 23–24
Abramson, L. 17
abuse: alcohol 66–67, 84, 96; child 115, 120, 144, 160, 162; persistent 58; sexual 32, 52, 56, 59, 65–66, 92–93
action stage 174
addiction 23, 60–68, 88, 145
adverse childhood experiences (ACEs) 82–83
Affluenza (James) 26
Agmon, M. 24
Agrawal, A. 61
Ainsworth, M. 43–44, 88–89, 91
Alloy, I. 17
All-Party Parliamentary Group 158
American Diagnostic and Statistical Manual 101
American Psychological Association 26, 124–125
Andersen, M. M. 8
anxiety 5, 7–9, 14, 15, 17, 43, 123–124
anxious-preoccupied insecure attachment style 89–90
Asmussen, K. 100
Attachment and Biobehavioral Catch-up (ABC) programme 97, 100
Attachment, Regulation and Competency (ARC) model 96, 99
attachment styles 89–90
attachment theory 100–101
attention deficit hyperactivity disorder (ADHD) 67, 167n3
autistic spectrum disorder (ASD) 53, 67, 79–80
avoidant-dismissive attachment style 89–90
Azjen, I. 173

Bacigalupe, A. 10
Baier, J. 144
Bandura, A. 175
Barlow, J. 99
Barnes, C. D. 118
Bastiani, A. 122
Baumeister, R. 120
Beck, A. 124
Becker, M. 170, 172
Belcher, A. 61
Bellosta-Batalla, M. 118
Benner, P. 114
Berkowitz, L. 54, 108
Bernard, K. 92
Bifulco, A. 21
Big Five theory 73–75, 80n3
Bigsby, E. 151
bioecological model 78–80, 82, 160, 161
Bitsika, V. 80
Blair, C. 143

Blair, T. 148
Blakemore, S. -J. 53
The Body Keeps the Score (van der Kolk) 124
Bopp, M. 147
Bowlby, J. 42–43, 87–88, 94, 161
Bremner, D. 55
Briquet, P. 105
British Association of Social Workers (BASW) 134
Bronfenbrenner, U. 77, 80, 96, 160–161, 164
Brooks, A. 16
Brooks, N. 113
Brown, J. 17
Brown, R. 10, 53, 122
burnout 126–129
Butwicka, A. 67
Bywaters, P. 160

Cacioppo, J. 26
Cameron, D. 148
Carr, A. 175
Caspi, A. 34
Centers for Disease Control and Prevention (CDC) 161–163
Chaffey, L. 115
Chandra, A. 145
Chapple, K. 145
Chase, D. 66
Cheshire, J. 144
Chess, S. 35
child development 34, 71, 77–78, 83, 89, 98–100, 160–161
Christ, G. 86
Christian, J. 23–24
Christiansen, S. G. 68
Christopher, S. 167
chronic stress 37–38, 119, 129
Claxton, G. 114

Cobner, R. 156, 176
Cochrane systematic review 170, 177n1
Cohen, F. 66
community action 176
community resilience 144–147
compassion 115–117; mindfulness 123–125
compassionate organisations 135–137
condition humana 5–6, 123, 135
Connolly, C. 64
contemplation stage 174
Cooley, C. H. 45–46
corruption 147–149
Costa, P. 74
craving 63
crime 153–156
criminal justice systems 154
cultural intolerance 10–12

Danese, A. 32, 35
Darzi, L. 139–140
Dearing, R. 94, 122
Deaton, A. 26
Decety, J. 109
Densen-Gerber, J. 66
depersonalisation 127
DiClemente, C. 174
disorganised attachment 90–100, 102n2
disrupted attachment 94, 101, 102n2
Doku, D. T. 68
Donaldson, L. 138
dopamine 62–65
Dorey, P. 27
Douglas, C. 111
Downey, L. 115
Dozier, M. 92, 97, 100
Drigas, A. 111–112
Dunedin Longitudinal Study 31

Index

Durkheim, E. 23, 66
Dweck, C. 12–13
Early Head Start 163
economic capital 146
Educational Welfare Officers 158
embarrassment 51
emotional: dysregulation 62, 82, 92, 96–97, 159; forgiveness 11; management 111
emotional intelligence 109–113; intuition as 113–115
emotion, development of 106–109
empathic recognition 111
empathy 40, 52, 112, 115–121
epigenetics 46–49, 78, 142, 159
Erisman, J. 114–115
Etherson, M. 122
Evans, N. 137
extrinsic motivation 150

FADS2 31
Fairchild, A. 151
Family Nurse Partnership (FNP) Programme 95–97, 99, 171
family resilience 84–87
Farrington, D. 156
Federal Aviation Administration 138
Feiden, W. 147, 149
Feldman-Summers, S. 120
Fernando, S. 34
Fishbein, M. 173
Fitzgerald, M. 100
Fitzgerald, S. 7
FKBP5 48
Francis Enquiry 132
Francis, R. 137
Frankenhuis, E. 90
Franz, M. 86
Fraser, A. 10

Freud, S. 105
Friedman, V. 23
Fritzon, K. 113
Fry, S. 173

Gambin, M. 119
Gartland, D. 142–143
gender 171
General Adaption Syndrome 36
general intelligence 103–106
George, C. 91–92, 95
Gilbert, P. 54, 115–116, 119, 121, 123
Glaser, D. 42
Glickson, J. 113
glucocorticoids 48, 50n2
Goddard, V. 136
Goleman, D. 109, 112
Goodman, R. 146–147, 177
Goodness of Fit 35, 79, 82
GOV.UK 131–132, 154, 156–157
Greenberg, D. 119
Gregory, F. 59
groupthink 165–166
guilt 51–52, 56, 59, 68n1, 120
Gunderson, J. G. 101
Gunnar, M. 99

habituation 60–61, 68n2
Hall, W. 62
Halmi, K. 122
Ham, C. 134
Hancock, M. 142
happiness 25–27
Harlow, E. 98
Harold, A. 87
Harris, V. 8
Hart, J. 177
Hartwig, A. 165
Harvard Medical School Grant Study 71–72

Haukaas, R. 125
Hawkley, L. 26
health belief model 170–172
Heinke, M. 112
helplessness 19
Herman, L. 93
High Commissioner for Human Rights 149
hippocampus 35, 38, 42, 55, 107, 125n1–125n2
Hobson, N. 16
Hodgdon, H. 99
Holmes, T. 21
Hölzel, B. 125
Hone, D. 118
honour-killings 54
human error 138–140
Hutchinson, P. 23–24
hyperarousal 56
hypothalamic-pituitary-adrenal axis (HPA) 36–38, 117

Incredible Years programme 162
Insel, T. 30
Institute for Fiscal Studies 148
inter-generational poverty 142–143, 159–164
International Classification of Diseases (ICD11) 56
International Monetary Fund 147–148
International Society of Traumatic Stress 87
intrinsic motivation 149–150
intrusion 56

Jachens, L. 131
James, O. 26
Janet, P. 56
Janis, I. 22, 165–166
Janz, N. 172

Jarret, C. 123
Job Demand-Control Model 128
Jones, E. 8
Joseph Rowntree Foundation 160
Just World Fallacy 29

Kagan, J. 32–33
Kagan, L. 21
Kahneman, D. 26
Kaminsky, Z. 48
Karasek, R. 128
Keiser-ACE programme 163
Kelly, G. 57
Keysers, C. 5
Kinman, G. 130–131, 133, 135, 137
Klein, G. 114
Kocovski, N. 125
Kohler-Evans, P. 118
Kordowitz, M. 135

Layard, R. 25–26
Leith, K. 120
Lepianka, D. 27
Lerner, M. 15
Lewin, K. 93–94
Lewis, H. B. 54
Lewis-Herman, J. 54–56, 92
Lewis, M. 109
limbic system 41, 45, 107, 110, 125n1
Liotti, G. 94–95
long-term addiction 64–65
Louis, W. 112
Louve, E. 13
Luna, F. 10
Lynskey, M. 61

McCoy, M. B. 5
McCrae, R. 74
McCrory, E. 41–42
MacDonald, K. 83–84

Index

McFarlane, C. 131
McGarvey, D. 19, 143, 145, 147, 176
MacKenzie, M. 125
Mackintosh, K. 118
McKenzie, S. 11
MacLean, P. 107
McVicar, D. 152
magnetic resonance imaging (MRI) techniques 59
maintenance stage 174
Mann, L. 22
Manstead, A. 11
Marcel, G. 8
Marin, A. 165
Martin, U. 10
Maslach Burnout Inventory 127
Maslach, C. 127
Mason, S. 66
Masten, A. 77
Masten, C. 53
Mate, G. 63–65
material capital 13, 143, 146
Mayer, J. 111
MBCT. *See* mindfulness-based cognitive therapy (MBCT)
Meaney, M. 47–48
Meinhardt, C. 129
Mental Health America 130
mentalisation 40–41, 45
Messer, E. 94
methylation 47–48
Miccoli, A. 83
Milgram, S. 140
Millers, W. 168–169, 172
mindfulness 123–125
mindfulness-based cognitive therapy (MBCT) 124–125
Moore, M. 138–139
Morina, N. 59
Morris, A. S. 83
Morris, D. 106
Moskowitz, J. 26
Mosteller, F. 28
motivation, problem of 149–152
Mowat, J. 23
Mueller, T. 62
Muller, K. 65

Nader, M. 63
National Health Service (NHS) 130, 134
Neff, K. 118, 122
negative self-evaluation 127
Neilsen, M. 8
Nelson, C. 99
The Neuroscience of Mindfulness Meditation (Tang) 125
Nielsen, S. 87
Noar, S. 150

occupational burnout 129–132
occupational stress 127
Office for National Statics 85
Ofsted 136, 141n2
Ohlmeier, M. 67
Okoli, J. 115
Olds, D. 96
organisational failings and burnout 132–135
Oxfam 144–145

Papoutsi, C. 112
Parent-Child Interaction Therapy programme 162
parenting 81–84
Parkes, C. M. 16
Peele, S. 66
Peeters, M. 131
Pereq, H. 34
perfectionism 122
personal exhaustion 127

Peterson, Z. 62
Petrich, D. 154
Philips, W. 118
Phoenix, O. 59
Piercy, C. 166
Piff, P. 26
Pika, S. 111
Pilling, J. 67
Pope, K. 120
Positive Psychology (Carr) 175
Positive Psychology Movement 72
post-traumatic stress disorder (PTSD) 55, 59
poverty 24–25; inter-generational 142–143, 159–164
powerlessness 20, 26–27
Power of Intuition (Klein) 114
pre-contemplation stage 174
Premack, D. 40
preparation stage 174
presenteeism 131, 135, 141n1
principles of change 168–170
Problem Solving in Teams and Groups (Janis) 166
Prochaska, J. 174
professional burnout 127
psychopathy 113, 125n3
Pulkinnen, L. 156

Rahe, R. 21
Ramirez, G. 165
randomised control trials (RCTs) 98–99
Raver, C. 143
Razer, M. 23
resilience 80n2, 136; attachment styles and 89–90; bioecological model 78–80; community 144–147; definitions of 73; disorganised attachment 95–100; family 84–87; history of 71–72; model of 76–77; parenting and 81–84; social support and 164–167
Rippon, G. 104, 112
rituals 15–16
Roberts, H. 95–96
Robling, M. 99
Robson, A. 177
Rogers, C. 83, 122
Rohmer, O. 13
Rollnick, S. 168–169, 172
Rose, L. M. 133
Rosenstock, I. 170
Rosenthal, L. 136
Rotenstein, L. 126–127
Rust, T. 19

SafeCare programme 162
Salovey, P. 111
Sameroff, A. 81
Samulowitz, A. 106
Sapolsky, R. 6, 36–37
SARS-CoV-2 pandemic 16, 29–30, 130
Schachter, S. 108
Schaufeli, W. 127–128, 131
Schimmel, J. 25
Schneir, F. 67
Scholes, P. 173
Scholte, W. 59
school exclusion 156–158
Schwarzer, R. 172
Sebastian, C. 53
secure attachment style 89
selective serotonin reuptake inhibitors (SSRIs) 63
self-compassion 117–118; and shame 121–123
self-efficacy 45, 74, 76, 90, 96, 98, 130, 150–151, 158, 160–161, 165, 172, 175
self-medication 65

Index

Seligman, M. 18–20, 57, 72
Selye, H. 36
The Sentencing Project 153
Shackman, A. 35
Shadd, M. 155
shame 52; self-compassion and 121–123; and vulnerability 51–54
Sharp, C. 119
Sharpley, C. 80
Shoesmith, S. 136
Siegrist, J. 128
Silva, P. 34
Simon, P. 11–12
Simpson, J. 90
Singer, J. 108
SKA2 48
Skinner, B. F. 105
Slater, T. 148
Sliter, M. 167
Smith, M. 122–123
social brain 40–44
social capital 146
social exclusion 23
social inclusion 22–23
social support 164–167
sociopathy 110, 113, 125n3
Solomon, J. 91–92, 95
Sonuga-Barke, E. 85
Sourander, A. 87
Southwick, S. 77
Spangle, G. 44
Spence, R. 21
Spicker, P. 146
Stages of Change model 174–175
Stewart-Richardson, D. N. 66
stigmatisation 147–149
Strange Situation Experiment 43–44
stress 20–21; and burnout 126–129; gene 48
Strohmeier, H. 59

Stuewig, J. 52
Sure Start Programme 95
Sussman, S. 61
Svarer, M. 152
Swanson, V. 173
Szymanski, D. 66

Tangney, J. 52, 94, 120–122
Tang, Y. -Y. 125
Tannenbaum, M. 151
Taylor, S. 17
Teitz, M. 145
theory of mind 40, 45, 109, 116
Theory of Reasoned Action model 173, 175
Thomas, A. 35
Tobi, E. 47
Todorov, A. 114
Toft, B. 166
tolerance 10–12, 63
Toussaint, L. 11
Transactional Model of Childhood Development 81
Transactional Theory of Stress 20
trauma 54–60, 65–66, 84, 86–87, 92–93, 95
traumatic maltreatment 92
Triad, D. 125n3
Trivedi, S. 139
Troubled Families Programme 27, 86, 159
trust and intimacy 87–88
Tull, M. 66
Turan, N. 115

Uher, R. 30
United Nations Educational, Scientific and Cultural Organisation (UNESCO) 3–4
Upshaw, M. 116

Van der Kolk, B. 55, 57, 124
The Victorian Mental Health Asylums 19
The Voices of the Poor 27
von Kanel, R. 129
vulnerability: addiction and 60–68; biological systems and 35–37; as *condition humana* 5–6; and cultural intolerance 10–12; definitions of 3–5; epigenetics and 46–49; fluid *vs.* fixed construct 12–13; happiness and 25–27; as heritable condition 30–32; management 14–17; poverty and 24–25; shame and 51–54; and social brain 40–44; trauma and 54–60; as weakness 7–10

Walsh, F. 84–85, 87
Wang, P. 30
Warrier, V. 112
Warshaw, M. 58
Watt, J. 115
Weiss, J. 18–19
Welfare Conditionality Project 153
welfare sanctions 152–153
Wellons, S. 113
Werner, E. 72

West, M. 128, 133, 137
White, J. 173
White, S. 92
Why Zebras Don't Get Ulcers (Sapolsky) 6
Wiehler, A. 117
Willis, J. 114
Wilson, W. 29
Wodehouse, P. G. 73
Woodruff, G. 40
World Bank 144
World Economic Forum 148
Wright, S. 152–153

Xu, X. 120

Yaacov, T. B. 113
Yehuda, R. 48–49
Youman, K. 52

Zapffe, P. W. 15
Zaugg, V. 170
Zhang, E. 5
Zier, J. 134
Zilberstein, K. 94
Zuckerman, M. 34